Who Should Die?

Who Should Die?

The Ethics of Killing in War

Edited by
RYAN JENKINS
MICHAEL ROBILLARD
and
BRADLEY JAY STRAWSER

OXFORD
UNIVERSITY PRESS

OXFORD
UNIVERSITY PRESS

Oxford University Press is a department of the University of Oxford. It furthers the University's objective of excellence in research, scholarship, and education by publishing worldwide. Oxford is a registered trade mark of Oxford University Press in the UK and certain other countries.

Published in the United States of America by Oxford University Press
198 Madison Avenue, New York, NY 10016, United States of America.

CIP data is on file at the Library of Congress
ISBN 978-0-19-049565-7

For all of those who shouldn't have died in war—combatants and noncombatants alike.

CONTENTS

FOREWORD

CÉCILE FABRE

As I am writing this, on Remembrance Sunday 2016, a Russian naval force has just moved into position off the coast of Syria, ready to assist President Assad in his fight against rebels and Islamist militants. The naval deployment is a prelude—it is thought—to ever more intense bombing campaigns. Close to 500,000 civilians have died since the conflict began in 2011. Meanwhile, Iraqi armed forces have just retaken the ancient city of Nimrud from Islamic State—at the costs of both civilians' and militants' lives.

I could go on. I won't: those facts are familiar enough—and all the more depressing to rehearse today, of all days. If nothing else, they tell us that, when all is said and done, the only important questions to be asked about war—*any* war—is who may and should die in it, why, and at whose hands.

At first sight, the question of who may and should die in war is easily answered: "*of course*, soldiers may die—that is their job, their role, is it not? And, *of course*, civilians may not die, or at least only as collateral damage—for they are innocent, are they not? And, *of course*, soldiers at whose hands other soldiers, and civilians, should die—for who else?"

And yet, as the philosophers whom R. Jenkins, M. Robillard, and B. J. Strawser have enlisted for this excellent volume make abundantly clear, there is nothing obvious about this. For consider.

Those soldiers may be fighting for a just cause: why should *they* die?

Perhaps they are fighting in an unjust war, but suppose that they give us the choice of surrendering to them as an alternative to being killed or that they are not responsible for their participation in that war or that they are morally responsible for it but would have faced very severe punishment for refusing to fight: why *should* they die?

As for those civilians, some of them may be supporting an unjust cause: so why should they *not* die? Indeed, some of them may be benefiting from the war—after all, if the United States, France, and their coalition partners succeed in defeating the Islamic State in Iraq and Syria, a great many civilians will survive who would otherwise die. So why *should* they not bear at least some of the risks of being killed by the coalition, if this could help the coalition's forces win the war?

As for who should do the killing, why should it be soldiers and not mobs of civilians intent on protecting themselves and their loved ones or properly designed automated weapons systems?

These points might read as rhetorical questions. They are not meant to be. Rather, they should be read as disquieting thoughts, which are addressed throughout the book with unstinting intellectual rigor and at times brutal honesty by some of the finest philosophers currently working on war.

The book, though, is not just a work of moral philosophy. Its pages resonate with deep compassion for war's victims and attest to the fact that it is possible to write about war in a relentlessly philosophical way without losing sight of the emotional valence of the subject matter. If only for that reason, it is an important book.

NOTES ON CONTRIBUTORS

Saba Bazargan-Forward is an associate professor at the University of California at San Diego. He currently works in normative ethics; he focuses on the morality of war, defensive violence, the bases of compensatory liability, and individual responsibility for collectively committed harms. He has also published papers on moral coercion, contingent pacifism, war profiteering, and territorial occupation. He is currently authoring a book combining these issues, and is a coeditor of a forthcoming Oxford University Press volume on the morality of war.

Yitzhak Benbaji is a professor of philosophy at Tel-Aviv University Law Faculty. His fields of interest are just war theory, political theory, theories of distributive justice, philosophy of language, and, more recently, the philosophy of law and of international law. He earned his PhD (summa cum laude) at the Hebrew University (2001), and he did postdoctoral research at the Institute for Advanced Study, Princeton (2000–2002). Before moving to Tel-Aviv University, he was a professor in the Philosophy Department and the Law Faculty at Bar-Ilan University (2002–2012). His publications in just war theory include "A Contractarian Account of the Crime of Aggression" in C. Fabre and S. Lazar (eds.) *The Morality of Defensive Wars* (Oxford University Press, 2015); "The Moral Power of Soldiers to Undertake the Duty of Obedience," *Ethics* (2011); "The War Convention and the Moral Division of Labour," *Philosophical Quarterly* (2009); and "A Defense of the Traditional War-Convention," *Ethics* (2008).

Susanne Burri is an assistant professor in the Department of Philosophy, Logic and Scientific Method at the London School of Economics and Political Science. She works on topics in normative ethics, political philosophy, and the philosophy of economics.

Lars Christie is a postdoctoral fellow at the Oxford Institute for Ethics, Law and Armed Conflict and a professorial fellow at ConceptLab at the University of

Oslo. He received his PhD from the University of Oslo in 2015 and his master's degree from Columbia University in 2005. Between 2006 and 2012 he worked in the Norwegian Foreign Ministry, serving as a diplomat both in Islamabad and in Jerusalem.

Kai Draper is professor and chair of philosophy at the University of Delaware. He writes on the significance of death, the ethics of self-defense and war, and the nature of evidence. His work has appeared in the *Philosophical Review, Philosophy and Public Affairs, Philosophical Studies, Nous, Philosophy and Phenomenological Research,* and other philosophical journals. His book *War and Individual Rights* was published in October 2015.

Cécile Fabre is a senior research fellow at All Souls College, Oxford. She has written extensively on distributive justice, democracy and rights, as well as the ethics of war. Her book *Cosmopolitan War* came out in 2012 (Oxford University Press). She is currently writing a monograph on the *jus post-bellum.*

Ryan Jenkins is an assistant professor of philosophy and a senior fellow at the Ethics + Emerging Sciences Group at California Polytechnic State University in San Luis Obispo. He studies normative ethics and applied ethics, especially military ethics and emerging technologies. He has published on autonomous weapons, autonomous vehicles, cyberwarfare, and just war theory in venues including *Ethics & International Affairs, Ethical Theory and Moral Practice,* and *Journal of Military Ethics.*

Leonard Kahn, PhD, teaches in the Department of Philosophy at Loyola University New Orleans. He is the editor of *Mill on Justice* (Palgrave, 2012), *Consequentialism and Environmental Ethics* (Routledge, 2013), and *John Stuart Mill's "On Liberty"* (Broadview, 2015); and he has published articles in *Philosophical Studies, Journal of Moral Philosophy, Ethical Theory & Moral Practice,* and *Ethics, Policy, and Environment.*

Stephen Kershnar is a Distinguished Teaching Professor of Philosophy at the State University of New York at Fredonia and an attorney. He focuses on applied ethics and political philosophy. He has authored over eighty articles and book chapters on such diverse topics as torture, affirmative action, God, pornography, hell, free will, adult–child sex, discrimination, the most valuable player, capitalism, equal opportunity, and the nature of pleasure. He is the author of seven books: *Pedophilia and Adult-Child Sex* (2015), *Gratitude Toward Veterans: A Philosophical Explanation of Why Americans Should Not Be Very Grateful to Veterans* (2014), *For Torture: A Right-Based Defense* (2012), *Desert and Virtue: A Theory of Intrinsic Value* (2010), *Sex, Discrimination, and Violence* (2009), *Justice for the Past* (2004), and *Desert, Retribution, and Torture* (2001).

Jeff McMahan is White's Professor of Moral Philosophy at Corpus Christi College at the University of Oxford. He works primarily in ethics and political philosophy and occasionally in metaphysics and legal theory.

Lionel K. McPherson is associate professor of philosophy at Tufts University. His publications, which range from political and social philosophy to ethics, include "Is Terrorism Distinctively Wrong?" (*Ethics*), "Deflating 'Race' " (*Journal of the American Philosophical Association*), and "Normativity and the Rejection of Rationalism" (*Journal of Philosophy*). In addition to writing again on political violence, he is completing a book, *The Afterlife of Race*, about racial identity, political solidarity, and black progress.

Michael Robillard is a postdoctoral research fellow at Oxford's Uehiro Center for Practical Ethics, working on the interface of collective responsibility and counterterrorism. He received his PhD in philosophy from the University of Connecticut in 2016; his MA in philosophy from the University of Victoria, British Columbia, in 2011; and his BS in philosophy from the US Military Academy in 2002. He was also a resident research fellow at the Stockdale Center for Ethical Leadership from 2015 to 2016. His research focuses on various topics in normative ethics to include exploitation and its relation to present-day military recruitment, war and its relation to future generations, and the ethics of emerging military technologies. He is an Iraq War veteran and former Army Airborne Ranger.

Bradley Jay Strawser is an associate professor of philosophy in the Defense Analysis Department at the Naval Postgraduate School in Monterey, California, and a research associate at Oxford University's Institute for Ethics, Law, and Armed Conflict. His research focus is primarily ethics and political philosophy, though he has also written on metaphysics, ancient philosophy, and human rights. He recently published *Binary Bullets: The Ethics of Cyberwarfare*, with Adam Henschke and Fritz Allhoff (Oxford University Press, 2016). He is presently working on *Outsourcing Duty: The Moral Exploitation of the Citizen-Soldier*, with Michael Robillard, and *The Bounds of Defense: Killing, Moral Responsibility, and War*, both of which are forthcoming from Oxford University Press.

David Whetham is reader in military ethics in the Defence Studies Department of King's College London. He is the director of the King's Centre for Military Ethics and delivers or coordinates the military ethics component of courses for between two and three thousand British and international officers a year at the UK's Joint Services Command and Staff College. He has held visiting fellowships at the Stockdale Center for Ethical Leadership, Annapolis, Maryland; the Centre for Defence Leadership and Ethics at the Australian Defence College in Canberra; and the University of Glasgow. Publications include *Ethics, Law* *and Military Operations* (Palgrave, 2010), *Just Wars and Moral Victories* (Brill, 2009), and, with Andrea Ellner and Paul Robinson (editors), *When Soldiers Say No: Selective Conscientious Objection in the Modern Military* (Ashgate, 2014). He is vice president of the European Chapter of the International Society for Military Ethics.

Who Should Die?

Editors' Introduction

RYAN JENKINS, MICHAEL ROBILLARD, AND BRADLEY JAY STRAWSER

A schism is under way in the military ethics community, and the concept of *liability* is the wedge. The question of who is liable to be killed in war—who should die?—has triggered an avalanche of debate at the heart of our understanding of the ethics of war. Until fairly recently, just who should be killed in war was either taken as a given or mostly ignored. But once the question of liability is on the table, an endless host of questions follows. Is war a unique moral context, and are special moral permissions thereby extended to its participants? Are all soldiers equally liable to be targeted in war—even those fighting for a just cause, such as those defending their homes against unjust aggression? Or are some soldiers more liable to harm than others? What mix of considerations informs the liability of individual soldiers: the objective justice of their cause, their individual past actions, what they could reasonably know about the war they fight in? How much risk are soldiers required to take when fighting, exposing themselves in order to minimize collateral damage, and how much risk are they allowed to shift onto noncombatants?

The contemporary philosophical study of military ethics was spurred in large part by Michael Walzer's impressive achievement, *Just and Unjust Wars* (1977). Walzer's is still the canonical treatment of many issues in just war theory; it is a mainstay of undergraduate and graduate teaching and required reading at many military academies. But the foundations of Walzer's view of just war have recently come under an onslaught of criticism, due in large part to this turn to liability—to investigating seriously which individuals can be justly harmed in war and which individuals cannot be. Scholars nurturing this nascent school of counter-thought have dubbed themselves "revisionists" and set themselves apart from the "traditionalist" just war theory advanced by Walzer. Though still inchoate—and not without its detractors—the revisionist view is now ascendant and has come to dominate the landscape within debates over the ethics of war. The standard bearers for this camp are some of the most important moral philosophers working today, such as Jeff McMahan, Cécile Fabre, and David Rodin. These scholars have brought to bear the instruments of analytic philosophy, sharpened and refined through the increasingly technical skirmishes of twentieth-century philosophy, and applied insights from more recent debates over moral epistemology and normative uncertainty in an attempt to articulate and specify the moral demands on soldiers in warfare.

Walzer's project in *Just and Unjust Wars* was to articulate what he calls the war convention: "the set of articulated norms, customs, professional codes, legal precepts, religious and philosophical principles, and reciprocal arrangements that shape our judgments of military conduct."[1] Walzer's work alternates between descriptive and normative ethics as he strains to systematize and clarify the inherited work of medieval casuists and early modern philosophers such as Anselm, Grotius, and Suarez. Walzer took care to make sure that his theory maintained a recognizable continuity with those earlier scholars, and he has usually been loath to abandon their ideas altogether. While his project is laudable for attempting to unify ideas originating in disparate eras and traditions of the ethics of war, the new challenges from the revisionist school—with individual liability to harm as the driving force—seek to expose weaknesses in the center of his theory, and it may not hold.

The Bifurcation of War

The first foundational claim of Walzer's *Just and Unjust Wars* is the stark division of the moral evaluation of warfare into two categories: the justice of initiating war (*jus ad bellum*) and the justice of waging war (*jus in bello*). War is judged twice, Walzer says: first, whether it was just to initiate the war and, second, whether the war is being prosecuted with only just means of fighting. Whatever the causes of war—whatever the circumstances surrounding a war's declaration—the moral constraints on waging war and conduct within war are identical and equally binding for both sides. Once war is declared, Walzer contends, we find ourselves in a special moral context where normally heinous actions—namely, wholesale, organized, and usually impersonal killing—are morally permitted and equally permitted on both sides. The army on the side of justice cannot claim special moral permissions, even in pursuit of its objectively good cause. This leads Walzer to famously argue, for instance, that though Erwin Rommel deployed his masterful tactics in the service of unspeakable evil, he himself and

[1] Michael Walzer, *Just and Unjust Wars* (New York: Basic Books, 1977), 44.

his subordinates are faultless (at least on that count). Walzer's view is anticipated by Shakespeare, writing hundreds of years earlier:

> . . . we know
> enough, if we know we are the king's subjects: if
> his cause be wrong, our obedience to the king wipes
> the crime of it out of us.[2]

Walzer argues that, while at most one side of a war has a just cause for fighting, the individual combatants during warfare are morally equal: they have equivalent dignity and equal rights which demand respect and fair treatment. Soldiers waive their rights to life by making themselves dangerous to the other side; but this is something that both sides do equally, insofar as the property of soldiers *being dangerous* toward one another is symmetrical. Because all soldiers are collectively involved in the profession of fighting against one another, each is similarly trained and equipped to do harm to the other side, and each is actively trying to do so, they are united in a common moral status. Despite the fact that many soldiers may be misled, coerced, drafted, or impressed into service, all of them are justly endangered because they have made themselves dangerous. Or so says the Walzerian tradition.

Justification and Liability

This notion that all soldiers share a similar moral status across both sides of a conflict is the second foundational claim of Walzer's just war theory. It is commonly known as the *moral equality of combatants* thesis, and it flows directly from his bifurcated view of war into distinct *jus ad bellum* and *jus in bello* spheres. Walzer's view is more permissive than the contrasting revisionist view in that even soldiers on the unjust side of a conflict are morally justified in fighting—this is to say, they do not wrong enemy soldiers when they kill them, even in the service of an unjust cause and even when they kill opposing soldiers who have only served on behalf of a just cause.[3] We may find this view sympathetic since we think it is inappropriate or crass to criticize the common soldiers fighting in a war they

[2] William Shakespeare, *King Henry V*, edited by John Henry Walter (London: Routledge, 1995), Bates in act IV, scene 1.

[3] Of course, it is not sufficient for being justified that one's action wrongs no one. (The Non-Identity Problem shows us that.) But we should also note that in war it can be wrong to fight for unjust goals even if one does not wrong the soldiers one kills. One may instead wrong those whom the soldiers might have protected. Our thanks to Jeff McMahan for this point.

had no part in initiating. The pervasive view for centuries has been that "theirs [is] not to reason why" a conflict is being waged and, for that matter, whether it is just.[4] Combine this with other social or economic pressures on soldiers and sophisticated domestic propaganda campaigns that frequently attend wars and it seems increasingly problematic to lay any blame at the feet of individual soldiers.

A distinction is useful here between *excuse* and *justification*. To say an act is justified is to say that it is morally permissible, that it is impervious to moral criticism, or that no one is wronged by it. We may think some acts, however, are unjustified and yet still *blameless*—for example, because the actor in question has a good excuse. Walzer's view does not make this claim about soldiers. Rather, the Walzerian-traditionalist view contends that soldiers on either side of a war are acting in ways that are justified, even if their cause is unjust. (This is only the case as long as they are obeying the rules of war and are not, for example, committing wanton crimes against humanity in the course of their service.) That is, their *mere participation* in an unjust war is not enough to implicate them in the injustice of the war itself. This is what is meant by the moral equality of combatants thesis. For Walzer, soldiers on both the just and unjust sides of a conflict are equally liable to be harmed and likewise equally justified in exercising their mutual rights of self-defense. Indeed, while there may be a moral asymmetry at the macro-level between states, on the micro-level, according to Walzer, the common soldiers on either side of the conflict share the same moral status based upon a mutual recognition that they are both equally "poor sods . . . trapped in a war they did not make."[5]

There is another possible view, adopted by some in the revisionist camp, which is that some soldiers' actions are objectively unjustified—such as those soldiers fighting for an unjust cause—but that the soldiers themselves are excused on account of the epistemic burdens or social pressures that have been

[4] The quotation is a nod to Tennyson's "Charge of the Light Brigade," in particular the second stanza:

> "Forward, the Light Brigade!"
> Was there a man dismayed?
> Not though the soldier knew
> Someone had blundered.
> Theirs not to make reply,
> Theirs not to reason why,
> Theirs but to do and die.
> Into the valley of Death
> Rode the six hundred.

Alfred Tennyson, *The Complete Poetical Works of Alfred Lord Tennyson, Poet Laureate,* edited by Anne Thackeray Ritchie (Troy, NY: H.B. Nims, 1885).

[5] Walzer, *Just and Unjust Wars,* 36–41 (quote 36).

mentioned. The crux of this disagreement is whether the usual actions of soldiers in war (such as killing other soldiers) are open to moral criticism in the first place. We can separate this question from the matter of how we ought to feel toward the soldiers themselves and whether they ought to be punished for their mere participation in an unjust war. Sometimes, out of an excess of psychological pressure, confusion, or cultural expectations, we are morally excused, even when performing actions that wrong others—actions we should not perform. The same may be true of soldiers fighting for an unjust cause.

However, once we head down this road we quickly depart from Walzerian orthodoxy. For now the focus is on the individual liability of the soldiers themselves, rather than a blanket equal liability applied to all combatants on both sides of a conflict. Such a focus is sensitive to the individual conditions of each soldier and attempts to take their moral rights as individuals seriously. Once the individual liability of soldiers becomes the focus of our investigation—once we ask *who should die* and ask that question in a meaningful way apart from mere participation in a war, regardless of the justice of the cause one serves—the moral equality of combatants thesis must be left behind. And this is precisely what the revisionist school does.[6]

For revisionists, many soldiers' actions are morally impermissible in virtue of their contribution to an unjust cause, and soldiers in battle are not equally liable to harm. Soldiers may be ex ante excused because the moral reasons that bear on the justice of a war are inaccessible to the average soldier, or if they are accessible, the epistemic cost of scrutinizing them is unreasonably burdensome. Or others may contend that some other excuse applies against a soldier's blameworthiness, such as coercion. In any case, the act of contributing to an unjust cause itself will remain. Since the unjust cause in question is the waging of an unjust war—and thereby killing people—a soldier's liability to defensive harm, in order to prevent the unjust action, quickly follows.

A standard definition of *liability to harm* would be helpful here. To say that a person is *liable to harm* means that the person is *not wronged* when he or she is harmed. If a person is liable to defensive harm in particular, then typically the person in question is in some way contributing to or carrying out an unjust, wrongful threat of harm to others *and* harming the person is both necessary and proportionate to stop that threat of wrongful harm. In such a case, if a person is liable to be harmed, harming that person is justified in order to prevent the

[6] It is important to note here that many philosophers think that a rejection of the moral equality of combatants will entail a rejection of the moral distinction between combatants and noncombatants as well. Such an entailment, however, is controversial as several philosophers have tried to preserve the distinction based upon other moral considerations such as associative duties to fellow citizens, causal proximity to violence, and one's position within social institutions.

unjust harm he or she poses. For example, if a man charges into a grocery store with a gun and begins unjustly shooting people at random, he would be liable to defensive harm. Imagine that a nearby police officer could pull out a gun and shoot the man as a necessary and proportionate means to stop his unjust harm to nonliable people. The police officer in such a case would be acting wholly justifiably—that is, harming a person who is liable to harm. The harm itself would be both instrumentally necessary to stopping the unjust threat of harm and proportionate to the wrong to be stopped, given that the shooter was posing a lethal threat to innocents.

It is important here to point out that the question of liability is critically different from the question of desert. To call someone liable to harm is to say that you do not *wrong* that person when he or she is harmed; that is, there is some objective justification for harming him or her. It may still be regrettable that the person is harmed, however. To say a person *deserves* to be harmed is a much stronger claim. That claim, depending on one's account of justice, could very well generate *a reason in favor* of harming that person. Many believe that it is good when people *get what they deserve*, even if what they deserve is to be harmed. (This explanation is often invoked in defense of the practice of punishment, for example.) However, it is not good, in itself, when people are treated in ways that they are *liable* to be treated. Regardless, to say that one is liable to harm is not to say that one deserves to be harmed. Liability is importantly instrumental in this way: one is only liable to defensive harm as it directly connects to the wrongdoing the defensive harm is meant to thwart. For example, one might be liable to harm in the moment when one is committing a crime and the crime could be stopped by force, but later, when such a person no longer poses a wrongful threat, that person would not be liable to such *defensive* harm, even though he or she may very well still be deserving of punishment.

This discussion leads us directly into the question of soldiers' liability to harm: what are the reasons that justify the use of potentially lethal force by one soldier against another soldier? For Walzer, the answer to this question was simple. Mere participation in a war makes one liable to lethal force solely in virtue of the threat one poses as a combatant. For McMahan, Fabre, Rodin, and their intellectual comrades in the revisionist school, this view can seem absurd—its justifications either implausible or resting on some mysterious metaphysics of morals. As McMahan remarks, once we expose these claims to the light of day, they can seem "obviously absurd."[7] Mere participation in the use of force cannot be enough to make one liable to harm, the revisionists demand. For if it was, every time force was *justly* used, that just party would become liable to

[7] Jeff McMahan, *Killing in War* (Oxford: Oxford University Press, 2009), vii.

harm as well. This would mean that every time a police officer, for example, used force to stop a violent criminal, the police officer would become liable to defensive harm from the criminal. But surely, the revisionist school cries out, that is preposterous.

Is War a Special Moral Context?

These "domestic" analogies (e.g., involving police and criminals) are a common resort of revisionists. But if war is a different kind of moral context from "everyday life," then within war liability to harm might function differently, and these analogies would not be helpful. Walzer's moral equality of combatants thesis seems to demand this. But for revisionists, the justifications for harming others are identical inside and outside of war, and special permissions are not bestowed simply on account of a person's membership in an army. It may strike them as ludicrous that an Allied soldier and a Nazi soldier are in identical moral positions when they kill an enemy and that neither of them does something wrong.

Normally, there are very few circumstances that make a person liable to harm; the most obvious of these is engaging in an unjust attack. The attacker's wrongful attack makes him or her liable to harm in order to stop the wrongful attack. If we apply this directly to war, the liability of normal soldiers to harm becomes complicated. Are only soldiers who are engaged in wrongful attacking liable to harm? And just how do we define a wrongful attack by a soldier in war? One answer seems natural: those soldiers waging war on behalf of an unjust cause are liable to be killed in order to thwart that unjust cause. But those soldiers fighting for a just cause, perhaps defending innocent people against aggression, are no more liable to harm than the police officer trying to stop the violent criminal. The most obvious and troubling result of this, if revisionists are right, is that a great deal of the killing that takes place in warfare, even the killing of combatants, is wrongful killing. Worse still, even much of the killing carried out by the just warriors (those soldiers fighting for a just cause), will end up being wrongful killing since many combatants on the unjust side do not actually contribute toward an unjust cause in any concrete way or are not immediately threatening soldiers on the just side when they are killed. That is to say that most warfare might well be nothing more than highly organized large-scale murder, with relatively few instances of harm to people who are actually liable. Still, if liability is to be taken seriously—if the question of *who should die* is given its due—the Walzerian claim that all soldiers in war are equally liable must be rejected, or so argue the revisionists.

Philosophers who follow Walzer have not been standing still while these criticisms against their view have unfurled. The talented heirs of Walzer's "traditionalist" view include Michael Skerker, Yitzhak Benbaji, and Daniel Statman, whose influential writings have buttressed Walzer's theory against revisionist challenges. One traditionalist response to criticisms of the moral equality of combatants and the bifurcation of war is to vest *institutions* with special moral status, rather than war itself. Institutions with morally justified purposes, they argue, may need to extend extraordinary moral permissions to their members in order to function efficiently and carry out just projects. Juries are a clear case of this: the members of a jury constitute a body that is endowed with novel permissions that no particular individual member has, nor does any random group of twelve individuals have, outside of their special institutional role. We extend these permissions to jurors because it is necessary for a larger institution, the justice system, to effectively pursue its just aims. Armies are perhaps the epitome of an institution that must extend special moral permissions to its constituents in order to efficiently serve its just purpose. If this is correct, then Walzer's view is vindicated, and soldiers on both sides of a war enjoy special moral permissions in virtue of their participation in institutions that are constituted for a just purpose.

This collection of essays continues to press this debate forward. The chapters contained within develop and explore many of the important threads that have come out of the question of *who should die* and initiate several new threads that must be resolved. Our hope is that this volume will contribute toward this important body of work that has unfolded over the past decade on the ethics of war.

In Chapter 1, "Liability to Deadly Force in War," Leonard Kahn observes that both conventionalists and anticonventionalists (or revisionists) rely heavily on rights in formulating their theories—witness several of the authors in this volume. Kahn criticizes both sides for trading on a theory of rights that is absolute and ignoring the possibility that some conditions might exist in war that defeat otherwise very strong rights. Even those who view rights as "trumps" accept that some outcomes are sufficiently morally significant to override the constraints that rights usually place on us. Once we move from absolute rights to defeasible rights, the door is opened to understand liability to killing through a new theory of prima facie duties. Kahn concludes by discussing the virtues of this theory, which he calls "minimal Rossianism"—namely, that it provides a "richer and more nuanced" picture of liability to deadly force.

In Chapter 2, "*Pre-emptive Rules and the Scope of Defensive Rights*," Yitzhak Benbaji defends a new theory of defensive harm, in which a victim is permitted to kill an innocent threat, if this is necessary for her survival. The theory confronts and resolves a so-called innocent threat paradoxes in a novel way: Benbaji suggests that both parties would have a right to *kill one another,* under certan epistemic conditions, when neither knows the liability of the other—even stronger, both may *in fact* be innocent. In these dire situations, we might not even be *obligated to investigate* the liability of our attackers to harm: we have a wide moral berth when defending our own lives.

In Chapter 3, "Do Some Soldiers Deserve to Die More Than Others? Selective Conscientious Objectors and Liability," David Whetham explores the ethical implication of selective conscientious objection. While many states recognize the rights of committed pacifists to refuse to fight, very few states are willing to allow their soldiers to refuse to fight if it is a *particular* conflict which they consider to be unjust. However, over the past ten years, this position has been increasingly challenged. Whetham explores the way that three different Western militaries currently deal with soldiers who refuse on ethical grounds to participate in a specific conflict in order to answer the question *Do soldiers from some states deserve to die more than others if those states fight unjust wars?*

In Chapter 4, "Defensive Liability: Four Common Mistakes," Kai Draper points out several conceptual mistakes being made in contemporary just war dialogues. One of these mistakes concerns a failure to understand the relationship between rights and liability. A second mistake concerns writers mischaracterizing the sort of responsibility that can generate liability while others overlook the relevance of comparative responsibility to the question of whether liability exists. The final group of mistakes is a product of the common assumption that defensive liability can be generated only by an objective threat of harm. This assumption leads to a failure to appreciate the role that risk must play in an adequate account of defensive liability, for the sort of risk that is relevant to the question of defensive liability is relative to an epistemic situation and so inherently subjective.

In Chapter 5, "Fighting for One's Self," Michael Robillard investigates a peculiar dilemma arising from third-party interveners' competing duties both to respect authorization and to enforce conditions of necessity. Indeed, even in cases in which a third-party intervener could defend an agent from an unjust aggressor more effectively and less harmfully, Robillard argues that there is still good reason (within limits) for third-party interveners to refrain from enforcing necessity and allowing or even encouraging agents to fight for themselves. Borrowing from Statman and Frowe, he argues that "defense of one's honor" can serve as an independent moral reason justifying one's use of defensive force, even in cases where conditions of necessity appear not to be met.

In Chapter 6, "An Axiomatic Theory of Just War: Forfeiture Theory," Stephen Kershnar provides a rights-forfeiture explanation for when a war is just and when it is morally permissible to kill. Except in the case where killing is necessary to avoid a catastrophe, argues Kershnar, only those who forfeit their rights are liable to be killed in wartime. Hence, at the heart of the theory is an account of when people forfeit their rights in general and in the particular context of wartime. This theory also has implications for which, if any, of the commonly cited restrictions on wartime killing (imminence, necessity, proportionality, and discrimination) are relevant.

In Chapter 7, "Dignity, Self-Respect, and Bloodless Invasions," Saba Bazargan asks *How much violence can we impose on those attempting to politically subjugate us?* According to Bazargan, "reductive individualism" answers this question by determining how much violence one can impose on an individual wrongly attempting to prevent one from political participation. Some have argued that the amount of violence one can permissibly impose in such situations is decidedly sublethal. Accordingly, this counterintuitive response has cast doubt on the reductive individualist project. Bazargan argues, however, that political subjugation involves an institutionally embodied form of disrespect that has been altogether missed. A proper appreciation of this sort of disrespect, he contends, morally permits much greater defensive violence against those attempting to politically subjugate us or others.

In Chapter 8, "What Is the Moral Problem with Killer Robots?," Susanne Burri focuses on the question of whether lethal autonomous robots are morally problematic *in principle*. Bracketing downstream worries about the potential for abuse, Burri scrutinizes four separate arguments that such robots are pro tanto impermissible and argues that none of these arguments are ultimately convincing. Having responded to these four arguments, Burri then moves on to offer an explanation as to how our duty to protect our own soldiers speaks in favor of developing such autonomous technology further.

In Chapter 9, "Distributing Death in Humanitarian Interventions," Lars Christie challenges McMahan's distinction between the immunity of mere civilian bystanders and the immunity of civilian beneficiaries of a just intervention. McMahan argues that the requirement on soldiers to take on risk to minimize collateral harm is less demanding when the risk of harm is to beneficiaries rather than to bystanders. *Contra* McMahan, Christie argues that the prospective beneficiaries' self-interested reason to accept a great cost to be rescued from an injustice does not alter how much of the cost they ought to carry. He further challenges McMahan's definition of beneficiary civilians, and he offers an alternative view which distinguishes between an ideal distribution of harm and permissible deviation.

In Chapter 10, "Legalism, Justice, and the War on Terrorism," Lionel K. McPherson critiques traditional just war theory's expression in law. Particularly, he challenges the permissibility of "collaterally" harming noncombatants through attacks traditionally deemed militarily legitimate. Moreover, he argues that instances of political violence that fall within the limits of the law of war take inadequate account of harm to noncombatants. If combating terrorism is to have any realistic chance of success, he argues, then we must give up legalistic approaches to *jus in bello*. This means fighting to a higher standard with respect to Muslim noncombatant casualties, even when conventional doctrine of double effect criteria are met.

Whichever side prevails in these debates, the arguments in this emerging field have already provided much appreciated clarity and care to the debates over just war theory. Moreover, these debates have real, practical upshot for the militaries, political leaders, and policymakers of the world—as well as every individual caught in the horrors of war. The debate between the revisionists and traditionalists has direct implications for how militaries should educate their soldiers, how they should formulate rules of engagement, and how they should wage war itself, among others. And these debates are, in fact, having such an impact as just war theory is taught in military academies and training courses throughout much of the world.

All of these chapters, each in its own way, point us toward a clearer and more nuanced understanding of the fundamental conceptual underpinnings related to the ethics of killing and war. And with such clarity new questions likewise emerge as our philosophical horizons expand to regions yet uncharted.

This collection has been a long labor of love, and we are deeply indebted to all of our excellent contributors for their work on their respective chapters; they each have our warmest thanks. We were indeed fortunate to be able to draw together the impressive cadre of authors for this volume. We especially wish to thank Jeff McMahan and Cécile Fabre for their guidance and mentorship as well as for writing the foreword and postscript to this collection. We also extend our deepest gratitude to Lucy Randall, Hannah Doyle, and their team at Oxford University Press for their unending encouragement and help in making this edited volume possible. A special thanks is owed to Jordan Rowley for his swift and meticulous assistance with editing. We also thank our home academic institutions for their support of this project: the Naval Postgraduate School, California Polytechnic State University in San Luis Obispo, and the University of Connecticut. We are further indebted to the Stockholm Center for the Ethics of War and Peace. It was at the center's annual conference in 2014 in Stockholm that the vision for this book was first conceived. Related to that, we would also be remiss if we did not thank our colleague and friend Dr. Knute L. Amrisk for his tireless efforts and inspiration. Finally, we would like to thank our families for their support and love.

References

McMahan, Jeff. *Killing in War*. Oxford: Oxford University Press, 2009.

Shakespeare, William. *King Henry V*. Edited by John Henry Walter. London: Routledge, 1995.

Tennyson, Alfred. *The Complete Poetical Works of Alfred Lord Tennyson, Poet Laureate*. Edited by Anne Thackeray Ritchie. Troy, NY: H.B. Nims, 1885.

Walzer, Michael. *Just and Unjust Wars*. Basic Books: New York, 1977.

1

Liability to Deadly Force in War

LEONARD KAHN

> What is overcoming the enemy? Always simply the destruction of his military force, whether it be by death, or wounds, or any means; whether it be completely or only to such a degree that he can no longer continue the contest; therefore as long as we set aside all special objects of combats, we may look upon the complete or partial destruction of the enemy as the only object of all combats.
>
> —Carl von Clausewitz[1]

> Death has a tendency to encourage a depressing view of war.
>
> —Donald Rumsfeld[2]

It is killing and death that make war unique—and uniquely terrible. Only in war do we kill each other in such great numbers and with such little regard for what we have done. Only in war does death come so often and so early in life for so many. Staggering examples from the last century are easy to educe: nearly 20 million were killed in World War I, and more than 60 million were killed in its successor. Smaller wars within and between states killed millions in China, the Soviet Union, Korea, Vietnam, India, Pakistan, Ethiopia, Cambodia, Afghanistan, and Sudan, as well as hundreds of thousands elsewhere. While some optimists, such as Steven Pinker, think that our future will see less war than our past, they run the risk of sounding like the foolish Monsieur Rivet in Balzac's *Cousin Bette*:

> [You] do not understand the times we live in; we are no longer barbarians. War is coming to an end, my dear mademoiselle; it went out with

[1] Carl von Clausewitz, *On War*, trans. J. J. Graham, ed. Anatol Rapoport (London: Penguin, 1968), 304.

[2] Quoted in Roger Cohen, "Rumsfeld Is Correct—The Truth Will Get Out," *New York Times*, June 7, 2006, accessed March 16, 2016, http://www.nytimes.com/iht/2006/06/07/world/IHT-07globalist.html.

> the Monarchy. This is the age of triumph for commerce, and industry, and middle-class prudence, such as were the making of Holland.[3]

Rivet's prediction has turned out poorly, and I suspect that Pinker's will as well.[4]

Yet the ubiquity of killing in war does not demonstrate that all, or even most, killing is morally permissible—far from it. So it is imperative that we ask *Which attempts to kill in war are morally permissible, and which are not?* Let us make this question a little more precise by saying that an entity, X, is liable to the use of deadly force by an agent, Y, in circumstances, C, if and only if, in C, Y is morally justified in intentionally killing X. In other words, if X is liable to the use of deadly force by Y in C, then Y does not act morally wrongly by intentionally killing X in C.[5] Our question, then, is this: *Who is liable to deadly force in war?*

This chapter is a contribution to the resolution of this difficult question. In the first two sections, I compare and contrast the conventionalist and anticonventionalist answers. Then, I turn my attention to something that conventionalists and anticonventionalists have in common: a strong reliance on the idea of rights. I contend that this reliance on rights fails sufficiently to advance our understanding of liability to deadly force in war. Finally, I outline an alternate approach that focuses on prima facie duties, and I explore some of its implications, arguing that it provides a more nuanced and more discriminating, though less general, account of liability to deadly force.

The Conventional View

What I shall call the *conventional view* provides an expedient point of departure for determining who is liable to deadly force in war. This view, as its name suggests, has been the dominant position in thinking about the ethics of war since the time of Thomas Aquinas, though in recent times it is most closely associated with Michael Walzer. But in order to avoid unnecessary entanglement with the details of any one philosopher's particular interpretation of the

[3] Honoré de Balzac, *Cousin Bette*, trans. Sylvia Raphael (Oxford: Oxford University Press, 2008), 74.

[4] For critiques of Pinker, see Peter Singer, "Is Violence History?" *New York Times*, October 6, 2011; James Q. Wilson, "Burying the Hatchet," *Wall Street Journal*, July 16, 2011; and John Gray, "Steven Pinker Is Wrong about Violence and War," *Guardian*, March 13, 2015, accessed July 19, 2016, https://www.theguardian.com/books/2015/mar/13/john-gray-steven-pinker-wrong-violence-war-declining.

[5] Note that being liable to deadly force does not mean one can be intentionally killed *in any manner whatsoever*. That I am subject to deadly force does not entail that I can, for instance, be tortured to death or infected with a lethal bioagent. The permissibility of means of the use of deadly force is a topic worth serious thought, but it is not my concern here, so I shall set it aside for now.

conventional view, I shall refer to a generic advocate of the conventional view as *the conventionalist.*

The conventional view has three main parts. The first of these parts is the distinction between combatants and noncombatants. Combatants are, first and foremost, soldiers who, in Walzer's words, are "a class set apart from the world of peaceful activity; they are trained to fight, provided with weapons, [and] required to fight on command." In Walzer's view, "the enterprise of this class [is war], and this fact radically separates the individual soldier from the civilians he leaves behind."[6] Noncombatants, in contrast, are understood negatively as those who fail to meet the conditions of combatants. This class embraces civilians, of course, but also includes soldiers who are incapacitated by wounds or disease, soldiers who are prisoners of war, and those members of the military who are primarily medical or religious personnel.[7]

The second main part of the conventional answer is what I shall call the *noncombatant immunity thesis*. Briefly put, noncombatants are not liable to deadly force in war. "A legitimate act of war," Walzer tells us, is one that does not violate the rights of people against whom it is directed," and a noncombatant "retains his rights" to not have deadly force used against him (or her).[8] This right[9] to not be intentionally killed is quite important and plays a large role in this chapter. Hence, it will be useful to have a detailed outline of the conventionalist's argument for the noncombatant immunity thesis, which I provide below.

1. X has a right not to be killed intentionally, if he or she has done nothing to invalidate this right.
2. Noncombatants have done nothing in war to invalidate their right not to be killed intentionally.
3. So noncombatants have a right not to be killed intentionally in war.

[6] Michael Walzer, *Just and Unjust Wars: A Moral Argument with Historical Illustrations*, 4th ed. (New York: Basic Books, 1977), 144. Though I concentrate here on Walzer's thinking, the distinction between combatants and noncombatants goes back at least as far as the *Pax Dei* of 989 CE. The distinction was elaborated in the thirteenth century by Raymond of Peñafort and Thomas Aquinas, in the fourteenth century by Christine de Pizan, and in the fifteenth century by Thomas Cajetan and Francisco de Vitoria. It remains a central part of most thinking about the ethics of war today.

[7] On this point, see especially Articles 12-15, 24-25, and 29 of the 1949 Geneva Convention as well as Michael Byers, *War Law: Understanding International Law and Armed Conflict* (New York: Grove Press, 2005), 115–135.

[8] Walzer, *Just and Unjust Wars*, 135–136. This idea also has antique heritage and can be traced back to Thomas Aquinas and Francisco de Vitoria.

[9] I am concerned only with *moral* rights—as opposed to, say, *legal* rights—in this chapter, but I shall take that as understood in order to avoid needless repetition of the word "moral." The same is true, mutatis mutandis, for duties, obligations, etc.

4. If Y's doing F violates one of X's rights, then Y is not morally justified (i.e., is morally wrong) in doing F.
5. So if someone's action violates a noncombatant's right not to be killed intentionally in war, then he or she is not morally justified (i.e., is morally wrong) in doing this action.
6. X is liable to the use of deadly force by another agent, Y, if and only if Y is morally justified in intentionally killing X.
7. Therefore, noncombatants are not liable to the use of deadly force in war.[10]

Let us call the foregoing the *noncombatant immunity argument.*

However, it is a matter of no small importance that the noncombatant immunity thesis allows for situations in which noncombatants may be *un*intentionally killed, provided that certain conditions are met. These conditions are usually understood in terms of the doctrine of double effect. As a result, even though noncombatants are not liable to deadly force in war, they can be killed if the act of killing them (1) is not bad itself, (2) the direct effect of the action is morally acceptable, (3) the intention of the agent is good (and, therefore, not the death of noncombatants), and (4) the good effects of the action outweigh the bad.[11]

The third and final part of the conventional answer is what I call the *moral equality of combatants thesis*. According to this thesis, all combatants are liable to deadly force, provided that the use of force obeys a short set of principles that will be discussed. Speaking for individual combatants, Walzer says, "They can try to kill me, and I can try to kill them. But it is wrong to cut the throats of their wounded or shoot them down when they are trying to surrender . . . war is still, somehow, a rule-governed activity, a world of permissions and prohibitions—and moral world, therefore, in the midst of hell."[12]

[10] Based on Walzer, *Just and Unjust Wars*, 138–151, and Brian Orend, *The Morality of War* (Toronto, Canada: Broadview Press, 2006), 105–149.

[11] Thomas Aquinas is the doctrine of double effect's intellectual father, but Francisco de Vitoria, Francisco Suarez, and Hugo Grotius also invoked versions of it in discussions of the ethics of war. More recently, see G. E. M. Anscombe, "War and Murder," in *Nuclear Weapons: A Catholic Response*, edited by Walter Stein (London: Sheep & War, 1961), 44–52; Walzer, *Just and Unjust Wars*, 151–159; and Frances Kamm, *The Moral Target: Aiming at Right Conduct in War and Other Conflicts* (Oxford: Oxford University Press, 2012), 24–80. Though the doctrine of double effect was long associated with the Catholic Church, it has developed into an essentially secular theory; see Philippa Foot, "The Problem of Abortion and the Doctrine of Double Effect," in *Virtues and Vices*, ed. Philippa Foot (Oxford: Oxford University Press, 2002), 19–20. My goals in this chapter do not involve a deep discussion of the doctrine, so I mention it here largely for the sake of setting it aside.

[12] Walzer, *Just and Unjust Wars*, 36. The moral equality of soldiers can be traced back to the fifth century CE in Augustine of Hippo, "Letter 189, to Boniface," in *The Ethics of War: Classic and Contemporary Readings*, ed. Gregory M. Reichberg, Henrik Syse, and Endre Begby (London: Blackwell, 2007), 74–75.

Let me take a moment to sketch the principles that are meant to constrain the actions of combatants, that is, the principles of *jus in bello* (justice in war). Typically, these principles require that the uses of force by combatants be proportional, discriminant, and necessary. Roughly speaking, the use of force is proportional just in case it does no more damage than is necessary to achieve its aim. The use of force is discriminate if and only if it targets combatants only,[13] and it is necessary when it takes as its end what is militarily essential but not otherwise.[14] It should now be clear why Walzer's examples of shooting combatants who are attempting to surrender or cutting the throats of combatants who are asleep are cases of immoral action, even though they take place in war and are undertaken against enemy combatants. For both actions fail the tests of proportionality since surrendering or sleeping enemy combatants can be made prisoners of war rather than killed. The moral equality of soldiers thesis does, then, place limits on how combatants can behave toward one another within war. However, according to the conventionalist, these limits are symmetric; they are the same for *all* combatants.

Of course, many issues that are relevant to the subject of this collection arise with regard to the conventional view, including, but not limited to, the following: How should we understand the details of the distinction between combatants and noncombatants? Why is this distinction thought to have moral importance? Are conscripts any less deserving of moral protection than noncombatants, or are they morally on a par with other willing combatants? What are the conditions under which noncombatants can be unintentionally killed? Why should it make any moral difference whether a person is killed intentionally or unintentionally? What are the moral obligations of a combatant if those

[13] Clearly, the principle of discrimination's raison d'être is the protection of noncombatants. But somewhat surprisingly to me it appears that one could wrong a combatant by violating it as well. Suppose that Hector and Achilles are both combatants. Hector wishes to kill Achilles, and he can do so in a way that does not violate either the principle of proportionality or the principle of necessity but only the principle of discrimination (since it would result in the death of ten noncombatants). If Hector successfully attacks Achilles, he wrongs not only the ten noncombatants that he kills but also Achilles, who would not otherwise have died. (I take it that this is true even if Achilles was using the noncombatants as human shields, though of course then Achilles would also be guilty of gross wrongdoing.)

[14] Concerns about proportionality and discrimination are given voice by Raymond of Peñafort and Thomas Aquinas as early as the thirteenth century. Concerns about necessity are a more modern phenomenon; for discussion see Walzer, *Just and Unjust Wars*, 144–149, and Kamm, *Moral Target*, 81–86. For recent discussion of these principles of *jus in bello*, see Nicholas Fotion, *War & Ethics: A New Just War Theory* (London: Continuum, 2007), 21–22, 36–39, and 115–121; Helen Frowe, *The Ethics of War and Peace: An Introduction* (London: Routledge, 2011), 82–83 and 103–112; and Steven P. Lee, *Ethics and War: An Introduction* (Cambridge: Cambridge University Press, 2012), 181–190 and 213–216.

attacking him or her violate the ethical principles that are supposed to constrain all of them? I touch on some of these issues in this chapter, but my concern with the moral equality of combatants is conceptually distinct from all of them.

The Anticonventionalist View

As we have seen, the conventionalist holds that noncombatants are not liable to the use of deadly force in war. But he or she also maintains that all combatants are liable to deadly force, so long as this force is constrained by the principles of *jus in bello*. Yet not everyone agrees with the conventionalist. Adherents of the *anticonventionalist view*, as I shall call it, accept the distinction between combatants and noncombatants as well as the immunity of noncombatants thesis but reject the moral equality of combatants thesis. The anticonventionalist view has had comparatively few adherents among war ethicists, but a remarkably diverse body of thinkers has captured its spirit. It is hard to imagine a more unlikely paring than Pascal and Voltaire. Yet it was Pascal who asked rhetorically, "Can anything be more ridiculous than that a man should have the right to kill me because he lives on the other side of the water, and because his ruler has a quarrel with mine, though I have none with him," while it was Voltaire who quipped that "It is forbidden to kill; therefore all murderers are punished unless they kill in large numbers and to the sound of trumpets."[15] The anticonventionalist's basic idea is clear enough: the mere fact that someone is a combatant in a war does not mean that the combatants whom he or she opposes become liable to deadly force against him or her. Something more than adherence to the principles of *jus in bello* is required to make it morally permissible to kill people, even if they too are combatants. And the mere fact that one is there on the orders of a king, a president, or a prime minister is not enough.

In order to get a deeper understanding of this basic idea, it will be useful to note that specialists in the ethics of war distinguish the principles of *jus ad bellum* (justice toward war) from the principles of *jus in bello*, discussed in the previous section. A state goes to war justly when and only when it adheres to all of the principles of *jus ad bellum*. While the details of these principles are beyond the reach of this chapter, suffice it to say that a state goes to war justly only if it does so in response to illegitimate aggression (just cause condition), with the intention to rectify this aggression (just intent condition), with a reasonable chance of doing so (reasonable chance of success condition), in a manner that is

[15] Blaise Pascal, *Pensées*, trans. A. J. Krailsheimer (London: Penguin, 1995), 16; Francois Voltaire, *Philosophical Dictionary*, trans. Theodore Besterman (London: Penguin, 1984), 322.

constrained by a concern to minimize harm (macro proportionality condition), and only as a last resort (last resort condition) and after war has been publically declared (public declaration condition) by a political body with the authority to do so (legitimate authority condition).[16]

For my purposes, what is vital to note is that according to the conventional view the question of whether or not one's state has gone to war justly plays no substantial role in determining whether a particular combatant is liable to deadly force in war. For example, according to the conventionalist, Hector, who is a combatant, is liable to the use of deadly force by an opposing combatant, Achilles, just in case Achilles's actions toward Hector do not transgress against the principles of proportionality, discrimination, and necessity. The question of whether Achilles's state has begun the war with Hector's state, for example, by aggressing against it unjustly—say, invading it without provocation—does not in any way place moral limits of Achilles's actions toward Hector, according to the moral equality of combatants thesis.

However matters might have seemed to Homer's audience, the moral equality of combatants thesis does seem deeply counterintuitive to some. It is not just that Greater Germany acted unjustly when it invaded Poland in 1938; its soldiers acted wrongly as well. The same seems true of imperial Japan and the members of its military in Manchuria in 1931 and in any number of similar wars. That, at any rate, is the reaction of anticonventionalists in the tradition of Pascal and Voltaire.

Nevertheless, it is not enough for an anticonventionalist to point out the counterintuitive results of the moral equality of combatants thesis. What is required is an *argument* against it. And, oddly enough, it is the conventionalist who provides the template for it with the argument for noncombatant immunity, discussed in the previous section. First, a terminological note: Let us call *just combatants* those combatants of a state that goes to war without violating the principles of *jus ad bellum*, and let us call *unjust combatants* the combatants of a state that goes to war while violating the principles of *jus ad bellum*. We can now outline the modification to the argument for noncombatant immunity as follows.

1. X has a right not to be killed intentionally, if he or she has done nothing to invalidate this right.
2. *Just combatants* have done nothing in war to invalidate the right not to be killed intentionally.
3. So *just combatants* have a right not to be killed intentionally in war.

[16] Lists like these are common enough, but see Martin L. Cook, *The Moral Warrior: Ethics and Service in the US Military* (Albany: State University of New York Press, 2004), 28; and J. Carl Ficarrotta, *Kantian Thinking about Military Ethics* (Burlington, VT: Ashgate, 2010), 108.

4. If Y's doing F violates one of X's rights, then Y is not morally justified (i.e., is morally wrong) in doing F.
5. So if someone's action violates a *just combatant's* right not to be killed intentionally in war, then he or she is not morally justified (i.e., is morally wrong) in doing this action.
6. X is liable to the use of deadly force by another agent, Y, if and only if Y is morally justified in intentionally killing X.
7. Therefore, *just combatants* are not liable to the use of deadly force in war.[17]

Call this the *argument for just combatant immunity*. It is worth pointing out in passing that anticonventionalists need not in any way reject the principles of *jus in bello* as restraints on the use of deadly force. Nothing about accepting the argument for just combatant immunity requires an anticonventionalist to embrace the idea that just combatants are free to use whatever means they deem necessary to wage war.[18] On the contrary, the anticonventionalist's point is simply that an unjust combatant acts wrongly even if he or she manages to act within the principles of *jus in bello* when attacking a just combatant.

Simply by substituting "just combatants" for "noncombatants," the anticonventionalist puts the conventionalist in a difficult position. The conventionalist cannot accept the conclusion of the argument for just combatant immunity since it makes the principles of *jus ad bellum* relevant to the matter of whether combatants are liable to deadly force in war, and, therefore, it is inconsistent with the moral equality of combatants thesis. So the conventionalist must find some grounds for showing that the argument for just combatant immunity is unsound. However, the argument for just combatant immunity shares its logical form as well as three of its six premises with the argument for noncombatant immunity. As a result, the conventionalist must choose between two disagreeable options. The first of these options is to show that there are good

[17] Based on Jeff McMahan, *Killing in War* (Oxford: Oxford University Press, 2009), 38–51. I have italicized the modifications to the argument for noncombatant immunity in order to emphasize how minor they are. McMahan's ultimate position is shrewder and subtler than the argument of his that I am adapting would suggest. I am oversimplifying somewhat in order to clarify the broad contours of the debate over liability to deadly force.

[18] One possible exception to this idea is the doctrine of supreme emergency, which permits just combatants to set aside the principles of *jus in bello* but only when doing so is the only way to avoid a widespread and serious violation of rights. But the doctrine of supreme emergency is highly controversial, and those who cast a sympathetic look in its direction tend to be conventionalists such as Walzer, *Just and Unjust Wars*, 245–274, and Orend, *Morality of War*, 140–159. Hence, anticonventionalists are unlikely to find common cause here.

grounds for rejecting premise 2, 3, or 5 of the argument for just combatant immunity that are not also good grounds for rejecting these premises in the argument for noncombatant immunity. Indeed, since premises 3 and 5 appear to follow directly from the conjunction of premise 2 and premises 1 and 4 that the argument for noncombatant immunity takes for granted, premise 2 is the only acceptable target for the conventionalist. The second option is to reject both the argument for noncombatant immunity and the argument for just combatant immunity and find some other basis for claiming that noncombatants are not liable to deadly force, a basis which does not also show that just combatants are not liable.

But the heart of the controversy between the conventionalist and the anticonventionalist is what we can call *the equivalence conditional*: if noncombatants have done nothing in war to invalidate the right not to be killed intentionally, then just combatants have done nothing in war to invalidate the right not to be killed intentionally. If the conventionalist can show that the equivalence conditional is false, then the anticonventionalist will lack a leg to stand on, and the moral equality of combatants thesis seems safe. Contrariwise, if the anticonventionalist can show that the equivalence conditional is true, then the conventionalist will be decisively on the defensive, and the moral equality of combatants will be vulnerable. It is with a smile, however, that we excuse ourselves from considering the truth or falsity of the equivalence conditional. We are hunting bigger game.

Ex Ante Rights Versus Ex Post Rights

What I wish to argue is that both the noncombatant immunity argument and the just combatant immunity argument are invalid and, therefore, unsound. The problem, to put it briefly, is that both of these arguments trade on an equivocation concerning the word *right*. Of course, no one will deny that the word *right* is subject to many interpretations, and attempting to present a full taxonomy of rights would likely be a full-time occupation. But my concern here is with a single critical distinction. I shall say that X has an ex ante right not to have F done to him or her by Y if and only if were Y to do F to X it would provide us with a prima facie (or contributory) reason to believe that Y had acted wrongly by violating X's claim not to have Y do F. And let us further say that X has an ex post right not to have F done to him or her by Y if and only if were Y to do F to X this would provide us with an ultima facie (or decisive) reason to believe that Y had acted wrongly by violating X's claim not to have Y do F. It should be clear that if X has an ex post right, then he or she also has a corresponding ex ante right since every ultima facie reason to believe that P is also a prima facie reason (undefeated).

However, the converse is not true. If X has an ex ante right, it does not follow that he or she has a corresponding ex post right.[19]

Since this distinction is rather abstract, let me illustrate it with what I admit is a rather hackneyed example. Suppose that Achilles has borrowed $100 from Odysseus on condition that he repay Odysseus by the end of the year. Clearly, if Achilles were to fail to repay Odysseus by the end of the year, then that fact would provide us with a prima facie reason to believe that Achilles has acted wrongly by violating Odysseus's claim not to have Achilles fail to repay the loan by the end of year. Hence, Odysseus has an ex ante right to be repaid by Achilles. But it does not follow, as we have just seen, that Odysseus has an ex post right to be repaid by Achilles. For our reason to believe that Achilles has acted wrongly by violating Odysseus's claim not to have Achilles fail to repay the loan by the end of year is only a prima facie reason, not an ultima facie reason. This prima facie reason might be defeated by further considerations, such as that Odysseus tricked or coerced Achilles into taking this loan from him. Or it might be defeated by the fact that Achilles did not repay the loan by the end of the year because he had died or because Odysseus had vanished and could not be repaid, or any number of other possibilities. What is vital here is that we cannot simply move from having a prima facie right to having an ultima facie right. This movement is possible only if there are no defeater conditions in place.

Now return to the first five premises of the noncombatant immunity argument.

1. X has a right not to be killed intentionally, if he or she has done nothing to invalidate this right.
2. Noncombatants have, ipso facto, done nothing in war to invalidate the right not to be killed intentionally.
3. So noncombatants have a right not to be killed intentionally in war.
4. If Y's doing F violates one of X's rights, then Y is not morally justified (i.e., is morally wrong) in doing F.
5. So if someone's action violates a noncombatant's right not to be killed intentionally in war, then he or she is not morally justified (i.e., is morally wrong) in doing this action.

[19] On the prima facie/ultima facie distinction see John R. Searle, "Prima Facie Reasons," in *Philosophical Subjects: Essays Presented to P. F. Strawson*, ed. Z. van Straaten (Oxford: Oxford University Press, 1980), 238–259; and Thomas D. Senor, "The Prima/Ultima Facie Justification Distinction in Epistemology," *Philosophy and Phenomenological Research* 56, no. 3 (1996): 551–553. I am especially keen to avoid characterizing the distinction among rights that I have in mind in terms of prima facie and ultima facie rights since I think that the difference here is merely epistemic. However, duties are another matter. See the discussion of prima facie duties later in this chapter, under "Prima Facie Duties and Liability to Deadly Force in War."

Begin by noting that premise 4 makes the connection between an act's being a violation of a right and an act's being morally wrong. This connection holds only if we understand the right in question as an ex post right, not as an ex ante right. As we have said, there are any number of ways in which Achilles might violate Odysseus's ex ante right to be paid back for his loan without thereby acting wrongly. Moreover, the truth of premise 5 relies on the same interpretation of "right" as meaning ex post right.

But now turn to premise 1. This premise is plausible only if it is understood as the view that everyone has an ex ante right not to be killed intentionally; that is, there is prima facie reason to believe that anyone has acted wrongly by violating anyone else's claim not to be killed intentionally. But premise 1 is highly dubious if it is understood as the view that everyone has an ex post right not to be killed intentionally unless he or she has done something to invalidate this right. For that would entail that one would act in a manner that is morally wrong by intentionally killing such an individual regardless of the circumstances.

There are at least two good reasons for thinking that it is false that all of us have an ex post right not to be killed intentionally. The first of these concerns conflicts of rights.[20] Achilles might have to choose between intentionally killing Hector or intentionally killing Odysseus, where neither Hector nor Odysseus has done anything to invalidate his right not to be intentionally killed. If we understand the right in question to be ex post rather than ex ante, then we are forced to say that Achilles would act morally wrongly no matter what he did. Barring a rejection of the "ought" implies "can" principle and an embrace of the idea of so-called tragic dilemmas,[21] that seems far-fetched; it seems highly unlikely that anyone who wanted to defend the noncombatant immunity argument from the charge of equivocation would want to go this far.

The second good reason for thinking that it is false that all of us have an ex post right not to be killed intentionally concerns the causal consequences of our actions. Talk of rights as "trumps"[22] has rhetorical value. Indeed, even utilitarians occasionally take advantage of it. After all, it was John Stuart Mill, not Robert Nozick or Ronald Dworkin, who wrote "If all mankind minus one, were of one opinion, and only one person were of the contrary opinion, mankind would be no more justified in silencing that one person, than he, if he had the

[20] Jeremy Waldron, "Rights in Conflict," *Ethics* 99, no. 3 (1989): 503–519; and Frances Kamm, *Intricate Ethics: Rights, Responsibilities, and Permissible Harms* (Oxford: Oxford University Press, 2007), 285–304.

[21] Ruth Barcan Marcus, "Moral Dilemmas and Consistency," *Journal of Philosophy* 77 (1980): 121–136.

[22] Ronald Dworkin, *Taking Rights Seriously* (Cambridge, MA: Harvard University Press, 1977), 153.

power, would be justified in silencing mankind."[23] But even advocates and allies of talk of rights as trumps admit that "tradeoffs of some claims on the one hand for increments of good, or anyway increments of advantage, on the other, *are* permissible."[24] And this is surely the case here too. Our ex ante right not to be killed intentionally should be taken seriously, but there are situations in which we must make trade-offs; and if the good to be attained is sufficiently great or, more importantly perhaps, the evil to be avoided is sufficiently appalling, then it is not morally wrong to intentionally kill someone. Hence, premise 1 is true only if we read "right" as an ex ante, not an ex post, right.

Similar considerations can be mustered in favor of understanding "right" in premise 2 and 3 as an ex ante rather than an ex post right. While noncombatants have, more or less by definition, done nothing in war to lose their right not to be killed intentionally, this right is ex ante for the same reasons that the general right not to be killed intentionally is an ex ante right. Moreover, premise 3 follows directly from premises 1 and 2. Since the only rights denoted in premises 1 and 2 are, as we have seen, ex ante rights, the right denoted in premise 3 must be ex ante as well.

Thus, the move in premises 1, 2, and 3 from an ex ante right not to be killed intentionally to, in premises 4 and 5, an ex post right not to be killed intentionally is illegitimate. The conjunction of the proposition that noncombatants have an ex ante right not to be killed in war (premise 3) and the proposition that if one's doing an action violates someone's ex post right, then one is not morally justified in doing this action (premise 4) does not entail if someone's action violates a noncombatant's right not to be killed intentionally in war, then he or she is not morally justified in doing this action (premise 5), as the noncombatant immunity argument requires if it is to be sound.

I will not belabor the details of the similar equivocation in the just combatant immunity argument. It was one of the advantages of the anticonventionalist's approach that he or she was able to help himself or herself to an argument for just combatant immunity that shared its logical form and most of its premises with the conventionalist's argument for noncombatant immunity. For, by doing so, he or she made it difficult for the conventionalist to refute the just combatant immunity argument without compromising his or her own position. But this

[23] John Stuart Mill, *On Liberty*, ed. Leonard Kahn (Toronto, Canada: Broadview Press, 2014), 59.

[24] Judith Jarvis Thomson, *The Realm of Rights* (Cambridge, MA: Harvard University Press, 1990) 174, italics in original. See also Thomas E. Hill, *Human Welfare and Moral Worth: Kantian Perspectives* (Oxford: Oxford University Press, 2002), 362–402. Among nonconsequentialists, Anscombe stands out for her unwillingness to take the consequences of actions seriously in situations where intentional killing of noncombatants is involved; G. E. M. Anscombe, "Modern Moral Philosophy," *Philosophy* 33, no. 124 (1958): 1–19.

stroke of genius has a downside. Since the argument for just combatant immunity and the argument for noncombatant immunity share a logical form, if one is invalid, then the other is as well—and for the same reasons.

Neither conventionalists nor anticonventionalists will be happy with my criticism of the noncombatant immunity argument, and anticonventionalists will also be displeased with my analysis of the just combatant immunity argument. One obvious response to learning that one has an invalid argument on one's hands is to tweak the logical form of the argument. Both the noncombatant immunity argument and the just combatant immunity argument are invalid because they move without justification from claims about ex ante to claims about ex post rights. But in principle it would be possible to try to modify either or both arguments in such a way that the move from ex ante rights to ex post rights was justified. In particular, one would need to show that there are no defeater conditions for the ex ante right in question. However, my primary purpose here has not been to show that either conventionalism or anticonventionalism can be vanquished with a single blow. Even badly thought-out philosophical positions are usually more resilient than that. Rather, my main aim is to make enough imaginative space to situate a rather different approach to the question of liability to deadly force in war, an approach to which I turn in the next section.

Prima Facie Duties and Liability to Deadly Force in War

Though the inspiration for this approach is W. D. Ross' theory of prima facie duties, I shall be selective about the elements of Ross's thinking that I appropriate, focusing on three main ideas. First, moral agents have a set of standing duties, each of which provides strong but not necessarily decisive reasons for action. Second, these duties can conflict with one another, and there is not ordering by which certain types of duties always defeat other types of duties. Indeed, it is only the presence of one duty that can defeat another, when it comes to determining what one is required to do, that is, what we have an ultima facie duty to do. Third, a list of these duties includes[25] the following:

- Duties of fidelity, which include duties to keep one's promises and duties not to lie

[25] W. D. Ross, *The Right and the Good* (Oxford: Oxford University Press, 1930), 16–47. Ross stresses that the duties on this list are subject to different descriptions that would change the number of duties and that this list might not be complete (p. 20). But it is as close to complete as it needs to be for the purposes of this discussion.

- Duties of reparation, which include duties to repair, to the extent possible, the bad consequences and/or the wrongfulness of one's actions
- Duties of gratitude, which include duties to return good to those who have benefited one in the past
- Duties of justice, which include duties to ensure a fair distribution of benefits and burdens
- Duties of beneficence, which include duties to improve others
- Duties of self-improvement, which include duties to improve oneself
- Duties of nonmaleficence, which include duties not to harm others

For the sake of convenience, I shall refer to someone who takes as a starting point these three aspects of Ross's theory of prima facie duties as a *minimal Rossian*. There are other aspects of Ross's theory of prima facie duties about which I remain neutral in this chapter. The most important of these are Ross's claim that our knowledge of these duties is self-evident and that these duties neither have nor need any deeper justification than themselves.[26] However, these features of Ross's theory play no role in my discussion of liability to deadly force in war, and the minimal Rossian is not committed to them, even if he or she is ultimately on the hook to provide a credible moral epistemology and normative foundations at some point.

How, then, does minimal Rossianism differ from the conventionalist and anticonventionalist views? It would be best for me to adumbrate a bit before diving into the details. Though minimal Rossians reject the noncombatant immunity thesis, they provide reason to think that noncombatants are *almost*

[26] On the self-evidence (or not) of prima facie duties, see Jonathan Dancy, "Intuitionism," in *A Companion to Ethics*, ed. Peter Singer (Oxford: Blackwell, 1990a), 411–420; Thomas Baldwin, "The Three Phases of Intuitionism," in *Ethical Intuitionism: Reevaluations*, ed. Philip Stratton-Lake (Oxford: Oxford University Press, 2002.), 92–112; Roger Crisp, "Sidgwick and the Boundaries of Intuitionism," in *Ethical Intuitionism: Reevaluations*, ed. Philip Stratton-Lake (Oxford: Oxford University Press, 2002), 56–75; Robert Audi, *The Good in the Right: A Theory of Intuition and Intrinsic Value* (Princeton, NJ: Princeton University Press, 2007), 40–79; and Thomas Hurka, *British Ethical Theorists from Sidgwick to Ewing* (Oxford: Oxford University Press, 2014), 108–127). On the underivative nature (or not) of prima facie duties, see Jonathan Dancy, "An Ethic of *Prima Facie* Duties," in *A Companion to Ethics*, ed. Peter Singer (Oxford: Blackwell, 1990b), 219–229, and "Has Anyone Ever Been a Non-Intuitionist?" in *Underivative Duties: British Moral Philosophers form Sidgwick to Ewing*, ed. Thomas Hurka (Oxford: Oxford University Press, 2011), 87–105; David McNaughton, "An Unconnected Heap of Duties?" in *Ethical Intuitionism: Reevaluations*, ed. Philip Stratton-Lake (Oxford: Oxford University Press, 2002), 76–91; Robert Shaver, "The Birth of Deontology," in *Underivative Duties: British Moral Philosophers from Sidgwick to Ewing*, ed. Thomas Hurka (Oxford: Oxford University Press, 2011), 126–149; and Hurka, *British Ethical Theorists*, 128–149. My own view is that prima facie duties are not self-evident and are best understood as having something akin to a rule-consequentialist basis, but that is a topic for another time.

never liable to deadly force in war, and they provide fairly clear conditions under which liability to deadly force is in order. Furthermore, minimal Rossians reject the just combatant immunity thesis as well. However, they provide a richer and more nuanced picture of liability to deadly force among combatants than either conventionalists or anticonventionalists do.

Let us begin with our duties of nonmaleficence and duties of justice. To kill someone is, inter alia, to harm one.[27] Hence, when it comes to liability to deadly force in war, both our duties of nonmaleficence and our duties of justice are in play. According to minimal Rossians, all combatants have a prima facie duty of nonmaleficence not to harm noncombatants, just combatants and even unjust combatants. Although it might initially sound strange to speak of a duty not to harm unjust combatants, we have already seen a similar idea with regard to the principles of *jus in bello*. Recall that the principle of proportionality prohibits excessive acts of violence against all combatants, including unjust combatants. This point is one on which both conventionalists and anticonventionalists agree, and there is no reason for a minimal Rossian to avoid joining the consensus. In fact, a minimal Rossian will maintain that it is our duty of nonmaleficence that explains, at least in part, why the principle of proportionality is a valid constraint on the actions of combatants. Importantly, the duty in question is only prima facie, not ultima facie. So minimal Rossians are also able to provide the groundwork for an explanation of why combatants can use deadly force despite the existence of a duty not to harm others. More on that point in a moment.

All combatants also have a prima facie duty of justice, that is, a duty to help to ensure a fair distribution of benefits and harms. This duty is relevant both to the combatant/noncombatant distinction and to the just combatant/unjust combatant distinction. To begin with, noncombatants are not, as Walzer pointed out, in the business of killing. All other things being equal, it is highly unlikely that they have done (or are doing) anything during war that warrants their death. So, all other things being equal, there is a duty of justice that requires combatants to refrain from subjecting them to deadly force. Hence, at least initially, minimal Rossians seem to be on the same page as both conventionalists and anticonventionalists.

[27] I do not deny that the harm of death is puzzling; see Thomas Nagel, "Death," in *Mortal Questions*, ed. Thomas Nagel (Cambridge: Cambridge University Press, 1979), 1–10; Fred Feldman, *Confrontations with the Reaper: A Philosophical Study of the Nature of Value of Death* (Oxford: Oxford University Press, 1992), 127–156; and Martha Nussbaum, *The Therapy of Desire: Theory and Practice in Hellenistic Ethics* (Princeton, NJ: Princeton University Press, 1994), 192–238. But like most people I don't doubt for a moment that death *is* a harm, and it would be disingenuous for me to proceed as if it weren't.

But it is not always the case that all things are equal. There are situations in war when noncombatants are morally responsible for unjustified harm and, by the same token, deserving of harm—or even death—themselves. One such class of example is civilian leaders who order war crimes and will continue to do so unless stopped. Minimal Rossianism allows us to explain why such noncombatants are liable to deadly force without trying to shoehorn civilian war criminals into the category of combatants. So while minimal Rossianism warrants a default assumption that noncombatants are not liable to deadly force in war, minimal Rossians are not committed to the noncombatant immunity thesis. In fact, as we shall see in a moment, they have far more flexibility when it comes to noncombatants than either conventionalists or anticonventionalists.

Matters are more complicated when it comes to the distinction between just combatants and unjust combatants. The mere fact that combatants are harming others does not, of course, show that a *fair* distribution of harms and benefits would involve returning harm to them. So, at least at a first glance, minimal Rossians appear to be closer to anticonventionalists than to conventionalists when it comes to the just combatant immunity thesis. Yet, as before, minimal Rossians have more tractability than either conventionalists or anticonventionalists on this point. One reason for this is that the distinction between just and unjust combatants is simply too crude. Recall that according to an anticonventionalist a combatant is just if he or she is a combatant of a state that goes to war without violating the principles of *jus ad bellum*, and he or she is an unjust combatant otherwise. However, it is in no way clear that our duties of justice require us to refrain from harming just combatants or that they permit us to harm unjust combatants, understood in this way. According to the anticonventionalist's way of drawing the distinction, one's status as a just/unjust combatant is almost entirely a function of the actions of one's state. But the actions of one's state are beyond the control of almost all combatants. So it is somewhat difficult to see why a combatant should be liable to deadly force because of something for which he or she bears no causal responsibility. Duties of justice require that we help to ensure a fair distribution of benefits and harms, and the fairness of such a distribution cannot be determined by something that lies beyond the abilities of a combatant to influence.

Nevertheless, there is room to accommodate the anticonventionalist's most plausible intuition: if one's state violates the principles of *jus ad bellum*, then one can in principle refuse to serve as a combatant for it. Is one obligated to do so? This question is difficult to answer from the point of view of a minimal Rossian since it requires paying attention to all of his or her prima facie duties and determining where his or her ultima facie duty lies. But it is clear that one's own duty on nonmaleficence counts strongly in favor of not harming others on behalf of a state that is acting unjustly. Not for nothing did Ross's Cambridge University counterpart suggest that the proper response to being forced to fight for a state that is going to war unjustly is suicide.[28]

I have already suggested that the just combatant/unjust combatant distinction is too crude to be of much help. For example, the principles of *jus ad bellum* require that a state not go to war unless it has a reasonable chance of success. But states sometimes violate this principle when fighting against much more powerful invading aggressors. It would be bizarre to think of the combatants of such a state as being unjust for this reason. While we often speak of wars as being either just or unjust, doing so is often misleading. This is the case since there are many ways in which a state can be either justified or unjustified when beginning a war, and there are many degrees to which a state can be justified or unjustified in doing so. The just/unjust combatant distinction simply runs roughshod over these subtleties. In contrast, the minimal Rossian's prima facie duty of justice is far more flexible and appears capable of dealing better with the messy reality of war.

Duties of nonmaleficence and duties of justice are not the only duties that are relevant to liability to deadly force in war. In principle, any of our prima facie duties can have salience. Consider also duties of fidelity. Combatants often promise to carry out the orders of their superior officers and civilian leadership (if it exists). Consider also duties of gratitude. Plausibly, combatants have obligations to their own states for goods they have received in the past, such as education and basic services. Since all of these duties hold prima facie it might appear that having a sufficiently strong duty of gratitude and/or duty of fidelity to a state could make it the case that a combatant was permitted or even obligated to use deadly force against an innocent noncombatant.

However, caution is warranted. It is open to a minimal Rossian to stipulate[29] that X has an ultima facie duty to do F at the behest of Y only if Y is permitted to order (or request, etc.) that F be done. Suppose that Agamemnon orders Achilles to kill Iphigenia, an innocent noncombatant. Achilles, let us say, has duties both of fidelity and of gratitude toward Agamemnon. Though there are circumstances in which these duties would count in favor Achilles killing Iphigenia, we must remember that Agamemnon himself has duties of nonmaleficence toward Iphigenia. And the fact that she is innocent means he also has duties of justice toward her. Unless there are other duties that defeat these duties of nonmaleficence and justice, Agamemnon must refrain both from harming Iphigenia and from bringing it about indirectly that she is harmed. Hence, Agamemnon is not

[28] C. D. Broad, "Ought We to Fight for Our Country?" in *Broad's Critical Essays in Moral Philosophy*, ed. David Cheney (London: George, Allen, & Unwin, 1971), 135.

[29] I say "stipulate" advisedly. My attempts to squeeze an argument rather than a stipulation into this chapter have not met with success, but I shall provide elsewhere at a later date.

permitted to order Achilles to kill Iphigenia, and, therefore, Achilles is neither required nor permitted to do so. But might it be the case that Agamemnon does in fact have other duties that defeat his duties of nonmaleficence and justice and, as a result, permit his ordering her to be killed? In principle, yes. Within a system of prima facie duties, there is nothing like the ex post rights discussed in this chapter. Perhaps the benefits that will result from Iphigenia's death are so great that they defeat his duties of nonmaleficence and justice. But in practice it is very unlikely that any of us will see circumstances in which killing an innocent person will bring about any benefits at all, much less enough benefits to justify killing him or her.

Our question was *Who is liable to deadly force in war?* As we have seen, both conventionalists and anticonventionalists agree that noncombatants are not and that unjust combatants are, provided that uses of deadly force are constrained by the principles of *jus in bello*. Conventionalists maintain that just combatants are also liable to deadly force under these constraints, while anticonventionalists deny that they are liable to deadly force at all. I have argued that both conventionalist and anticonventionalist attempts to answer this question are far from perfect since they rely on what appears to me to be unsound arguments. Though these arguments might be patched up, there is reason to look elsewhere for an answer to our question. Minimal Rossians reject both the noncombatant immunity thesis and the just combatant immunity thesis, though they argue that our prima facie duties of nonmaleficence and of justice provide an overwhelmingly strong default case against using deadly force against noncombatants. Minimal Rossians cut a more ambiguous figure vis-à-vis just combatants. They reject the moral significance assigned to the just combatant/unjust combatant distinction and urge a highly nuanced view of the permissibility of using deadly force against combatants, a view that is sensitive to not only our duties of nonmaleficence and justice but also our duties of fidelity and gratitude. What minimal Rossians have to say about the morality of killing combatants in war would certainly not fit on a postcard. Unlike conventionalists and anticonventionalists, minimal Rossians believe there is nothing that can be said about the use of deadly force against combatants without a clear understanding of their duties that goes beyond their mere status as combatants. That said, minimal Rossians do not go so far as Lord Illingworth who, in Oscar Wilde's *A Woman of No Importance* quipped, "intellectual generalities are always interesting, but generalities in morals mean absolutely nothing."[30] However, minimal Rossians certainly offer less abstract guidance regarding liability to deadly force in war, while giving us a useful

[30] Oscar Wilde, *A Woman of No Importance* (London: Penguin, 1996), 45.

framework for moral deliberation on this topic, a framework that sometimes provides greater sensitivity to moral gradations than are offered by conventionalism and anticonventionalism.

References

Anscombe, G. E. M. "Modern Moral Philosophy." *Philosophy* 33, no. 124 (1958): 1–19.

Anscombe, G. E. M. "War and Murder." In *Nuclear Weapons: A Catholic Response*, edited by Walter Stein, 44–52. London: Sheep & War, 1961.

Aquinas, Thomas. *Summa Theologica*. Kindle ed. Translated by Fathers of the English Dominican Province. New York: Benziger Brothers, 2012.

Audi, Robert. *The Good in the Right: A Theory of Intuition and Intrinsic Value*. Princeton, NJ: Princeton University Press, 2007.

Augustine of Hippo. "Letter 189, to Boniface." In *The Ethics of War: Classic and Contemporary Readings*, edited by Gregory M. Reichberg, Henrik Syse, and Endre Begby, 74–75. London: Blackwell, 2007.

Baldwin, Thomas. "The Three Phases of Intuitionism." In *Ethical Intuitionism: Reevaluations*, edited by Philip Stratton-Lake, 92–112. Oxford: Oxford University Press, 2002.

Broad, C. D. "Ought We to Fight for Our Country?" In *Broad's Critical Essays in Moral Philosophy*, edited by David Cheney, 124–135. London: George, Allen, & Unwin, 1971.

Byers, Michael. *War Law: Understanding International Law and Armed Conflict*. New York: Grove Press, 2005.

Cajetan, Thomas. "Commentary on '*Summa Theologicae*.'" In *The Ethics of War: Classic and Contemporary Readings*, edited by Gregory M. Reichberg, Henrik Syse, and Endre Begby, 240–250. London: Blackwell, 2005.

Cohen, Roger. "Rumsfeld Is Correct—The Truth Will Get Out." *New York Times*, June 7, 2006. Accessed March 16, 2016. http://www.nytimes.com/iht/2006/06/07/world/IHT-07globalist.html.

Cook, Martin L. *The Moral Warrior: Ethics and Service in the US Military*. Albany: State University of New York Press, 2004.

Crisp, Roger. "Sidgwick and the Boundaries of Intuitionism." In *Ethical Intuitionism: Reevaluations*, edited by Philip Stratton-Lake, 56–75. Oxford: Oxford University Press, 2002.

Dancy, Jonathan. "Intuitionism." In *A Companion to Ethics*, edited by Peter Singer, 411–420. Oxford: Blackwell, 1990a.

Dancy, Jonathan. "An Ethic of *Prima Facie* Duties." In *A Companion to Ethics*, edited by Peter Singer, 219–229. Oxford: Blackwell, 1990b.

Dancy, Jonathan. "Has Anyone Ever Been a Non-Intuitionist?" In *Underivative Duties: British Moral Philosophers form Sidgwick to Ewing*, edited by Thomas Hurka, 87–105. Oxford: Oxford University Press, 2011.

de Balzac, Honoré. *Cousin Bette*. Translated by Sylvia Raphael. Oxford: Oxford University Press, 2008.

de Pizan, Christine. "The Book of Deeds, Arms, and Chivalry." In *The Ethics of War: Classic and Contemporary Readings*, edited by Gregory M. Reichberg, Henrik Syse, and Endre Begby, 210–226. London: Blackwell, 2006.

de Vitoria, Francisco. "*De Jure Belli Hispanorum in Barbarous*." In *The Ethics of War: Classic and Contemporary Readings*, edited by Gregory M. Reichberg, Henrik Syse, and Endre Begby, 308–332. London: Blackwell, 2006.

Dworkin, Ronald. *Taking Rights Seriously*. Cambridge, MA: Harvard University Press, 1977.

Feldman, Fred. *Confrontations with the Reaper: A Philosophical Study of the Nature of Value of Death*. Oxford: Oxford University Press, 1992.

Ficarrotta, J. Carl. *Kantian Thinking about Military Ethics*. Burlington, VT: Ashgate, 2010.

Foot, Philippa. "The Problem of Abortion and the Doctrine of Double Effect." In *Virtues and Vices*, edited by Philippa Foot, 18–32. Oxford: Oxford University Press, 2002.

Fotion, Nicholas. *War & Ethics: A New Just War Theory*. London: Continuum, 2007.

Frowe, Helen. *The Ethics of War and Peace: An Introduction*. London: Routledge, 2011.

Gray, John. "Steven Pinker Is Wrong about Violence and War." *Guardian*, March 13, 2015. Accessed July 19, 2016. https://www.theguardian.com/books/2015/mar/13/john-gray-steven-pinker-wrong-violence-war-declining.

Hill, Thomas E. *Human Welfare and Moral Worth: Kantian Perspectives*. Oxford: Oxford University Press, 2002.

Hurka, Thomas. *British Ethical Theorists from Sidgwick to Ewing*. Oxford: Oxford University Press, 2014.

Kamm, Frances. *Intricate Ethics: Rights, Responsibilities, and Permissible Harms*. Oxford: Oxford University Press, 2007.

Kamm, Frances. *The Moral Target: Aiming at Right Conduct in War and Other Conflicts*. Oxford: Oxford University Press, 2012.

Lee, Steven P. *Ethics and War: An Introduction*. Cambridge: Cambridge University Press, 2012.

Marcus, Ruth Barcan. "Moral Dilemmas and Consistency." *Journal of Philosophy* 77 (1980): 121–136.

McMahan, Jeff. *Killing in War*. Oxford: Oxford University Press, 2009.

McNaughton, David. "An Unconnected Heap of Duties?" In *Ethical Intuitionism: Reevaluations*, edited by Philip Stratton-Lake, 76–91. Oxford: Oxford University Press, 2002.

Mill, John Stuart. *On Liberty*. Edited by Leonard Kahn. Toronto, Canada: Broadview Press, 2014.

Nagel, Thomas. "Death." In *Mortal Questions*, edited by Thomas Nagel, 1–10. Cambridge: Cambridge University Press, 1979.

Nussbaum, Martha. *The Therapy of Desire: Theory and Practice in Hellenistic Ethics*. Princeton, NJ: Princeton University Press, 1994.

Orend, Brian. *The Morality of War*. Toronto, Canada: Broadview Press, 2006.

Pascal, Blaise. *Pensées*. Translated by A. J. Krailsheimer. London: Penguin, 1995.

Raymond of Peñafort. "Summa de Casibus Poenitentiae." In *The Ethics of War: Classic and Contemporary Readings*, edited by Gregory M. Reichberg, Henrik Syse, and Endre Begby, 131–147. London: Blackwell, 2006.

Ross, W. D. *The Right and the Good*. Oxford: Oxford University Press, 1930.

Searle, John R. "Prima Facie Reasons." In *Philosophical Subjects: Essays Presented to P. F. Strawson*, edited by Z. van Straaten, 238–260. Oxford: Oxford University Press, 1980.

Senor, Thomas D. "The Prima/Ultima Facie Justification Distinction in Epistemology." *Philosophy and Phenomenological Research* 56, no. 3 (1996): 551–566.

Shaver, Robert. "The Birth of Deontology." In *Underivative Duties: British Moral Philosophers from Sidgwick to Ewing*, edited by Thomas Hurka, 126–145. Oxford: Oxford University Press, 2011.

Singer, Peter. "Is Violence History?" *New York Times*, October 6, 2011.

Thomson, Judith Jarvis. *The Realm of Rights*. Cambridge, MA: Harvard University Press, 1990.

Voltaire, Francois. *Philosophical Dictionary*. Translated by Theodore Besterman. London: Penguin, 1984.

von Clausewitz, Carl. *On War*. Translated by J. J. Graham and edited by Anatol Rapoport. London: Penguin, 1968.

Waldron, Jeremy. "Rights in Conflict." *Ethics* 99, no. 3 (1989): 503–519.

Walzer, Michael. *Just and Unjust Wars: A Moral Argument with Historical Illustrations*. 4th Edition. New York: Basic Books, 1977.

Wilde, Oscar. *A Woman of No Importance*. London: Penguin, 1996.

Wilson, James Q. "Burying the Hatchet." *Wall Street Journal*, July 16, 2011.

2

Pre-emptive Rules and the Scope of Defensive Rights

YITZHAK BENBAJI

This essay advances a morality of defensive harm, which I call "Rule-SD." Rule-SD resolves in a new way two types of difficult cases. It entails that if certain conditions are met, a defender has the right to kill a man who is innocently falling on her, if this is necessary for her survival. Moreover, Rule-SD yields the "free competition resolution" in some symmetrical cases; it implies that two people who innocently threaten each other, whose position vis-à-vis each other is identical in every factual and (therefore) normative respect, might have a right to kill each other if necessary for their survival.

Rule-SD's core claim is that a defender's right of self-defense might arise from a "pre-emptive rule" rather than from facts about the liability of the attacker. In cases I call "one versus one (or less) self-defense circumstances" (or sometimes "the designated circumstances"), the defender might be subject to a rule that permits self-preference; the rules states that if certain conditions are met, a defender might treat the innocent attacker (or threatener) as if he were liable to necessary defensive harm. The rule further allows her to disregard some of the interests of innocent bystanders. (The permission is restricted. The rule permits self-preference as long as it does not foreseeably or intentionally harm bystanders by using force against them, cheating them, stealing from them, or any other illicit [but well defined] means.) Being subject to the rule that permits "restricted self-preference," the defender is exempted from the duty to ascertain that the attacker is indeed liable as well as from taking into account nonviolent, indirect harms to bystanders.

The normative basis of Rule-SD is twofold. First, Rule-SD appeals to a Razian conception of rules as pre-emptive reasons.[1] Under the designated

[1] Joseph Raz, *Practical Reason and Norms* (Princeton, NJ: Princeton University Press, 1990), 38ff; and *The Morality of Freedom* (Oxford: Oxford University Press, 1986), 39ff.

circumstances, the rule that permits restricted self-preference is normally justified in the sense that the defender might follow it, instead of deliberating on the merits of the case and responding to the first-order reasons this deliberation would have exposed. In particular, the rule grounds a reason to follow it *and* a reason not to be guided by the first-order reasons which the rule mediates. The other normative basis that underlies Rule-SD is the liability view of defensive harm, which has been elaborated in the last two decades, primarily by Jeff McMahan.[2] Put very simply, attacker A is liable to intentional killing if killing A is a necessary and proportionate means to avert an unjustified threat T and if A is *sufficiently* responsible for T; incidental harm to bystanders might be justified if it is proportionate, that is, if it is a lesser evil.

Now, Rule-SD establishes the pre-emptive rule which allows the defender's restricted self-preference in one versus one circumstances on the following *empirical* generalizations. First, threatening individuals are usually (but *not* always) at least minimally culpable for the threat they pose; hence, the liability view entails that these individuals are typically liable to defensive harm. Moreover, usually, if the defensive harm to the threatener is necessary and the incidental harm to bystanders is nonviolent and indirect (like causing loss to the attacker's dependents), the defensive harm is proportionate. Second, ordinary defenders facing one versus one circumstances are under stress; their deliberative capacities are limited. Moreover, exempting them from the duty to make sure that their attacker is liable to defensive harm and from taking into account nonviolent indirect harms to bystanders will enable them to be more effective in promoting their self-interest. That is, in most cases, the exemption will allow them to be more effective in doing the right thing.[3]

Rule-SD thus implies that if the following epistemic conditions are met, an ordinary defender facing the designated circumstances is subject to a pre-emptive rule that permits restricted self-preference: first, the defender does not know whether the attacker or threatener is liable to killing and does not know whether the nonviolent indirect harm to bystanders is proportionate; second, the defender justifiably believes that making sure that the attacker is liable to killing and that the incidental harm to bystanders is a lesser evil would be difficult and costly for him or her.

[2] Jeff McMahan, "The Ethics of Killing in War," *Ethics* 114 (2004): 693–733; "Self-Defense and the Problem of the Innocent Attacker," *Ethics* 104 (1994): 252–290, and elsewhere.

[3] As B. J. Strawser points out, we might worry that the risk of doing wrong here is significant enough such that it might warrant a cautionary principle against the kind of pre-emptive rule that I advocate. So just how much "most" actually is will matter. It would also matter how difficult and costly it usually is to make sure that an attacker is liable.

I noted that Rule-SD resolves innocent threat cases in a novel way. The following is a typical innocent threat case.[4]

> *Innocent Threat*: A defender realizes that a man is falling on him. Unless the falling man is blown to pieces, he will crush the defender to death. The man's falling is faultless and involuntary.

Existing moral theories offer at least three different resolutions of innocent threat cases. According to "free competition theories," both sides lose their right not to be attacked by each other but, nevertheless, they retain their right of self-defense: the defender might kill the falling man, whereas the falling man can use a gun, should he have one handy, to prevent the defender from killing him.[5] Second, according to the "fair procedure theories," in cases where the unavoidable harm is indivisible and the parties are morally equal, the parties ought to find a fair mechanism for resolving the conflict.[6] Innocent threat cases provoke a third response, according to which the defender has a right to defensively harm the falling man while the falling man has *no* right to fight back.[7]

I noted that Rule-SD offers a novel resolution to symmetrical cases. In those cases the vital interests of the parties are in conflict and their position vis-à-vis each other is identical in every factual and (therefore) normative respect. While the "free competition" view is not self-evidently obvious to all even in a symmetrical case like *Bear*, many believe it to be the only plausible resolution of this type of case.

> *Bear*: You and I are running away from a bear that is chasing us. The bear is faster and more powerful than both of us, but it needs only one of us for

[4] Cf., Judith J. Thomson, "Self-Defense," *Philosophy & Public Affairs* 20 (1991): 283–310. I discuss innocent threat and symmetrical cases in Yitzhak Benbaji, "A Defense of the Traditional War-Convention," *Ethics* 118 (2008): 464–495. The present essay offers a novel rule-based morality of harm that implies different resolutions of these cases from the ones offered in the former publication. This change results from the thought-provoking discussion in Victor Tadros, *The Ends of Harm* (Oxford: Oxford University Press, 2011), 197–216.

[5] Benbaji, "Defense of the Traditional War-Convention"; Nancy Davis, "Abortion and Self-Defense," *Philosophy & Public Affairs* 13 (1984): 192–193; Jonathan Quong, "Killing in Self-Defense," *Ethics* 119 (2009): 507–537.

[6] The argument advanced in Gerhard Øverland, "Contractual Killing," *Ethics* 115 (2005): 692–720, suggests such a fair procedure solution. For related discussions, Susanne Burri, "The Toss-Up Between a Profiting, Innocent Threat and His Victim," *The Journal of Political Philosophy* 23 (2015): 146–165. Bradley J. Strawser, *The Bounds of Defense: Killing, Moral Responsibility, and War* (forthcoming).

[7] For example, Thomson, "Self-Defense"; Helen Frowe, "Equating Innocent Threats and Bystanders," *Journal of Applied Philosophy* 25 (2008): 277–290.

> dinner, so either you or I will be the bear's food but not both. Whether you or I survive depends on who is faster. We do not have to outrun the bear to ensure our survival; all we need to do is to outrun each other.[8]

The competition ought to be fair: I can put on my own running shoes to gain speed but cannot toss yours into the fire to slow you down. Mutatis mutandis, the same is true of you.

In contrast, it is the fair procedure intuition that governs the resolution of another symmetrical case, *Flotsam.*

> *Flotsam*: You and I are trapped on a sinking piece of flotsam, and soon we will be submerged in the high sea where we will drown almost immediately. The flotsam can support the weight of either one of us but not both.[9]

Here, the parties should find a fair mechanism for resolving their conflict, for instance, tossing a coin.

Rule-SD supports free competition in innocent threat cases where both parties are subject to the self-preference rule. However, unlike free competition theories, under Rule-SD, restricted self-preference is permissible only if the epistemic conditions are met: the defender does not know whether the attacker is liable and is justified in assuming that it would be costly and difficult to gain this piece of knowledge.

Rule-SD draws a distinction between *Bear*-like and *Flotsam*-like cases in which the epistemic conditions are met. Restricted self-preference (and, therefore, free competition) is permissible for *uncertain* deliberators in *Bear* but not in *Flotsam.* In both cases, we do not threaten each other. We are threatened by "nature"; we are bystanders vis-à-vis the threat. In *Flotsam,* however, free competition involves *use of force;* I should push you into the water in order to survive. Hence, the restricted self-preference rule, which does not allow use of force against bystanders, does not apply to this case. In *Bear,* self-preference meets the restrictions: by outrunning you I do not use force against you. I merely indirectly and nonviolently harm you. Hence, I am governed by a rule that permits self-preference.

I will proceed as follows. In the first two sections that follow, I present and criticize two alternative accounts of defensive harm: a partialist account of the right of self-defense recently elaborated by Jonathan Quong and the "autonomist" analysis of symmetrical cases recently developed by Victor Tadros. In the

[8] Tadros, *Ends of Harm,* 209–211. Note that this is *not* the classic case of ducking harm as defined in C. Broose and R. A. Sorensen, "Ducking Harm," *Journal of Philosophy* 85 (1988): 115–134.

[9] Tadros, *Ends of Harm,* 203.

third section, I present Rule-SD and offer a novel analysis of innocent threat cases. The final section enriches Rule-SD and then uses it to resolve *Bear* and *Flotsam*.

The Partialist Account of Defensive Harm

Rule-SD is an impartialist morality of defensive harm: the rights a defender possesses are grounded in the agent-neutral reasons that apply to him or her. According to "partialism," the main rival of this view, impartialism overlooks a crucial element of the morality of defensive harm: egocentric reasons ground the moral permissions we have in various types of circumstances, in particular, self-defense circumstances.[10] In this section I briefly present a partialist account of the right to defensive harm; I then show that partialism faces a deep difficulty.

As I understand it, partialism asserts that since "egocentric reasons" have moral weight, "egocentric behavior" might be permissible or justified in some circumstances. I should therefore say more about these concepts. A simple example of an egocentric reason is the fact that the pain I am experiencing is bad for me. This fact is a prima facie reason for me to eliminate this pain.[11] Now, if I deserve the pain, my reason to eliminate it is *merely* egocentric. In such a case, others have no reason to relieve my pain and might even have a reason to prevent me from ridding myself of it.[12]

My reason is egocentric in virtue of the fact that its specification requires a pronominal back reference to me: that the pain is bad *for me* is a reason *for me*—but for no one else—to rid myself of it. Similarly, I have a reason to defend myself from a just attack, even if I am a culpable attacker, and therefore liable to defensive killing. My self-interest grounds an agent-relative reason to defend myself, while others have an agent-neutral reason to prevent me from doing so.

The notions of agent-neutrality and agent-relativity allow for a characterization of impartiality and impartial behavior, on the one hand, and egocentric behavior, on the other. An impartial agent cares about his or her interests to the extent that those interests are impartially important. In contrast, an egocentric

[10] A version of partialism is developed in Quong, "Killing in Self-Defense."

[11] The term "agent relativity" was coined in T. Nagel, *The Possibility of Altruism* (Princeton, NJ: Princeton University Press, 1970). My characterization of it is drawn from P. Pettit "Universality Without Utilitarianism," *Mind* 96 (1987): 74–82. For illuminating discussion, see, Michael Ridge, "Reasons for Action: Agent-Neutral vs. Agent-Relative," *The Stanford Encyclopaedia of Philosophy* (Winter 2011 Edition), ed. Edward N. Zalta, http://plato.stanford.edu/archives/win2011/entries/reasons-agent/.

[12] See Christine M. Korsgaard, "The Reasons We Can Share: An Attack on the Distinction Between Agent-Relative and Agent-Neutral Values," *Social Philosophy and Policy* 10 (1993): 24–51.

(or partial) agent cares about protecting and promoting his or her own interests more than about protecting and promoting strangers' interests, merely because of his or her special relation to his or her own interests. Obviously, egocentric agents are able to overcome their self-love. An agent acts impartially if he or she is guided solely by agent-neutral reasons; the mere fact that an action might also promote his or her interests rather than someone else's may not have had any impact on his or her choice. An agent exhibits egocentric behavior if his or her action is motivated also by egocentric reasons; his or her action is *strongly* egocentric if it is solely motivated by such reasons.

The partialist morality of defensive harm attaches moral significance to egocentric reasons. Suppose I am threatened by a person who is falling on me by no fault of his or her own. Partialists would usually deem the self-interest I have in my own life sufficient to grant me permission to kill the falling person in self-defense; *I* possess a right of self-defense, but my right does not extend to anyone else. In other words, my right of self-defense does not imply a right of other-defense: a third party has no right to kill the falling person in my defense.

Partialism must address questions such as the number of innocent attackers the defender is permitted to kill in order to survive and whether defensive killing is permissible when killing the attacker will yield fatal consequences for many others. In solving this problem, they assume that agent-neutral reasons can be weighed against agent-relative ones. If the (morally weighted) costs the defender would bear had she avoided harming the attacker are sufficiently low, the agent-neutral reasons against harming the attacker outweigh the agent-relative reasons in favor of such harm. Indeed, in innocent threat cases, agent-relative values are sufficiently weighty to break the tie: the defender has the right of self-defense—she has the right to prefer herself—merely because of the importance of her life to her.[13]

The difficulty partialism faces is simple: why is it that the preference that people have for their own well-being does not ground a similar set of permissions when killing bystanders is necessary for their survival?[14] Why is it impermissible to kill the bystander in *Innocent Bystander*?

> *Innocent Bystander*: A defender realizes that a man is falling on her and is about to crush her. The defender can block the falling man by using a bystander as a human shield, in which case the bystander would be crushed to death.

[13] Quong, *Killing in Self-Defense*, 514–523.

[14] Cf. Tadros, *Ends of* Harm, 209. Tadros raises this difficulty regarding Quong's partialist distinction between doing and allowing.

Partialists might respond as follows: the agent-relative values involved in *Innocent Threat* are just as weighty as the agent-relative values involved in *Innocent Bystander*. Yet, despite the moral reason one has to prefer one's own life, self-preference in *Innocent Bystander* is impermissible because manipulatively killing the bystander is more seriously wrong than the eliminative killing of attackers/threateners.

But this response seems to fail; the prohibition on self-preference seems to be much more straightforward than partialism would like us to believe: a defender has *no moral reason to prefer herself* over the bystander in *Innocent Bystander*. Indeed, a proponent of this view, Jonathan Quong, realizes that the agent-relative value can ground a moral right of self-defense only if it can be objectively, rather than subjectively, specified. He insists that "there is an objective sense in which each person may permissibly attach much greater weight to their own life in comparison to the lives of others."[15] He would acknowledge that a sadist who genuinely needs to cause pain to someone has *no* moral reason to cause pain to anyone. Acting on such a reason is malicious, precisely because of the nature of sadistic needs.[16] But, I submit, the same might be true of many cases of eliminative killing: I have no *moral* reason to kill you even if I genuinely need something you own and I cannot attain it unless I kill you. Partialists cannot explain this conviction.

Consider partialism's implication in a less trivial case: a bank robber, who initially was a potential attacker but is now a liable defender; as things stand, the guard of the bank threatens the robber's life. Partialism asserts that if necessary for his or her survival, the robber has a moral reason to kill the guard. Partialism means by this that the robber has *some* moral reason to kill the guard. It does not follow that this reason wins out—the moral reasons against killing the guard outweigh the reason for killing him.

But even this weak claim seems false: the fact that the robber has an interest in his or her own life—an interest that constitutes the robber's agent-relative reason to attach greater weight to his or her own life—doesn't seem to give the robber any *moral* reasons at all to kill the guard. For the very fact that the robber is liable to killing seems to imply that even if he or she has a reason to attach greater weight to his or her own life, in these circumstances, he or she has no *moral* reason to do so. The prohibition on killing bystanders in self-preservation is similar: despite the partialist claim to the contrary, there is *no* moral reason that speaks in its favor.

[15] Quong, *Killing in Self-Defense*, 517.

[16] Note, though, that sadism is not *intrinsically* bad. If a person meets his or her sadistic needs by watching horror movies, we might have a moral reason to provide him or her with such movies.

Quong might argue in response that egocentric reasons need not always have moral weight—they need not weigh against every other conflicting moral consideration—for it to be the case that these types of reasons sometimes have moral weight. Sometimes, under clearly delineated circumstances, considerations of the type ". . . it would be me . . ." are morally weighty. Alas, this line of argument might be effective, only if Quong can offer a plausible explanation as to why in some circumstances egocentric reasons are "suddenly" weightless.

The morality I advance in this chapter—Rule-SD—maintains that egocentric reasons as such are morally insignificant. It therefore concurs that under self-defense circumstances, the special relationship between the defender and his or her interests is morally irrelevant. Yet, Rule-SD implies that while partialism is wrong, the verdicts it advances in innocent threat cases are mostly correct: ordinary uninformed defenders have the right to exhibit egocentric behavior (i.e., to kill their attackers if necessary) even where they could have easily known that their attackers are not liable to defensive harm but justifiably believe that they cannot gain this piece of knowledge.

Beforehand, I will discuss *Bear* and *Flotsam*, the symmetrical cases that motivate Rule-SD, and the autonomist resolution of these cases.

Symmetrical Cases and the Autonomist Morality of Harm

It should come as no surprise that some symmetrical cases are resolved by free competition and others by fair procedure. The following *Crash* cases are an example.

> *Crash$_1$*: Following the instructions of a negligent inspector, two agents are driving two trains toward each other on the same track. A total-loss crash where both drivers are killed is bound to happen, unless one driver stops the other by using deadly force. Cooperative fair procedure is impossible as the drivers cannot communicate with each other. A noncooperative randomization—where one of the drivers, or both, flips a coin in order to decide whether to use lethal force against the other driver—would increase the chance that both drivers will avoid action and end up dead. In general, then, anything other than mutual defensive action will increase the likelihood that the drivers will be killed.

Certainly, free competition is permissible since it is the only way to prevent the suboptimal outcome in which both drivers are killed. Compare, however, *Crash*$_1$ to *Crash*$_2$:

> *Crash*$_2$: Like *Crash*$_1$, except that noncooperative randomization would increase the chance that one of the drivers survives as mutual defensive action is most likely to cause the drivers to kill each other.

The key normative consideration in each *Crash* case is aggregation. The same outcome-based considerations that support a free competition resolution in *Crash*$_1$ justify a fair procedure resolution in *Crash*$_2$. Any morality of defensive harm, according to which the defender's choice is prima facie justifiable if it minimizes harm to innocents, easily distinguishes between *Crash*$_1$ and *Crash*$_2$. In contrast, the symmetrical cases under discussion, *Bear* and *Flotsam*, resist an aggregation-based analysis; instead, in these cases the key normative consideration is fairness in the distribution of harm of a *given* size.

Common-sense morality distinguishes between *Bear* and *Flotsam* for reasons related to self-ownership. While both of us have an equal claim on the flotsam, I have an exclusive claim on my person and on my physical and mental abilities. As far as I do not exercise violence against you, use anything that belongs to you, or interfere with your affairs by coercion, deception, etc., it is permissible for me to take advantage of my powers and the things that I own in order to secure my survival. Therefore, I am allowed to run as fast as I can in *Bear* but not to push you in *Flotsam*. Another common-sense difference between these cases relates to the killing/letting die distinction. While your death in *Bear* is not the usual case of letting die (as by outrunning you I actively divert the bear to you), this is no killing either. I do not directly attack you. But in freely competing on the flotsam, we directly attack each other. The feeling that a coin flip is needed emerges from the common-sense morality requirement to avoid a direct attack.

Why do these differences matter?[17] Probably, they somehow imply that, as an autonomous agent, I am free to outrun you but I am not free to push you from the raft. Victor Tadros's systematic analysis of "the means principle" is an attempt to elucidate this autonomist reasoning. For Tadros, the means principle is violated where one incorporates others into one's plans and projects in a harmful way or where one manipulates others to serve one's own ends.[18] This

[17] For a related autonomist argument for the distinction, see Fiona Wollard, "If This Is My Body . . . : A Defence of the Doctrine of Doing and Allowing," *Pacific Philosophical Quarterly* 94 (2013): 315–341.

[18] Tadros, *Ends of Harm*, 140.

principle asserts that using a person as a means to another's end is fundamentally wrong because it disrespectfully offends his or her standing as an independent person.[19] The use of one's internal resources (viz., one's own body and talents) in pursuance of one's goals is permissible, unless this use interferes with another person's autonomy.

The means principle underlies some of the killing/letting die contrasts: harmful action usually interferes with the victim's autonomy, while harmful omission does not. If one harmfully attacks another person or if one harmfully uses another person's vital resources, one fails to treat him or her as an autonomous person who is entitled to set his or her own projects and plans. But if one is not subject to the duty to help, letting another person die does not amount to disrespecting that person.

In *Bear*, my running away is not disrespectful, despite being very harmful. This is because, first, the parties whose interests conflict with each other maintain no normatively significant special relationship (such as, say, parent to child). Second, the stakes are high: I could have rescued you but only at a great cost to myself. Finally, I am not under duty to bring about an equal distribution of chances to survive even if such an outcome is fairer and therefore impersonally better. In short, while by running as fast as I can I harm you, I do not use you or interfere with your autonomy in any way; thus, so the argument goes, I do not treat you disrespectfully. Or as Tadros puts it,

> Suppose that morality required me to toss a coin in *Bear*. That would require me, were I to lose, to sacrifice myself to save you. . . . But if that were so, morality would require one of us, the person who loses the toss, to make himself available as a means to save the other at the cost of his life. This would threaten the idea that each person is independent

[19] This idea is deeply related to the nonconsequentialist moralities of T. M. Scanlon, Arthur Ripstein, and Jay Wallace: T. M. Scanlon, *What We Owe to Each Other* (Cambridge, MA: Harvard University Press, 1998); Arthur Ripstein, "Authority and Coercion," *Philosophy and Public Affairs* 32 (2004): 2–35, and "Beyond the Harm Principle," *Philosophy and Public Affairs* 34 (2006): 215–245; R. Jay Wallace, "The Deontic Structure of Morality," in *Thinking About Reasons: Themes From the Philosophy of Jonathan Dancy*, ed. David Bakhurst, Margaret Olivia Little, and Brad Hooker (Oxford: Oxford University Press, 2013), 137–167. These versions of nonconsequentialism analyze morality in terms of bipolar rights and duties. For the seminal analysis, see Ernest Weinrib, *The Idea of Private Law* (Cambridge, MA: Harvard University Press, 1995); Michael Thompson, "What Is It to Wrong Someone? A Puzzle About Justice," in *Reason and Value*, edited by R. Jay Wallace, Philip Pettit, Samuel Scheffler, and Michael Smith, 333–384 (New York: Oxford University Press, 2004); and Stephen Darwall, *The Second-Person Standpoint* (Cambridge, MA: Harvard University Press, 2006).

> of every other in determining which projects and goals, amongst those that are valuable, to value and pursue.[20]

If I am required to agree to a fair procedure in *Bear* and sacrifice my life if I lose, then, according to Tadros, I am forced to be used as a means for realizing fairness. A morality that requires such a sacrifice is coercive and, as such, inconsistent with the means principle; it fails to recognize its addressee's autonomous personhood.

Thus, the autonomist framework, in symmetrical cases, is consciously insensitive to considerations of fairness. Suppose that I was paired with a particularly slower runner or I was paired with a handicapped person who can barely limp along, much less run. In those cases the other runner was eaten by the bear due to brute bad luck; the difference between me and that person is obviously unfair. Why should the brute luck fact of whoever happens to be faster be that upon which our lives hinge? No good answer is forthcoming, and still, according to the autonomist resolution of *Bear*, I am allowed to use my person and resources in order to advance important interests, even if this is unfair.

Still, Tadros's autonomist resolution of *Bear* and *Flotsam* faces a straightforward difficulty: he rightly observes that by running as fast as I can I do not use you as a means, but I still use you in avoiding the bear. I run as fast as I can in order to divert the bear to you: had you not been around, my running away would be pointless. I adopt the running strategy precisely because I hope that you are slower than I am. This plan seems to amount to a violation of the means principle.

The description offered here does not contradict Tadros's observation that a requirement to self-sacrifice might also violate my autonomy. The idea that in exceptional cases autonomy rights can conflict with each other is familiar.[21] In order to complete the argument against the fair procedure resolution in *Bear*, Tadros should explain why this resolution is inferior to free competition.

Tadros might answer that free competition in *Bear* is nonviolent and does not directly involve the other. But this answer is incomplete without explaining why direct involvement and the use of force matter. The fact that I exercise no violence in outrunning you seems irrelevant, from the perspective of the autonomist (means principle–based) morality Tadros employs.

[20] Tadros, *Ends of Harm*, 210–211.

[21] Jeremy Waldron, "Rights in Conflict." *Ethics* 99 (1989): 503–519.

A Pre-emptive Rule-Based Morality of Self-Defense

A Pre-emptive Rule Morality of Harm

The theory I advance in this section—Rule-SD—is a three-layered morality of defensive harm. It is composed of (1) a theory of the rights of fully informed defenders (and fully informed third parties); (2) prospectivism: a decision theoretic theory of the rights possessed by fully rational but uncertain, incompletely informed, defenders; (3) a Razian theory of "normally justified" rules that mediate (and therefore preempt rather than undermine) the reasons that apply to ordinary (i.e., less than fully rational) uninformed defenders.

Consider the first layer. A fully informed defender is justified in exercising defensive force if and only if in doing so he or she minimizes and fairly distributes the harm the attacker is about to inflict. Thus, if harming the attacker enforces fairness in the distribution of harm, the attacker is liable to defensive harm. I will follow Jeff McMahan in assuming that the attacker's degree of responsibility for a threat determines how the harm he or she is about to cause ought to be distributed. If the attacker is fully culpable for the threat, it would be fair if he or she would bear all of the necessary harm; if his or her responsibility for the threat is minimal, it would be fair if the harm were distributed more equally.[22] As an impartialist position, Rule-SD asserts that people who constitute a threat by, say, faultlessly falling on the defender—viz., they constitute a threat but not through their agency—are not liable to defensive harm; a fully informed defender has no right to kill the falling man. Probably, if one of the two must die, they ought to flip a coin in order to decide who will survive. Similarly, if in *Bear* and *Flotsam* the parties are fully informed, they should decide who is to survive by a fair procedure.[23]

[22] These propositions are endorsed in Philip Montague, "Self-Defense and Choosing Among Lives," *Philosophical Studies*, 40 (1981): 207–219; and "Self-Defense, Culpability, and Distributive Justice," *Law and Philosophy*, 29 (2010): 75–91; McMahan develops two different versions of this view in "Self-Defense and the Problem of the Innocent Attacker," in "Ethics of Killing in War," and in "The Basis of Moral Liability to Defensive Killing," *Philosophical Issues* 15 (2005): 386–405, as well as other places. Compare Michael Otsuka, "Killing the Innocent in Self-Defense," *Philosophy & Public Affairs* 23 (1994): 74–94; Suzanne Uniacke, *Permissible Killing: The Self-Defence Justification of Homicide* (Cambridge: Cambridge University Press, 1994).

[23] As Susanne Burri points out to me, my presentation leaves many questions open. First, the Otsuka argument against fair procedure in the innocent threat case: if I act to kill the falling man, I am responsible for my actions, whereas he is not responsible for falling toward me; hence, there is an asymmetry that means the harm should befall me (see his "Killing the Innocent in Self-Defense"). Second, what if fairness and minimization conflict: I can either inflict significant harm on the falling man or allow him to inflict a small harm on me? Does minimization take priority over fair distribution? These and other questions should not concern us here.

The second layer of the morality of harm addresses the problem of uncertainty, by overcoming the fact-relative morality/evidence-relative morality distinction.[24] Let me illustrate through *Falling Man with Defender's Uncertainty*:

> *Falling Man with Defender's Uncertainty*: A man Y is faultlessly and involuntarily falling on a defender, X; unless Y is blown to pieces, he will crush X to death. The defender X falsely but justifiably believes that Y is culpable for the threat he is posing. That is, X justifiably believes that the falling man Y is liable to defensive killing: she has evidence that indicates an 85% chance that the falling man is liable.

Consider a decision theoretic presentation of this case. The defender has only two options, {*Self-Preference*, ~ *Self-Preference*}, whose possible values are presented as follows:

Innocent Threat	*pr*	Good Outcome	*pr*	Bad Outcome
Self-Preference	.85	1 = U (defender survives thanks to killing a liable attacker)	.15	−1 = U (defender survives due to killing an innocent attacker)
~ *Self-Preference*	.15	1 = U (defender dies because she did not kill an innocent attacker)	.85	−1 = U (defender is killed because she did not kill a liable attacker)

Since the attacker is innocent,

$$U(\sim\textit{Self-Preference}) = U\begin{pmatrix}\text{defender dies because she did}\\ \text{not kill an innocent attacker}\end{pmatrix} = 1$$

$$U(\sim\textit{Self-Preference}) = U\begin{pmatrix}\text{defender survives due to}\\ \text{killing an innocent attacker}\end{pmatrix} = -1.$$

[24] For the distinction between fact-relative morality and evidence-relative morality, Derek Parfit, *On What Matters* (Oxford: Oxford University Press, 2011), chap. 7, and the discussion of those distinctions in Tadros, *Ends of Harm*, chap. 10. It is challenged in Frank Jackson, "Decision-Theoretic Consequentialism and the Nearest and Dearest Objection," *Ethics* 101 (1991): 461–482, and Michael J. Zimmerman, *Living with Uncertainty: The Moral Significance of Ignorance* (Cambridge: Cambridge University Press, 2008).

As U(*Self-Preference*) < U(~*Self-Preference*), a fully informed defender ought not to kill the falling man in self-defense.

What about the uncertain defender? Suppose that as far as the defender ought to know, the probability that the attacker is liable is .85; that is, the probability that the good effect of *Self-Preference* will come about is .85 (or, more formally, *pr*[Good/*Self-Preference*] = .85) and therefore *pr*(Bad/*Self-Preference*) = .15. If so,

$$U_e(\textit{Self-Preference}) = pr(\text{Good}/\textit{Self-Preference})\cdot U(\text{Good}) + pr(\text{Bad}/\textit{Self-Preference})\cdot U(\text{Bad}) = .85\cdot 1 + .15(-1) = .7$$

$$U_e(\sim\textit{Self-Preference}) = pr(\text{Good}/\sim\textit{Self-Preference}).U(\text{Good}) + pr(\text{Bad}/\sim\textit{Self-Preference}).\ U(\text{Bad}) = .15 - .85. = -.7$$

While the actual value of ~*Self-Preference* is greater than the actual value of *Self-Preference* (U[*Self-Preference*] < U[~*Self-Preference*]), the expected value of *Self-Preference* is greater than the expected value of ~*Self-Preference* (U_e[~*Self-Preference*] < U_e[*Self-Preference*]).

What should the uncertain defender do? A Parfit-style treatment asserts that defensively killing the falling man in *Falling Man with Defender's Uncertainty* is impermissible in the fact-relative sense because the falling man is not liable to defensive harm. Now, X, the defender, is incompletely informed, and X's belief that the attacker is liable has been formed on the basis of adequately researched evidence. If such research results in a belief that the attacker is most probably liable to harm, defensive killing is permissible in the "evidence-relative sense." For Parfit, the fact-relative justification and the evidence-relative justification are both valid and irreducible to each other.

In contrast, prospectivism (viz., the second layer of Rule-SD) offers a single concept of the rightness of action that follows from a general theory of uncertainty in ethics, developed by Frank Jackson and in more detail by Michael Zimmerman.[25] The fully rational yet uncertain deliberator ought to

[25] Jackson: "I hereby stipulate that what I mean from here on by 'ought' . . . was the ought most immediately relevant to action, the ought which I urged it to be the primary business of an ethical theory to deliver. When we act we must perforce use what is available to us at the time, not what may be available to us in the future or what is available to someone else, and least of all not what

maximize *expected* value.[26] Thus, if U_e(~*Self-Preference*) < U_e(*Self-Preference*), X's self-preference is permissible, even if it involves the killing of a nonliable person.

To understand the difference between prospectivism and the Parfit-style approach to uncertainty, consider a fully informed third party Z, who knows that the falling man Y is not liable to killing; Z can prevent X from killing Y by neutralizing X's gun (rather than by directly harming X). In doing so, Z allows Y to fall on X and crush her to death. Under the Parfit-style approach, X's killing is permissible merely in the evidence-relative sense, so by neutralizing X's gun Z can prevent an action which is in fact impermissible. Thus, Z's intervention has two consequences: Y would faultlessly (and therefore not impermissibly) crush X to death and X would fail to impermissibly kill innocent Y. Since Z can prevent X's fact-relative wrongdoing by neutralizing X's gun (rather than by killing or wounding X), Z ought to intervene.

In contrast, according to prospectivism, in the case just described, Z has no reason to prevent X's defensive action and thereby Z has no reason to allow Y to fall on her and crush her to death. After all, X's defensive killing is permissible since it maximizes expected moral utility. Hence, her status has not been compromised due to this killing. True, had X been fully informed: killing Y would have been a violation of her duty. Since X is not fully informed, her killing is permissible.

The distinction I offer above between the Parfit-style and the prospectivist treatments of uncertainty does not rest on the false assumption that if it is permissible for X to V, then it is not permissible for Z to interfere with X's V-ing. In many cases where Z knows something that X does not, it is permissible for Z to prevent X from doing what would be X's mistake had X been fully informed. The point here is different: X does not become *liable* to Z's harmful action in virtue of killing a nonliable man if her killing is permissible (according to prospectivism). That is, she does not become liable merely in virtue of the fact that had she been fully informed; she should have acted differently. Unlike the Parfit approach, which renders X's action wrongful in the fact-relative sense, prospectivism implies that X's defensive killing is permissible in every sense and infers from this fact that X cannot become liable to harm in virtue of permissibly killing nonliable Y.

is available to a God-like being who knows everything about what would, will, and did happen" ("Decision-Theoretic Consequentialism," 472).

[26] Seth Lazar "In Dubious Battle: Uncertainty and the Ethics of Killing," *Philosophical Studies* (2012): 1–25 offers a "deontologized" construal of Frank Jackson's decision theoretic consequentialism. (Lazar does accept the fact-relative/evidence-relative distinction.)

The second layer of Rule-SD entails the possibility of conflicting moral permissions. To see why, consider the following:

> *Falling Man with Defender's and Attacker's Uncertainty*: Like *Falling Man with Defender's Uncertainty* but in addition the falling man Y has a gun and can kill X before X kills him; Y justifiably but falsely believes that X knows that Y is not liable: they both have evidence that indicates an 85% chance that the other party is liable.

Where both fully rational parties justifiably believe each other to be liable to defensive harm, both are justified in defending themselves against each other: despite being innocent, both lost the right not to be attacked by each other but retain the right of self-defense.[27]

The Third Layer: A Pre-emptive Self-Preference Rule

The third layer of Rule-SD utilizes Joseph Raz's distinction between first-order and second-order reasons. The first-order reasons that apply to ordinary defenders in central self-defense cases might not be the only reasons they have. Ordinary defenders might be subject to a rule that functions as a second-order reason or, more particularly, as a pre-emptive reason. Saying that a person is subject to a rule that instructs/permits V-ing might mean that this person ought to/might V, instead of deliberating on whether V-ing is supported by the balance of the first-order reasons that apply to her in the circumstances.

A rule grounds a valid pre-emptive reason if it is "normally justified." A rule that instructs or allows its addressee to V is normally justified if following the rule—instead of deliberating on whether V-ing is supported by the balance of the first-order reasons—would enhance the conformity of the addressee to these reasons. Typically, rules are normally justified in circumstances in which the cost of comprehensive deliberation is high, the deliberative circumstances are poor, and the action supported by the rule would also be the most likely result of a suitably idealized comprehensive deliberation.[28]

[27] The second layer of Rule-SD cuts across the consequentialist/nonconsequentialist division; both camps might agree that under circumstances of self-defense, fairness in the distribution of harm is of crucial importance. Both camps might agree that the uncertain defender should maximize the chances that fairness in the distribution of harm would be realized.

[28] A pre-emptive reason is a second-order reason to exclude some first-order reasons from deliberation. Such reasons neither override nor conflict with first-order reasons. Rather, they determine which considerations are to be excluded from the calculation of the balance of first-order reasons. The rule to which Rule-SD subjects ordinary defenders is, in fact, a "protected reason": a protected reason to φ at T is the combination of (1) a first-order reason to φ at T and (2) a pre-emptive

The third layer of Rule-SD asserts that the permissions involved in some central self-defense cases emerge from the rule to which the defender is subject, rather than from the first-order moral reasons that apply to her according to prospectivism (the second layer). This core claim can be illustrated by *Falling Man with Defender's Uncertainty*.

According to prospectivism (of the second layer), if X is uncertain but fully rational, X has the right to act in self-defense if X justifiably but falsely believes that Y is liable. In such a case U(*Self-Preference*) < U(~*Self-Preference*)—because Defender X kills an innocent threatener Y; nevertheless, U_e(~*Self-Preference*) < U_e(*Self-Preference*), the killing is permissible.

The third layer takes this idea a step further. Suppose that as a result of X's limitations, X ought to follow a pre-emptive rule that permits self-preference, instead of carrying out the procedure recommended by prospectivism. If so, X has the right to act in self-defense, even where U_e(*Self-Preference*) < U_e(~*Self-Preference*). Thus, a fully informed third party Z has no reason to allow Y to crush X to death by forcing inaction on X, even if, had X been fully rational, X could have known that Y is not liable.

The third layer is based on an empirical speculation about ordinary defenders. This speculation is composed, in turn, of three empirical generalizations regarding cases in which the defender is threatened by one attacker or by a wild animal ("the designated circumstances"). Typically, under the designated circumstances, (1) the attacker/threatener (if there is one) is at least minimally culpable for the threat he poses and therefore liable to defensive harm and (2) the deliberative circumstances are poor so that the ordinary defender is under stress (i.e., not fully rational). Her deliberation would significantly deviate from ideal deliberation. In fact, ordinary people have a terrible track record in calculating likely consequences and correctly inferring the decision theoretic morality that

reason to disregard some of the first-order reasons that bear on the choice at T. See Raz, *Morality of Freedom*, 39ff. For an illuminating discussion of Raz's views, see Scott Shapiro, "Authority" in *The Oxford Handbook of Jurisprudence and Philosophy of Law*, ed. Scott Shapiro and Julius Coleman (Oxford: Oxford University Press, 2004), 382–439.

Raz's conception of the normal justification of rules has been criticized from various angles. See a summary in Shapiro, "Authority," sect. IV (which includes a clear presentation of Michael S. Moore, "Authority, Law and Razian Reasons," *Southern California Law Review* 62 (1989): 866–867. Cf. Chaim Gans, "Mandatory Rules and Exclusionary Reasons," *Philosophia* 15 (1986): 373–396, and William A. Edmundson, "Rethinking Exclusionary Reasons," *Law and Philosophy* 12 (1993): 329–343.

The Razian analysis of pre-emptive rules employed here might be replaced without losing much. For interesting alternatives, see Stephen Perry, "Second Order Reasons, Uncertainty and Legal Theory," *Southern California Law Review* 62 (1989): 932–957; and Fred Schauer, *Playing by the Rules: An Examination of Rule-Based Decision-Making in Law and in Life* (Oxford: Clarendon Press, 1991), 88–93. I do not try to defend the Razian view of authority here, nor do I try to defend the modifications of his views offered by Perry and Schauer.

governs stressful circumstances. In following a well-designed rule instead of directly maximizing expected moral value they are more likely to imitate ideal deliberators. And (3) the defensive actions of a defender under stress are more effective if she exhibits strong egocentrism, viz., disregards any agent neutral reasons that apply to her.

If the first generalization is true, most one versus one cases are such that the fully informed defender has a right to harm the attacker in self-defense. It follows that according to prospectivism fully rational but uncertain defenders have a right to defensively harm their attackers, due to the high probability that the attackers are liable to defensive harm. Indeed, under the empirical generalization adopted here, rational but not fully informed defenders may permissibly defend themselves in some falling man cases since mostly their false belief that the falling man is liable to harm will be supported by the defender's evidence.

Enter the second and third generalizations: ordinary deliberation on the merits of one versus one self-defense cases is usually both very different from ideal deliberation and costly. Ordinary defenders are under stress, and, therefore, their beliefs as to the liability of the attacker are biased. Furthermore, allowing defenders to exhibit egocentric behavior rather than respond to the agent-neutral reasons that apply to them is more likely to lead them to do (what Rule-SD's second layer defines to be) the right thing. A defender who invests all of her available resources in defending her interests but invests nothing in making sure that defending her interests is the correct thing to do (i.e., supported by the balance of agent-neutral reasons) is actually more likely to do the right thing.

Rule-SD infers from these generalizations that the defender is subject to the "self-preference rule":

> The rule of restricted self-preference in self-defense: A defender can promote her own interests by harming the attacker in one vs. one (or less) self-defense cases, provided that (a) the defender is morally innocent vis-à-vis the threat imposed on her; (b) has no immediately available or obvious evidence that indicates that the attacker is not liable to defensive harm; (c) (to be completed.)[29]

Arguably, if the generalizations listed above are all true *and* ordinary defenders can easily identify one versus one self-defense cases and follow the self-preference rule, the rule is normally justified. It mediates the first-order reasons that, according to prospectivism of the second layer, apply to ordinary defenders

[29] The third part of the rule concerns harm inflicted on bystanders. I will develop it in the next section.

in these circumstances. As such, the self-preference rule grounds a pre-emptive reason: allowing the defender to follow it and exempting her from attending to first-order agent-neutral reasons would enable the defender to promote her interests more effectively and thus be more successful at doing the right thing. This permission to exhibit strongly egocentric behavior is likely to enhance the defender's conformity to the agent-neutral reasons that apply to her in the designated circumstances. Therefore, the self-preference rule grounds a permission to exhibit egocentric behavior (viz., to disregard agent-neural reasons) without abandoning the conviction that morality is intrinsically related to impartiality. Thus, although egocentric reasons are of no moral significance, the agent is permitted to exhibit egocentrism because it is likely to bring about the best outcome impartially considered.

Prospectivism and the pre-emptive rule morality of the third layer are neutral between consequentialism and nonconsequentialism. Whatever the reasons that apply to the defender in the designated circumstances—they might follow from facts about consequences (per the consequentialist formulation) or from facts about autonomy and respect (per nonconsequentialism)—subjection to the self-preference rule usually enhances the defender's conformity with these reasons.[30]

[30] Having said that, I tend to read Rule-SD as a consequentialist doctrine sensitive to both aggregate welfare and fair distribution. Despite appearances to the contrary, Rule-SD is not an instance of the common version of rule consequentialism ("An act is wrong if it is forbidden by the code of rules whose internalization by the overwhelming majority of everyone everywhere . . . has maximum expected value": Brad Hooker, *Ideal Code, Real World: A Rule-Consequentialist Theory of Morality* (Oxford: Oxford University Press, 2000a), 32. According to Rule-SD, the following rule is permissible because subjection to this rule is likely to enhance compliance of the *individual* with the demands of act consequentialism, in each circumstance he or she faces. The rule's belonging to the "ideal code" has no role in determining the rightness of the action, according to Rule-SD.

Now, Rule-SD might be read as an instance of indirect consequentialism. *Direct* consequentialism is "usually construed as holding that an act's moral permissibility depends on a comparison of that act's consequences with the consequences of alternative acts open to the agent. *Indirect* consequentialism judges an act permissible if and only if it accords with motivation, dispositions, rules and kind of conscience that are favoured by the consequentialist assessment": Brad Hooker, "Impartiality, Predictability and Indirect Consequentialism," in *Well-Being and Morality: Essays in Honour of James Griffin*, ed. Roger Crisp and Brad Hooker (Oxford University Press, 2000b), 130. I prefer a different reading of Rule-SD. It asserts that the self-preference rule to which Rule-SD subjects ordinary defenders functions like future-directed decisions: "Future-directed decisions are . . . tools for the non-manipulative, intrapersonal division of deliberative labor over time. A future-directed decision to φ gives rise to a defeasible exclusionary reason to φ. This reason is grounded on the default authority that is normally granted to one's prior self as an 'expert' deliberator": Luca Ferrero, "Decisions, Diachronic Autonomy & the Division of Deliberative Labor," *Philosopher's Imprint* 10 (2010): 7. Subjection to the self-preference rule is a way to overcome a predictable limitation at the time of action. In light of those limitations, the agent should decide to follow a normally justified rule because this decision maximizes the expected value of the future choice at the time of the decision.

Rule-SD Versus Partialism, or Four Payoffs of Rule-SD

Four interesting implications of Rule-SD are immediately apparent. First, like partialism, it allows egocentric behavior in *some* innocent threat cases. In one versus one circumstances the defender is entitled to disregard (some of the) agent-neutral reasons that apply to her. Prospectivism further implies that even a nonviolent intervention of a third party, whose goal is preventing defensive killing, has no moral justification, despite the fact that the falling man is not liable to this defensive killing.

Second, like partialism, the self-preference rule permits defensive harm in some of the rare cases in which a defender under stress could have easily known that the attacker is totally innocent and therefore not liable to defensive harm. Suppose an ordinary defender does not know that the attacker is innocent and that she could easily gain knowledge about the liability of the attacker. This defender *might be* subject to the self-preference rule as well in case she does not know that she can gain the knowledge about the nature of the threat. Then, she might follow the self-preference rule instead of deliberating on the merits of the case. Being subject to this rule, she is exempted from the duty to assess the probability that her attacker is liable to defensive harm. Thus, under prospectivism of the second layer, killing an attacker whose innocence can easily be known is indistinguishable from killing an innocent bystander. Yet, Rule-SD insists that given the normal justification of the self-preference rule to which ordinary defenders are subject, defensive harming against a person who could have been known to be an innocent attacker can at least in principle be permissible.

Third, unlike partialism, Rule-SD does not permit a defender to kill attackers or threateners who are already known to her to be innocent. Further, the rule does not exempt a defender who knows that deliberation on the merits of the case is easily doable from conducting it. Rather, it merely exempts a stressed defender who lacks these pieces of knowledge from conducting an investigation into the attacker's liability. Thus, Rule-SD yields an asymmetry between fully rational but uninformed defenders and uninformed *ordinary* defenders.

Fourth, Rule-SD supports the intuition that egocentric reasons can only function as tiebreakers in one versus one self-defense cases. This is because the empirical generalizations that justify a rule permitting egocentric behavior in these cases are untrue of more complicated cases. Suppose the costs the defender would bear should she avoid killing the attacker are sufficiently low. In

For the limited, biased defender, the way to maximize expected value is to subject oneself to a rule *before* limitations and biases take hold. Accordingly, deliberators ought to follow a rule only if they justifiably believe that deliberation on the merits of the case at the time of action won't bring about better results.

such a case, the benefit she secures by defensively killing an attacker is less likely to justify self-preference. As a consequentialist would put it, even if the attacker is fully culpable for the threat he poses, an outcome whereby the attacker is killed and the defender's minor interest is protected is worse than an outcome in which the attacker stays alive and the defender suffers minor harm. The nonconsequentialist articulation of Rule-SD might analyze this situation in different terms but would reach the same conclusion.

Suppose the aggregate costs the defender needs to inflict in order to survive are higher than they are in one versus one cases. Consider, for example, a modification of *Innocent Threat* where the defender is threatened by a large number of trapped elevator passengers. As opposed to the culpability/innocence of attackers, in this self-defense case the number of falling persons is a visible feature of the case, such that even defenders under stress can grasp it. Hence, treating a self-preference rule as a pre-emptive reason is less likely to lead the defender to make the right choice, impartially considered.

Self-preference is likely to be impartially justified in one versus one cases also because, usually, an ordinary defender is certain that she is innocent vis-à-vis the threat imposed on her but has no easy way to determine the degree to which the attacker is responsible for the threat he is posing. This asymmetry yields only minor impact on the first-order moral reasons in one versus many self-defense cases. Put, again, in terms of consequences, an outcome in which the innocent defender is killed and ten minimally culpable attackers survive might be preferable to an outcome in which the ten are killed and the single defender survives. Before following the self-preference rule, defenders should try to make sure that they are indeed facing a one versus one self-defense case governed by this rule.

Innocent Threats/Innocent Bystanders, *Bear/Flotsam*, and the Pre-emptive Rules Morality of Harm

Free competition in *Flotsam* involves use of force, while free competition in *Bear* does not. This difference seems insignificant from standard consequentialist perspectives. Moreover, this difference seems insignificant from deontological perspectives that centralize the means principle. This section argues that, properly enriched, Rule-SD explains the moral significance of violence in these cases and, thus, successfully draws a plausible distinction between versions of *Bear* and *Flotsam*.

Consider two distinctions and the empirical generalizations associated with them. The first is the attackers/bystanders distinction: unlike attackers, bystanders are not likely to be liable to defensive harm. The second is between violent and nonviolent harms: other things being equal, violence is more likely to cause harm than other types of action. In light of these generalizations, the rule of self-preference offered above would be normally justified only if it sharply restricts the permission to self-preference. The rule allows self-preference and exempts the ordinary defender from attending to agent-neutral reasons, only if the harm to bystanders is unlikely to be disproportionate.[31] Typically, a harm is likely to be disproportionate if it results from violent and direct involvement.

> The rule of self-preference in self-defense: a defender can promote her own interests in one vs. one (or less) self-defense cases . . . as far as (c) she does not foreseeably or intentionally harm bystanders by using force against them, cheating them, stealing from them, or any other illicit (but well defined) means.

The restriction is designed to impede the undesirable foreseeable effects of egocentric behavior in designated circumstances, without forcing the defender to overcome his partiality.

These restrictions are *not* prohibitions. The self-preference rule does *not prohibit* killing bystanders or cheating or stealing from them. Rather, it states that *if*, in order to survive, the defender must violently harm bystanders, she is not exempted from deliberating on the merits of the case. Violently harming bystanders and, especially, stealing from them might be justified by lesser evil considerations; the permission to do or allow these harms can never be grounded in the self-preference rule. Thus, Rule-SD is consistent with the view which asserts that if intentionally inflicting serious harm on bystanders is necessary for the defender's survival, the defender is permitted to inflict it, as far as she makes sure that the inflicted harm is a lesser evil.[32]

[31] Put in terms coined by Jeff McMahan, in the designated circumstances, reasons grounded in *narrow proportionality* are pre-empted by the self-preference rule. (Narrow proportionality determines the size of harm to which the attacker/threatener is liable in proportion to the degree to which he is responsible for the threat he poses). For this distinction between narrow proportionality (that usually concerns harms inflicted intentionally) and wide proportionality (that usually concern harms inflicted foreseeably but unintentionally on bystanders), see Jeff McMahan, *Killing in War* (Oxford: Clarendon, 2009), sec. 1.3.

[32] As Ryan Jenkins pointed out in personal communication, I am permitted to steal from innocent bystanders to defend myself. Suppose you and I are running away from the bear, and I tip over a picnic basket that I find in someone else's campsite. I thereby destroy someone else's property. But by doing so, I save both your life and mine as the bear focuses its attention on the food from the basket. Surely this is permissible. In fact, it seems obviously preferable to the two of us running until one of us is exhausted and then mauled.

Interestingly, permissible egocentrism in the free market is restricted in the same way. Every individual is allowed to choose the most advantageous employment for whatever capital he or she can command. According to the free market myth, this rule enhances conformity to agent-neutral reasons: the egocentric agent is led to prefer the employment that is most advantageous to society. And yet, permissible egocentrism is constrained: as its undesirable effects are immediate and certain, robbery is prohibited even if it provides advantageous employment to some people. The same is true of enslavement. The regime restricts egocentric agents operating within the free market by ruling out clearly undesirable activities, without imposing on them a duty to be impartial.

Rule-SD offers a very simple resolutions of various *Bear*-like cases. They are all a one versus less than one self-defense case, in which both parties face a wild animal threat. Initially, the parties, you and I, do not threaten each other: I am a bystander vis-à-vis the threat imposed on you and, mutatis mutandis, the same is true of you. Supposedly, if it is part of a plan to divert the threat to another innocent bystander, running away in *Bear* is impermissible. Under a means principle–based morality, no first-order difference exists between diverting the threat posed by the bear by running as fast as one can and diverting it by using force against the other party.

But consider a *Bear*-like case—*Bear with Uncertainty*—in which we are both subject to the self-preference rule because we are unaware of the idiosyncratic features of the case. All we initially know is that the bear threatens us. What follows from our subjection to the self-preference rule is that we are allowed to exhibit strong egocentrism as long as we respect the restrictions specified by the third part of the rule. That is, we are allowed to run as fast as we can without taking each other's interests into account, insofar as we do not use force against bystanders, cheat them, steal from them, or act in any other illicit way toward them.

True, it turns out that in running away from the bear, I violate the means principle; I divert the bear to you, and (we assume that) diverting the threat by running away is just as wrong as using force against bystanders. Yet, *Bear with Uncertainty* is one of the unusual cases governed by the self-preference rule. When facing a threat by wild animals, the right choice of the uncertain defender is most probably to run away; impartial deliberation on the merits of the case will likely amount to a waste of time (the most precious resource in such situations). Being subject to the self-preference rule, I have a pre-emptive reason not to respond to agent-neutral reasons, so I do not have to make sure that I do not use you as a means. Mutatis mutandis, the same is true of you: you are allowed to run as fast as you can and in fact to prevent me from doing what I am at liberty to do. Unbeknown to us, these permissions conflict with each other: I am allowed to divert the bear to you, and you are allowed to prevent me from doing so. Thus,

Rule-SD implies that I am permitted to run from the bear *only* if it is not obvious to me that I use you in avoiding the bear.

Turn to *Flotsam*. In the relevant sense, we are both bystanders vis-à-vis the threat imposed on us; we are threatened by drowning in the deep waters rather than by each other. Perhaps, in another sense, we do threaten each other by virtue of our presence on the flotsam, which cannot carry us both. Still, the self-preference rule would treat us as bystanders because there is no presumption that a person who poses a threat by being on the *Flotsam* is minimally culpable for this threat, and therefore, there is no presumption that he or she is liable to defensive harm. Being subject to the self-preference rule, we are allowed to exhibit strong egocentrism, as long as it does not involve using force against bystanders.

Yet, in this case, mutual egocentric behavior entails violence, which the strong partiality rule does not allow.[33] If the parties in *Flotsam* are subject to no other pre-emptive rule, they should resolve their conflict by deliberating on the merits of the case they are facing. Considered on its merits, according to any view that relates morality to impartiality, fair procedure seems to be the only acceptable resolution of this case.

The resolutions of *Bear with Uncertainty* and *Flotsam* offered by the pre-emptive rule morality of harm are consistent with the claim that, considered on their merits, the cases are indistinguishable. All Rule-SD does (and can do) is provide a second-order distinction between these cases, which implies that the parties might be subject to the self-preference rule in *Bear*-like cases that involve uncertainty but never in *Flotsam*-like cases.

Conclusion

Rule-SD asserts that ordinary defenders facing one versus one (or less) self-defense circumstances are subject to a pre-emptive rule allowing them to defensively harm attackers and exempting them from conducting research into whether the attacker is liable to defensive killing. Rule-SD explains why uncertain, ordinary deliberators might have conflicting moral permissions in innocent threat cases and symmetrical cases like *Bear* (where X is permitted to kill Y in self-defense, while Y is permitted to prevent X from doing so). Moreover, the

[33] As Susanne Burri noted in a personal communication, it might be thought that the self-preference rule does not prohibit the parties to hang on to the flotsam, see who drowns faster; and if the other person drowns faster, I get to live because the flotsam will then support me. However, this might seem less like free competition and more like fair procedure to determine who should live, especially because of the restraint that the parties exhibit and their tacit agreement not to use force.

way the rule distinguishes between bystanders and attackers and between violent and nonviolent harms enables Rule-SD to draw a plausible moral distinction between different symmetrical cases like *Bear* and *Flotsam.*

References

Benbaji, Yitzhak. "A Defense of the Traditional War-Convention." *Ethics* 118 (2008): 464–495.

Broose, C., and R. A. Sorensen. "Ducking Harm." *Journal of Philosophy* 85 (1988): 115–134.

Burri, Susanne. "The Toss-Up Between a Profiting, Innocent Threat and His Victim." *Journal of Political Philosophy* 23 (2015): 146–165.

Darwall, Stephen. *The Second-Person Standpoint.* Cambridge, MA: Harvard University Press, 2006.

Davis, Nancy. "Abortion and Self-Defense." *Philosophy & Public Affairs* 13 (1984): 175–207.

Edmundson, William A. "Rethinking Exclusionary Reasons." *Law and Philosophy* 12 (1993): 329–343.

Ferrero, Luca. "Decisions, Diachronic Autonomy & the Division of Deliberative Labor." *Philosopher's Imprint* 10 (2010): 1–23.

Frowe, Helen. "Equating Innocent Threats and Bystanders." *Journal of Applied Philosophy* 25 (2008): 277–290.

Gans, Chaim. "Mandatory Rules and Exclusionary Reasons." *Philosophia* 15 (1986): 373–396.

Hooker, Brad. *Ideal Code, Real World: A Rule-Consequentialist Theory of Morality.* Oxford: Oxford University Press, 2000a.

Hooker, Brad. "Impartiality, Predictability and Indirect Consequentialism." In *Well-Being and Morality: Essays in Honour of James Griffin,* edited by Roger Crisp and Brad Hooker, 129–142. Oxford: Oxford University Press, 2000b.

Jackson, Frank. "Decision-Theoretic Consequentialism and the Nearest and Dearest Objection." *Ethics* 101 (1991): 461–482.

Korsgaard, Christine M. "The Reasons We Can Share: An Attack on the Distinction Between Agent-Relative and Agent-Neutral Values." *Social Philosophy and Policy* 10 (1993): 24–51.

Lazar, Seth. "In Dubious Battle: Uncertainty and the Ethics of Killing." *Philosophical Studies* (2012): 1–25.

McMahan, Jeff. "Self-Defense and the Problem of the Innocent Attacker." *Ethics* 104 (1994): 252–290.

McMahan, Jeff. "The Ethics of Killing in War." *Ethics* 114 (2004): 693–753.

McMahan, Jeff. "The Basis of Moral Liability to Defensive Killing." *Philosophical Issues* 15 (2005): 386–405.

McMahan, Jeff. *Killing in War.* Oxford: Clarendon Press, 2009.

Montague, Philip. "Self-Defense and Choosing Among Lives." *Philosophical Studies* 40 (1981): 207–219.

Montague, Philip. "Self-Defense, Culpability, and Distributive Justice." *Law and Philosophy* 29 (2010): 75–91.

Moore, Michael S. "Authority, Law and Razian Reasons." *Southern California Law Review* 62 (1989): 866–867.

Nagel, T. *The Possibility of Altruism.* Princeton, NJ: Princeton University Press, 1970.

Otsuka, Michael. "Killing the Innocent in Self-Defense." *Philosophy & Public Affairs* 23 (1994): 74–94.

Øverland, Gerhard. "Contractual Killing." *Ethics* 115 (2005): 692–720.

Parfit, Derek. *On What Matters.* Oxford: Oxford University Press, 2011.

Perry, Stephen. "Second Order Reasons, Uncertainty and Legal Theory." *Southern California Law Review* 62 (1989): 932–957.

Pettit, P. "Universality Without Utilitarianism." *Mind* 96 (1987): 74–82.

Quong, Jonathan. "Killing in Self-Defense." *Ethics* 119 (2009): 507–537.
Raz, Joseph. *The Morality of Freedom*. Oxford: Oxford University Press, 1986.
Raz, Joseph. *Practical Reason and Norms*. Princeton, NJ: Princeton University Press, 1990.
Ridge, Michael. "Reasons for Action: Agent-Neutral vs. Agent-Relative." In *The Stanford Encyclopaedia of Philosophy*, edited by Edward N. Zalta. Winter 2011 edition. http://plato.stanford.edu/archives/win2011/entries/reasons-agent/.
Ripstein, Arthur. "Authority and Coercion." *Philosophy and Public Affairs* 32 (2004): 2–35.
Ripstein, Arthur. "Beyond the Harm Principle." *Philosophy and Public Affairs* 34 (2006): 215–245.
Scanlon, T. M. *What We Owe to Each Other*. Cambridge: Harvard University Press, 1998.
Schauer, Fred. *Playing by the Rules: An Examination of Rule-Based Decision-Making in Law and in Life*. Oxford: Clarendon Press, 1991.
Shapiro, Scott. "Authority." In *The Oxford Handbook of Jurisprudence and Philosophy of Law*, edited by Jules Coleman and Scott Shapiro, 382–439. Oxford: Oxford University Press, 2004.
Strawser, Bradley J. *The Bounds of Defense: Killing, Moral Responsibility, and War*. New York: Oxford University Press, forthcoming.
Tadros, Victor. *The Ends of Harm*. Oxford: Oxford University Press, 2011.
Thomson, Judith J. "Self-Defense." *Philosophy & Public Affairs* 20, no. 4 (1991): 283–310.
Thompson, Michael. "What Is It to Wrong Someone? A Puzzle About Justice." In *Reason and Value*, edited by R. Jay Wallace, Philip Pettit, Samuel Scheffler, and Michael Smith, 333–384. Oxford: Clarendon Press, 2006.
Uniacke, Suzanne. *Permissible Killing: The Self-Defence Justification of Homicide*. Cambridge: Cambridge University Press, 1994.
Waldron, Jeremy. "Rights in Conflict." *Ethics* 99 (1989): 503–519.
Wallace, R. Jay. "The Deontic Structure of Morality." In *Thinking About Reasons: Themes From the Philosophy of Jonathan Dancy*, edited by David Bakhurst, Margaret Olivia Little, and Brad Hooker, 137–167. Oxford: Oxford University Press, 2013.
Weinrib, Ernest. *The Idea of Private Law*. Cambridge, MA: Harvard University Press, 1995.
Wollard, Fiona. "If This Is My body . . .: A Defence of the Doctrine of Doing and Allowing." *Pacific Philosophical Quarterly* 94 (2013): 315–341.
Zimmerman, Michael J. *Living with Uncertainty: The Moral Significance of Ignorance*. Cambridge: Cambridge University Press, 2008.

3

Do Some Soldiers Deserve to Die More Than Others?

Selective Conscientious Objectors and Liability

DAVID WHETHAM

Introduction

Those who have an objection to warfare can be divided into two distinct groups: those who object to all forms of warfare, regardless of how noble the cause is—therefore "general" conscientious objectors—and those who do not object to warfare in principle but *object to a specific war* for ethical, religious, or cultural reasons—selective conscientious objectors.[1] Merely objecting to a particular conflict is not enough to belong to this category. Somebody who believes that a particular war is counterproductive, stupid, or just plain bad foreign policy does not qualify as a conscientious objector. Someone must believe that the war is morally, not just politically, wrong, and that his or her participation in it would therefore be contrary to his or her conscience.[2]

The issue of selective conscientious objection was not a significant concern on the public radar until fairly recently. The end of the Cold War ushered in a new era of apparently discretionary conflicts, or "wars of choice," not necessary easily identified with national survival or even core national interests.[3] These appear to pose different ethical and legal challenges for democracies when

[1] For the sake of simplicity, this chapter will use *soldier* as a generic term to reflect members of the armed forces.

[2] Andrea Ellner, Paul Robinson, and David Whetham, "Sometime They'll Give a War and Nobody Will Come," in *When Soldiers Say No: Selective Conscientious Objection in the Modern Military*, ed. Andrea Ellner, Paul Robinson, and David Whetham (Farnham, UK: Ashgate, 2014a), 5.

[3] David Whetham, "Introduction: Purpose, Content and Structure," in *Ethics, Law and Military Operations*, ed. David Whetham (Basingstoke, UK: Palgrave Macmillan, 2010), 1–9.

compared to wars of national survival. Due to the existential threat posed by the two sides, the Cold War offered a fairly clear ethical backdrop. However, the relative uncertainties of the post–Cold War period have led to an increasing fascination with the subject of military ethics around the world and raised questions relating to the nature of contemporary military service on behalf of democratic communities. The catalyst for much of this thinking was the controversial decision to invade Iraq in 2003. The scale of the public protests was unprecedented, dwarfing even those related to Vietnam. A coordinated day of protest around the world in February 2003 involved more than 600 cities and has been described as the "largest protest event in human history."[4] Official police figures conservatively put the attendance at the antiwar march in London as in excess of 750,000 people, making it the largest demonstration the United Kingdom has ever seen.[5] However, despite the level of opposition, the war still went ahead. With such a background, it is hardly surprising that public and then academic interest turned to the question of when it is right or wrong for an individual to participate in a conflict the justice of which he or she is not certain about.[6]

Old Wine in New Bottles

Of course, the question as to whether soldiers should be expected to examine their consciences before fighting in the name of a particular cause is not a new one. As far back as Augustine it was understood that all rulers had an obligation to maintain the peace and that it was this obligation that gave them the right and duty to wage war in order to maintain that peace.[7] Subjects were *obliged* to participate in such activities for the common good, but they were not expected to question, let alone challenge, the ruler's position. This attitude led to a very clear separation of moral responsibility—it was the ruler who would face any divine retribution for waging an unjust war rather than the soldiers, who were simply obeying their orders to participate in it. This moral separation stood even if a soldier had doubts about the justness of the cause.[8] For example, Vitoria, writing in the mid-sixteenth century, argued for the necessity of this distinction for the

[4] Stefaan Walgrave and Dieter Rucht, eds., *The World Says No to War: Demonstrations Against the War on Iraq* (Minneapolis: University of Minnesota Press, 2010), xiii.

[5] The BBC estimated that around a million attended: "Anti-War Rally Makes Its Mark," BBC News, February 19, 2003, http://news.bbc.co.uk/1/hi/uk/2767761.stm.

[6] For an in-depth treatment of the subject, see Ellner, Robinson, and Whetham, eds., *When Soldiers Say No.*

[7] Augustine, *Against Faustus the Manichean*, in *Augustine: Political Writings*, trans. Michael W. Tkacz and Douglas Kries, ed. Ernest L. Fortin and Douglas Kries (Indianapolis: Hackett, 1994), 222.

[8] Alex J. Bellamy, *Just Wars: From Cicero to Iraq* (Cambridge: Polity Press, 2006), 28.

defense of the realm: "if subjects cannot serve in war except they are first satisfied of its justice, the State would fall into grave peril."[9]

The individual soldier was therefore expected, on moral as well as practical grounds, to give the leaders the benefit of the doubt. That didn't mean unqualified obedience of course. Vitoria also argued that it was possible that someone could be faced with "arguments and proofs of the injustice of war so powerful, that even citizens and subjects . . . may not use ignorance as an excuse for serving as soldiers . . . if the war seems patently unjust to the subject, he must not fight, even if he is ordered to do so by the prince."[10] If one was simply *unsure* about the situation, then one's duty was to obey the king because it could be safely assumed that he was in a better position to judge. However, *knowingly* doing the wrong thing crosses a moral boundary. Some things are so clearly wrong that one cannot simply dismiss the moral concerns by relying on an assumption that others know best. While Francisco De Vitoria (1483–1546) was writing nearly 500 years ago, "this is a theme that still has clear contemporary relevance."[11] Today, the idea that a soldier is expected to disobey a blatantly illegal order is widely accepted. As the Nuremberg trials demonstrate, there are ethical and legal lines that it is so wrong to cross that one cannot claim the defense of following superior orders.[12] However, it also widely accepted that it is not up to the soldier to question the policy of his or her government. There is a perceived difference between a local level, where soldiers are expected to exercise their moral autonomy and refuse to do the wrong thing, and the higher level dominated by government policy regarding the decision to go to war. At this level there is an epistemic consideration about what individual soldiers can realistically be expected to know about. The traditional assumption is that most soldiers are simply not in a position to know all the relevant facts about their government's decision to go to war and so are incapable of reaching a suitably informed judgment on the justice or injustice of the war.

On this theme, Vitoria argued that senior military commanders do have a specific professional responsibility to "speak truth to power" and examine the justice of a war, even if necessary, to try to avert a conflict that is unjust

[9] Quoted in Michael Walzer, *Just and Unjust Wars: A Moral Argument with Historical Illustrations*, 2nd ed. (New York: Basic Books, 1992), 39.

[10] Vitoria, "On the Law of War," in *The Ethics of War: Classic and Contemporary Readings*, ed. Gregory M. Reichberg, Henrik Syse, and Endre Begby (Oxford: Blackwell, 2006), 318–319.

[11] David Whetham, "The Just War Tradition: A Pragmatic Compromise," in *Ethics, Law and Military Operations*, ed. David Whetham (Basingstoke, UK: Palgrave Macmillan, 2010), 65–89.

[12] George R. Lucas, "Advice and Dissent: The Uniform Perspective," *Journal of Military Ethics* 8, no, 2 (2009): 141–161.

by providing appropriate advice to the ruler.[13] However, even with this qualification, Francisco Suarez (1548–1617) argued they are still expected to salute and execute the state's orders if their arguments are unsuccessful.[14] It is this expectation of service and the assumption that the state knows best that inform the basis of the moral equality of combatants—that soldiers on both sides are in the same moral position of assuming their own side is just—that has underpinned our traditional understanding of moral responsibility on war. According to this view, this is why soldiers on both sides of the battle—just and unjust in an objective sense—are morally permitted to fight and should be treated equally as a result.

Contemporary Challenges

In recent years, this traditional "default" position has started to come under increasing pressure. Some argue that the context has fundamentally changed. Modern soldiers are better educated and far better informed than their predecessors. Access to media means that only those who choose not to find out about the world remain in a state of ignorance about the moral rights and wrongs of a conflict, and surely if one chooses not to ask questions, then one cannot be said to remain blameless.[15] At the same time, things like the "dodgy dossier" of fabricated evidence for justifying the 2003 Gulf War challenge traditional attitudes toward deference and the idea that our leaders "know best."[16] Democratic societies, mindful of the horrors of the past, want to be confident that their soldiers are not moral automata. Around the world, military training and educational institutions spend time and effort in ensuring that they produce individuals capable of making appropriate ethical decisions in and outside of times of conflict.[17] Taken together, this changed context seems "incompatible with claims that the

[13] McMaster argues that there was an abdication of responsibility by American military leadership during the Vietnam War in precisely this area. H. R. McMaster, *Dereliction of Duty: Johnson, McNamara, the Joint Chiefs of Staff, and the Lies that Led to Vietnam* (New York: Harper Perennial, 1998).

[14] See Whetham, "Just War Tradition," 74. See also Lucas, "Advice and Dissent."

[15] See Dan Zupan, "Selective Conscientious Objection and the Just Society," in *When Soldiers Say No: Selective Conscientious Objection in the Modern Military*, ed. Andrea Ellner, Paul Robinson, and David Whetham (Farnham, UK: Ashgate, 2014), for an account of the limits of what can be expected on an epistemic level by soldiers committed at short notice to an operation.

[16] Richard Norton-Taylor, "Iraq Dossier Drawn Up to Make Case for War—Intelligence Officer," *Guardian*, May 12, 2011, http://www.theguardian.com/world/2011/may/12/iraq-dossier-case-for-war.

[17] See, for example, Don Carrick, James Connolly, and Paul Robinson, eds., *Ethics Education for Irregular Warfare* (Farnham, UK: Ashgate, 2009).

same soldiers must ignore their consciences regarding the justice of the wars in which they fight."[18] Rather, their critical faculties should be engaged in order to ensure that their consciences can be properly satisfied before they embark on military action.

Such considerations have led some, like Jeff McMahan, to argue that today soldiers have a duty to ensure that they are genuinely on the right side of a conflict:

> The wrong that is involved in fighting in an unjust war is very serious; it is the wrong of intentionally killing people who are doing nothing more than defending themselves and other innocent people from threats of wrongful harm.[19]

Opposing sides in a war cannot both be just in an objective sense, and yet the legitimate use of force requires that the innocent are not deliberately attacked. Just war revisionists have asked how it is justifiable to apply the principal of moral equality when one side (at least) must be in the wrong. As one of the leading thinkers in this movement, McMahan constructs a sophisticated logic about the moral risks associated with participating in an unjust conflict, with one of the implications being that *all* combatants have a duty to assure *themselves* of the justice of their cause (and by implication not obey orders to fight until they have done so) because otherwise one risks attacking and killing objectively innocent people—innocent because they are in the right and you are in the wrong.

Effectively, the burden of proof has changed from Vitoria's day. One cannot, and indeed must not, simply grant the prince (or the state) the benefit of the doubt because killing people who do not deserve to die is such a terrible wrong. *Seen in such a way*, it is difficult to see how military personnel who are engaged in fighting an unjust war can be excused from responsibility for fighting in such a war. Brian Orend suggests that we may decide that they are not as fully culpable as those who actually make the decision to go to war, but they might still be considered minor accomplices to a major crime: certainly, they are not fully responsible for the *jus ad bellum* violations involved in engaging in the war in the first place, but they are also not totally blameless.[20]

[18] Ellner, Robinson, Whetham, "Sometime They'll Give a War," 4.

[19] Jeff McMahan, *Killing in War* (Oxford: Oxford University Press, 2009), 132. With subtle variations, this position is supported by David Rodin, "Justifying Harm," *Ethics* 122 (2011): 109.

[20] Brian Orend, *The Morality of War* (Toronto, Canada: Broadview, 2006), 109.

Implications in the Real World

Just war revisionists argue that one cannot be excused from knowingly doing wrong on the basis of "he told me to do it," even if the "he" is the state. At the same time, being forced to do something because the cost of disobedience is high would appear to be some sort of blame mitigation or excuse. While perhaps not completely blameless, if I commit a murder only because there is another party holding a gun to my own head, one would have to assume that I am less responsible than if I do it of my own free will. This would appear to be akin to Orend's point about the accomplice above.

Of course, modern democratic states involved in discretionary conflicts do not enforce their will by means of a firing squad. However, that does not mean that those individuals who refuse to follow orders on the grounds of conscience are treated the same across those different states. Presumably, the easier it is to disobey, the more culpability one bears for doing the wrong thing. So, for example, if there is a formal mechanism by which one may "opt out" without detriment, someone who chose to do the wrong thing would surely be more morally culpable than someone else who faced jail time if they dissented and so reluctantly chose to participate out of fear of the consequences for himself or herself and his or her family.

So how are selective conscientious objectors treated in different places? The rest of this chapter will briefly look at how various forms of conscientious objection by professionals in all-volunteer militaries have been acknowledged or dealt with in the United States, Germany, and the United Kingdom. Along with many other democratic countries, all of these states accept that pacifists who object to all wars in principle should not be required to fight at all. However, the way that these three states deal with those who do not object to *all* wars but rather believe that participation in a *specific conflict* is wrong is heavily influenced by their different political systems, historical backgrounds, and legal traditions. This leads to the intriguing idea that soldiers who knowingly participate in an unjust war are more or less morally responsible depending upon the degree of moral autonomy they are institutionally sanctioned to exhibit. So, for example, if a state permits a great deal of freedom in exercising one's moral autonomy and imposes no sanction for refusing one's service, then presumably one is considered more morally culpable if one chooses to fight in that state's unjust war. The greater the penalty or cost of saying "no," the less culpable the soldier is for the wrong he or she goes on to commit by fighting in an unjust war. It is therefore possible that soldiers fighting an unjust war on behalf of some states may be more morally responsible and are therefore more liable to be killed than those soldiers fighting an unjust war on behalf of another state.

The United States

The United States acknowledges in law that even with an all-volunteer force, someone who joins the military may develop ideas and beliefs that subsequently turn out to be incompatible with military service.[21] In such circumstances, as long as applicants can demonstrate that their new position is related to a traditional religious belief or set of overarching ethical or moral beliefs rather than political, sociological, or purely personal ethical grounds, they can apply for conscientious objector status. If this is granted, they have to leave the military.[22] However, while this is a theoretical possibility, taking such a path is not easy. Applicants are passively or actively discouraged, and there is little transparency about how one should go about starting the process.[23] Due to the barriers put in their way, most of those who might wish to "never apply for conscientious objector status. Some of them go AWOL [Absent Without Leave], some can prove medical reasons or some may challenge their enlistment agreements."[24] For example, Specialist Augustine Augayo joined the Army in 2003 but disliked handling weapons. After deploying to Iraq as a medic, he applied for conscientious objector status but found himself on guard duty rather than deployed on noncombatant tasks while his application was considered, then rejected. Despite being decorated for his service, he eventually went AWOL, deserted, and was ultimately discharged with bad conduct, his conscientious objection never being formally acknowledged.[25] Although only a single example, this demonstrates how difficult it can be for someone to refuse to fight on ethical grounds.

The problem of what to do in the face of moral questions becomes even more acute for those who have not changed their beliefs about war as a whole but come to view a specific conflict as immoral or illegal. There are no formal legitimate options available in between, on the one hand, becoming a complete

[21] While there is no draft in the United States, it is also true that the level of inducements to sign up to military service (college tuition fees, signing-on bonuses, etc.) may mean that, for some volunteers, the free choice is not absolute.

[22] Andrea Ellner, "War Resisters in the US and Britain—Supporting the Case for a Right to Selective Conscientious Objection?" in *When Soldiers Say No: Selective Conscientious Objection in the Modern Military*, ed. Andrea Ellner, Paul Robinson, and David Whetham (Abingdon-on-Thames, UK: Routledge, 2014).

[23] Ellner, "War Resisters in the US and Britain," 216.

[24] Bill Galvin of the US Center on Conscience and War, quoted in Jane O'Brien, "The Soldiers Who Can No Longer Fight," BBC News, March 4, 2009, http://news.bbc.co.uk/1/hi/world/americas/7900059.stm.

[25] Marjorie Cohn and Kathleen Gilberd, *Rules of Disengagement—The Politics and Honor of Military Dissent* (Sausalito, CA: PoliPointPress, 2009), 32f. Cited in Ellner, "War Resisters in the US and Britain," 216.

conscientious objector and renouncing participation in all war and, on the other hand, accepting that wherever your state sends you, you must obey.[26] Drawing on evidence from people who have worked with resisters, Ellner highlights that this "all or nothing" problem must have played a part in the huge increases in the numbers of those who failed to follow orders to train, deploy, redeploy, or rejoin their unit after leave in the years following the start of the Iraq War.[27] Claiming conscientious objector status might have helped some of these, but for many others, this would have been a dishonest or even dishonorable route as they had not changed their mind or beliefs about *all* war and still accepted that in some situations fighting is a legitimate option to defend one's state. An example of this would be T. J. Buonomo—a graduate of the US Air Force Academy and former Army officer who discussed his critical views of the Iraq War with fellow officers, speaking up about "illegal policies and actions."[28] This led to him being investigated and eventually administratively discharged. Even had he wished to take the conscientious objection route, it would not have been available to him as he supported (and wished to be deployed to) the intervention in Afghanistan—it was the war in Iraq that he believed to be wrong.

Buonomo believed he was not court-martialed because of a fear of the publicity that a freedom of speech defense would have provoked. However, the "poster child" of selective conscientious objection, Lt. Ehren Watada, US Army 5th Battalion, 20th Infantry Regiment, was handled rather differently.[29] In 2006, Watada refused to deploy to Iraq with his unit, becoming the first US commissioned officer to refuse such orders. His decision was based on his belief that the war was illegal in that it violated the US Constitution and the War Powers Act, as well as the United Nations Charter, the Geneva Conventions, and the Nuremberg principles banning wars of aggression and, thus, that following such orders would make him a party to war crimes.[30] Any official or institutional preference for keeping the story confined or controlled was made impossible by Watada's public stance. Following his refusal to deploy in Iraq, Watada spoke at a number of public functions and gave media interviews in order to explain his actions. Each time this happened, he followed established rules for military

[26] The only exception would be very senior officers who can choose to retire early, whether that be over an issue of conscience or something else, although again the way that such retirements are recorded makes building a clear idea of the scale very difficult to determine. My thanks to Martin Cook for pointing out this particular exception.

[27] Ellner, "War Resisters in the US and Britain," 320.

[28] Buff Whitman-Bradley, Sarah Lazare, and Cynthia Whitman-Bradley, eds., *About Face—Military Resisters Turn Against War* (Oakland, CA: PM Press, 2011), 148.

[29] Lucas, "Advice and Dissent."

[30] Hal Bernton, "Officer at Fort Lewis calls Iraq war illegal, refuses order to go," *Seattle Times*, June 7, 2006, http://old.seattletimes.com/html/iraq/2003044627_nogo7m.html.

personnel making statements in public, notifying his commanding officer, wearing civilian clothes rather than uniform, and making it clear that he was only expressing his own personal views.

Whether this publicity at a difficult political time was the reason that Watada was court-martialed or not, he was initially charged with seven offenses under the Uniform Code of Military Justice, with three of these—"missing movement" and two charges of "conduct unbecoming an officer and a gentleman"—proceeding to trial. The judge presiding over the court-martial got to the heart of the issue before the trial had even begun by ruling that the issue of whether the war was legal was a political question "not suitable for judicial consideration"![31] This had the effect of ruling the order to deploy as lawful and prevented Watada's defense counsel from presenting any evidence that would question the legality of the conflict.[32]

His court-martial eventually ended up being declared a mistrial due to the prosecution case being built upon inadmissible self-incriminating statements Watada had made. A second court-martial was set in 2008 amid arguments about double jeopardy. Army spokesperson Joe Piek made it clear that they were going to continue pursuing Watada through the courts on any of the original seven counts if they could: "The one element that concerns us most is that this case has always been and will forever be about a soldier—in this case, a lieutenant, a commissioned officer—who refused orders to deploy."[33] However, the Army eventually dropped the case in 2009, and Watada was discharged on October 2, three and a half years after raising his objection.

Like Buonomo, Watada was not a conscientious objector as defined in the rules because he did not object to *all* wars (he was also happy to be posted to Afghanistan, for example). He was objecting to being sent to fight in a specific conflict and found himself being prosecuted through the courts as a result. If these cases can be considered representative of broader policy, the US government clearly has no intention of allowing individual service members to "pick and choose which obligations they fulfil."[34] Exercising moral autonomy with

[31] See the chapter "Power and Authority—Giving and Following Orders," in Stephen Coleman, *Military Ethics: An Introduction with Case Studies* (New York: Oxford University Press, 2012).

[32] Although it is beyond the scope of this chapter, it is worth noting that Watada's arguments were based on legal arguments rather than necessarily moral ones. Some of the reasons that a sharp distinction cannot be maintained between the two realms can be found in Henry Shue, "Do We Need a Morality of War?" in *Just and Unjust Warriors: The Moral and Legal Status of Soldiers*, edited by David Rodin and Henry Shue (Oxford: Oxford University Press, 2010), 106–111.

[33] Quoted in Jeremy Brecher and Brendan Smith, "The Trials of Ehren Watada," *The Nation*, June 1, 2009.

[34] Andrea Ellner, Paul Robinson, & David Whetham, "The Practice and Philosophy of Selective Conscientious Objection," in *When Soldiers Say No: Selective Conscientious Objection in the*

respect to *which* wars a soldier feels he or she should fight in is not something that is acceptable within this system and comes with a cost to those seeking to exercise such autonomy. Democracy does not extend into the barracks.

The Federal Republic of Germany

On the face of it, the German context provides for quite a contrast to that in the United States. Total defeat and the fall of the Nazi regime at the end of the Second World War led to the adoption of a completely new German constitution in 1949. This "Basic Law for the Federal Republic of Germany" sought to draw a clear line under the atrocities carried out by obedient German soldiers in the previous war. It guaranteed all Germans certain fundamental human rights: the right to freedom of faith and conscience as well as the right to refuse to perform military service if this was against that conscience. At the time of the introduction of this law, many feared that such a provision would forever neuter the ability of the German state to defend itself and its people. However, although controversial, it was included despite objections relating to the security of the state because of the recent memory of the "mass slumber of conscience" in which millions of Germans simply said "orders are orders, and killed in view of that."[35]

Even as national service was introduced following the war to ensure that the nation's military remained representative of wider society, a right to conscientious objection was enshrined in the very fabric of the new state. Everybody could avail themselves of their right—whether conscript, regular, or reservist. It recognized that everybody could change their mind or, through education or new beliefs, come to hold a belief that was incompatible with armed service. In such circumstances, the individual could not be compelled to serve. Of course, to exercise such a right was not automatic. Someone claiming such an ethical position would be legally obliged to have his or her conscience explored and rigorously tested by a board of examiners who were in a position to grant or reject the soldier's motion for conscientious objection. The board of examiners would be looking for evidence of a genuine shift in beliefs to a position where taking up

Modern Military, ed. Andrea Ellner, Paul Robinson, and David Whetham (Abingdon-on-Thames, UK: Routledge, 2014b), 246.

[35] Fritz Eberhard, quoted in Jürgen Rose, "Conscience in Lieu of Obedience: Cases of Selective Conscientious Objection in the German Bundeswehr," in *When Soldiers Say No: Selective Conscientious Objection in the Modern Military*, ed. Andrea Ellner, Paul Robinson, and David Whetham (Abingdon-on-Thames, UK: Routledge, 2014), 177. One of the drivers for this was a desire to recognize those who had been executed for refusing to serve the Nazi war machine.

arms was going to be incompatible with the fundamental freedom of conscience enshrined in German law. One can see such ideas enshrined in the German military concept of *Innere Führung*, or "inner leadership," of the citizen in uniform where, unlike the traditional view expressed above, "democracy *does not* end at the barrack's gate."[36]

The right for anyone to become a genuine conscientious objector was therefore clear. This position was not, however, generally understood to be a right to *selective* conscientious objection. One did not have a right to choose which wars one participated in—just the right to reject participation in *all* wars. This "bounded" or restrictive interpretation of the German Basic Law was demonstrated in 2003 when disciplinary proceedings were started against Major Florian Pfaff for refusing to contribute to a software program that had the potential to be used directly or indirectly to provide logistical support for the war in Iraq—a war that Major Pfaff believed was an illegal war of aggression.[37] Once combat operations had begun, Major Pfaff informed his superiors that he would not obey any orders, if by executing them he would become guilty of collaborating in the "murderous occupation of Iraq by the US (and others)."[38] In February 2004, he was found guilty of insubordination and disobedience and demoted to the rank of captain. What happened next was significant on many levels—an appeal was immediately lodged, and in 2005 a higher court overturned the decision of the original court-martial. Major Pfaff was instead provided with an absolute discharge. The judges stated that "In case of a conflict between conscience and legal obligation the freedom of conscience is 'inviolable.'"[39]

The implications of what was effectively a test case were not immediately felt—the findings of an obscure court-martial appeal were not highlighted, and the government chose to call it an isolated case with no real attention being paid to any wider relevance for the military or society as a whole.[40] In 2007, however, the issue arose again in a way that could not be quietly dismissed when Lt. Colonel Jürgen Rose made an official request to be exempted from anything to

[36] Wolf Graf von Baudissin, quoted in Rose, "Conscience in Lieu of Obedience," 181.

[37] This and the next case are explored in some depth in Rose, "Conscience in Lieu of Obedience," 186ff.

[38] Florian Pfaff, quoted from Second Senate for Military Jurisdiction of the Federal Administration Court, June 21, 2005, BVerwG 2 WD 12.04, 103 http://www.bverwg.de/entscheidungen/pdf/210605U2WD12.04.0.pdf.

[39] Bundesverwaltungsgericht, *op. cit.*, 106.

[40] The case of the German fighter pilots who had refused to participate in Suppression of Enemy Air Defence missions in 1999 had also been allowed to quietly disappear—the military choosing to avoid disciplinary action for fear of the negative publicity that might have resulted at a politically delicate time. See Jürgen Rose, "Gehorsam bis zum Hindukusch?" *S&F Sicherheit und Frieden* 22, no. 3 (2004): 134–135.

do with deploying Tornado aircraft to Afghanistan due to "grave reservations with respect to constitutional, international, criminal and international criminal law."[41] The constitutional angle led to a complaint being lodged with the Federal Constitutional Court, guaranteeing widespread media coverage in Germany. This case could not be downplayed or ignored, but perhaps in light of the 2005 ruling, the German government chose not to prosecute this particular case by court-martial. Rose was simply moved to another division instead, thus removing him from the cause of the problem.

While, of course, the legal position could be tested once again, such recent constitutional developments in Germany appear to demonstrate that, unlike in many other states, the right to reject participation in a specific conflict that one disagrees with *on moral grounds* does not become suspended just because someone joins the military. The same basic constitutional principles remain applicable to everyone, soldier or civilian, regular or reservist, conscript or volunteer. While selective conscientious objection is not explicitly recognized as a term, and of course the German state could seek to amend or challenge the situation again in court, the Basic Laws at the heart of the German constitution do appear to privilege individual conscience in a way that effectively means that a refusal to serve in a particular conflict on moral grounds both exists and can be exercised without risking punishment.

The United Kingdom

The policy position in the United Kingdom appears much like the position of the United States; while military personnel can appeal to leave the military if they become conscientious objectors to all wars, the United Kingdom does not recognize a right to object to serving in a specific conflict. In the United Kingdom, it appears as if "conscientious objection to military service has been a rare event."[42] However, Ellner points to the fact that the United Kingdom keeps no publically available official statistics on applications, making a straightforward assessment rather difficult.[43] The Ministry of Defence's response to a Member of Parliament's argument in 2006 that over a thousand British military personnel had deserted

[41] Jürgen Rose, "Aufklären, damit die anderen bomben können. Dokumentation. Antrag des Oberstleutnants Jürgen Rose, von allen dienstlichen Aufgaben bei einem Tornado-Einsatz in Afghanistan entbunden zu werden," *Freitag—Die Ost-West-Wochenzeitung*, March 23, 2007, 7.

[42] Stephen Deakin, "Conscientious Objection to Military Service in Britain," in *When Soldiers Say No: Selective Conscientious Objection in the Modern Military*, ed. Andrea Ellner, Paul Robinson, and David Whetham (Abingdon-on-Thames, UK: Routledge, 2014), 116.

[43] Ellner, "War Resisters in the US and Britain," 215.

since the start of the Iraq War because they "questioned the morality and legality of the occupation" was to say that soldiers currently missing were considered "absent without leave" and that they would have to be court-martialed before it was possible to find them guilty of desertion.[44] Yet, for a variety of reasons, very few cases actually reached that stage, perhaps demonstrating the "skill with which the Ministry of Defence handled any such issues" in order to avoid fuss and disruption.[45] Officers who resign their commissions over a point of principle may also be rare, but whether the resignation is over equipment shortages or policy decisions, the way the numbers are recorded, again, makes interpretation difficult.[46]

While the right to object to serving in a specific conflict is not recognized, in practice there is a difference between the officially stated position and what actually happens. While the official position looks very similar to that of the United States, the actual policy may be closer to that of Germany (although it would be very difficult to find an official statement in either country to this effect). Just as Germany's historical context shaped its attitude toward conscience and military service, for the United Kingdom it was the experience of the Great War that set the tone for the following century. Consistent with its history, Britain began the war relying exclusively on an all-volunteer force, but the unprecedented scale of the First World War quickly led to pressure to introduce conscription. The Military Service Act of 1916 was controversial and needed to be steered carefully through Parliament in the face of a divided cabinet and country. The act permitted exception to conscripted service to be made on the grounds of conscience, although it did not, "perhaps could not," define this.[47] Either way, this "formal acknowledgement of the possibility of conscientious objection to military service has shaped British thinking and policy . . . ever since."[48] Of the 5 million men who served in the war, approximately half were conscripts. Out of this enormous number, according to official figures, only 16,000 refused and were found supporting noncombat roles to play in the war instead. A minority of 985 who, due to strong religious or political beliefs, refused to do anything that might aid the war effort, found themselves in prison instead, often subject to hard labor and solitary confinement. Perhaps surprisingly, as many of these

[44] "At least 1,000 UK Soldiers Desert," BBC News, May 28, 2006, http://news.bbc.co.uk/1/hi/uk/5024104.stm Cited in Deakin, "Conscientious Objection," 124.

[45] Deakin, "Conscientious Objection," 131.

[46] Deakin notes that, in effect, the processes of resigning one's commission and claiming conscientious objection are very similar due to the time it takes (12–18 months) and the requirement that one is still expected to deploy to a combat zone if required during that period. Deakin, "Conscientious Objection," 134.

[47] Deakin, "Conscientious Objection," 117.

[48] Deakin, "Conscientious Objection," 117.

were well connected and capable of publicizing their views, controversy followed this policy even in the middle of a war.[49] Amid the government embarrassment, a very British compromise was reached where many of these were released on health grounds. The fact that despite accusations of cowardice from some quarters, some of those people ended up in high positions within public service or even in the Houses of Parliament indicates the way that these people were viewed as principled objectors, by some at least. As the country entered World War Two, Prime Minister Chamberlain exemplified British attitudes to conscientious objection when he said,

> We learned something about this in the Great War and I think we found that it was both a useless and exasperating waste of time and effort to force such people to act in a manner which was contrary to their principles.[50]

The British position on conscientious objection was thus a practical one combined with a fear of challenge to the official consensus that might result in official embarrassment.

The United Kingdom returned to an all-volunteer force in 1970 but retained this general approach even though the perceived need for conscientious objection, universal or selective, was less of an issue but one that still occurred from time to time. Today, the established route for raising questions of conscience is still to bring them up with one's commanding officer. If the case is considered genuine, the soldier may be discharged from the military on compassionate grounds. "The evidence suggests that such resignations and discharges are mainly handled without acrimony and through established administrative procedures."[51] For example, Trooper Ben Griffin served in Iraq with the elite Special Air Service and came to the considered view that the war was both illegal and immoral and that the British people had been deliberately misled by their politicians. Rather than making a public protest, he explained his position to his commanding officer, expecting to be court-martialed for refusing to return to Iraq. However, to his surprise, he was permitted to leave with an unblemished military record *and* a glowing testimonial stating that he possessed the "strength and character to genuinely have the courage of his convictions."[52] Deakin gives

[49] John Rae, *Conscience and Politics* (London: Oxford University Press, 1970), 201. Cited in Deakin, "Conscientious Objection," 117.

[50] Prime Minister Chamberlain quoted in Denis Hayes, *Conscription Conflict* (London: Sheppard Press, 1949), 242–243.

[51] Deakin, "Conscientious Objection," 120.

[52] Sean Rayment, "I Didn't Join the British Army to Conduct American Foreign Policy," *Daily Telegraph*, March 12, 2006, http://www.telegraph.co.uk/news/uknews/1512767/

other historical examples of cases being handled in very similar ways, with soldiers who raise points of conscience being allowed either to leave or to continue their service in a different way, removed from the area or policy that caused them moral problems.[53]

That does not, of course, mean that the United Kingdom's approach is always consistent. Perhaps unsurprisingly, as it is not an officially stated policy, people with similar arguments may find themselves treated differently within the system, which prefers to employ "internal administrative procedures to deal with issues in this area."[54] An example may be that of Michael Lyons, who was court-martialed for refusing to take part in predeployment rifle training. He had requested a noncombat role and had been assigned medical duties. However, medical personnel may carry weapons for both personnel defense and that of their patients, thus the requirement for weapons training even in this role. Lyons had two requests for conscientious objection turned down, and he was eventually dismissed from the Royal Navy and sentenced to seven months detention by his court-martial.[55] On the face of it, this appears to demonstrate a clear inconsistency; but looked at in another way, the reason Griffin was treated differently from Lyons was the way he went about it, using "the military system of his chain of command to quietly make his protest" rather than refusing an order in predeployment training.[56] The cases that go to court-martial in the United Kingdom seem to be those where the individual "has refused legitimate orders and then pressed their case as a matter of conscientious objection," rather than doing things quietly and without fuss.[57]

What becomes very clear from the evidence is that the British military regards this as a practical rather than moral issue and has consistently "shown no interest in deliberating over anyone's conscience." As long as the issue is kept as a private matter, it tends to be accommodated, employing an approach "characterised by common sense administrative leniency."[58] If one chooses to make the issue public or politicize it, then courts-martial follow. This has also been consistent through history—when Captain Douglas-Home refused to take part in an attack on a French town in 1944 because he believed an aspect of the war policy was wrong and that this particular attack would lead to excessive and

I-didnt-join-the-British-Army-to-conduct-American-foreign-policy.html. Cited in Deakin, "Conscientious Objection," 125.

[53] Deakin, "Conscientious Objection," 119–130.

[54] Deakin, "Conscientious Objection," 119–130.

[55] "Navy Afghan War Objector Michael Lyons Detained," BBC News, July 5, 2011, http://www.bbc.co.uk/news/uk-england-devon-14028167.

[56] Deakin, "Conscientious Objection," 135. Deakin refers to other similar cases (e.g., 184–185).

[57] Deakin, "Conscientious Objection," 134.

[58] Deakin, "Conscientious Objection," 136.

disproportionate civilian casualties, the official response was to move him away from the fighting (and, of course, those doing the fighting). This would probably have been the end of it if Douglas-Home had not written to a newspaper publicizing the incident, leading to a court-martial and prison sentence.[59] Sixty years later, in 2006, Flight Lieutenant Malcolm Kendall-Smith was court-martialed for refusing to return to Iraq, claiming that the war was illegal and he did not wish to participate in an "act of aggression."[60] Just as in the US case of Watada, Kendall-Smith was not permitted to challenge the legality of the war in his court-martial, although by 2005 the legal situation had been transformed anyway by a clear United Nations mandate, presumably making the government confident of avoiding embarrassment in this area. Kendall-Smith had also already been to Iraq, had come back without making any objections known at the time, and was seen by the court as just wanting to avoid redeployment there. He was sent to prison for eight months and ordered to pay £20,000 toward his defense costs, the judge wishing to send a clear warning to others that "those who wear the Queen's uniform cannot pick and choose which orders they will obey."[61]

Conclusion

The United States, United Kingdom, and Germany exhibit similar attitudes to those in their military service who develop genuine moral objections to war. While the processes may vary, and it may be easier or harder to actually apply for in practice, in principle at least, those who renounce war completely have an acknowledged right to leave the military. On the face of it, two of the three states also have the same attitude to dealing with *selective* conscientious objection, where it is not war in general that is being objected to but a specific campaign, conflict, or war. Both the United Kingdom and the United States reject such a right as being incompatible with the discipline necessary for a professional military force charged with defending the state, a position the German state also adhered to until very recently. However, when translated into practice, each state actually deals with selective conscientious objectors in different ways.

[59] William Douglas-Home, *Sins of Commission* (Salisbury, MD: Michael Russell, 1985), 60–63. Cited in Deakin, "Conscientious Objection," 134.

[60] "RAF Doctor Jailed over Iraq Refusal," *Guardian*, April 13, 2006, http://www.guardian.co.uk/uk/2006/apr/13/military.iraq.

[61] "Prisoner of Conscience: RAF Doctor Who Refused Iraq Service Is Jailed," *Independent*, April 14, 2006, http://www.independent.co.uk/news/uk/crime/prisoner-of-conscience-raf-doctor-who-refused-iraq-service-is-jailed-474090.html.

The US position in reality appears very close to its stated policy on paper—it applies an "all or nothing" interpretation of conscientious objection. Nothing short of an outright rejection of all conflict is enough to qualify for this right, and unless one is a senior officer who can take early retirement, there are many practical obstacles in the way for anybody trying to go down this route. One must either lie and claim to have become a pacifist or face the very real possibility of court-martial and imprisonment as the trial court is not going to take into account what it considers to be policy-level questions because the state is assumed to know best when it comes to decisions of war and peace.

While Germany does not explicitly recognize such a right as a policy either, according to recent legal developments, the 1949 Basic Law for the Federal Republic of Germany written in the aftermath of World War Two can be, and has been, interpreted in such a way as to privilege individual conscience over *any* military order (perhaps in accordance with its original intent). It is too soon to say if Lt. Colonel Jürgen Rose will be followed by others, also claiming a right to selective conscientious objector status, or if the German state will seek to test the 2005 ruling. At this moment in time, however, as the German state enters a new military era containing the type of out-of-area deployments that would have been inconceivable only a generation ago, selective conscientious objection appears to be a real option for German soldiers who may disagree with their country's choice of war on moral grounds.

Just as with the other two countries examined, the United Kingdom's practice on selective conscientious objection has been shaped by historical, political, and very pragmatic factors, occupying a middle ground "neither completely opposing it nor fully endorsing it as an official right."[62] Individual beliefs are accommodated as long as public or policy embarrassment is avoided and operational effectiveness is not compromised. Regarding the latter point, a theme that runs throughout British military history in this area is the desire to keep those with stated conscientious objections away from the rest of the troops. This can be achieved by letting them leave the service or, as in Germany, simply by giving them a different deployment or task that distances them from the issue that gave cause for concern—the very practical rationale being that if someone doesn't want to fight, it is better not to have him or her on the front line at all as he or she will only undermine the effectiveness of the rest of the unit.

Even this brief exploration of the issue highlights that this is not a problem that is going to disappear. Nor is it a problem exclusively for the three states used as the case studies here—this is a challenge to any democratic state concerned

[62] Ellner, Robinson, and Whetham, "Practice and Philosophy of Selective Conscientious Objection," 242.

with legitimacy and may explain the apparent fear that the governments of all three countries have had when exposing their own policy decisions to legal test in court. Fear of negative publicity and bad headlines is always going to be a factor, with the media constituting "the crux of the legitimization process, framing discourse about the just character and rightfulness of both cause and conduct of whatever action is taken."[63] As governments seek to intervene in conflicts that are not clearly identifiable with national survival or even core national interests, the importance of ensuring legitimacy and therefore "buy in" from the population and support in the wider international community is not something that will diminish. It remains to be seen how such legitimization will be affected by the choice to recognize or deny the moral autonomy of those who are sent to be instruments of state policy.

There are obviously questions about how far democratic states should encourage and/or permit dissent among their servants and how far individual moral autonomy should be accepted at an institutional level. However, while those debates continue, we are left trying to work out some of the real-world implications of the just war revisionist position. This chapter has quite deliberately chosen to exclude epistemic questions. Whether or not someone actually does know that what he or she is doing is wrong or that the war that he or she is fighting in is manifestly unjust is itself an extremely complex question and needs to be properly considered by just war revisionists rather than simply assumed if their arguments about individual accountability are to have practical effect.[64] However, putting this profound problem aside for now, the idea that soldiers on the objectively unjust side of a conflict have collectively forfeited their right to not be deliberately harmed is untenable if looking at the group as a homogenous moral entity. Different people on the unjust side of a conflict will be motivated by different factors. Some may believe in what they are doing, some may feel it is wrong but feel compelled to act due to the sanctions they will otherwise face, and some may know it is wrong but are happy to go along with it anyway. If the moral quality of an action, the culpability of those involved and therefore their liability to defensive harm, is shaped by the intention of those carrying it out, these different motivations matter.

Such a collective culpability position fails to account for the complexities of the real world and the difference in context between different regimes. The cost of "saying no" and refusing to participate in what is perceived as an unjust conflict is not the same, even between three liberal democratic states in the same

[63] James Gow, *Defending the West* (Cambridge: Polity Press, 2005), 136.

[64] For a discussion on this topic, see David Whetham, "My Country, Right or Wrong: If the Cause Is Just, Is Anything Allowed?" in *Ashgate Research Companion to Military Ethics*, ed. James Turner Johnson and Eric D. Patterson (Farnham, UK: Ashgate, 2015), 283–294.

alliance structure. If one were to include a state with more onerous sanctions for dissent, perhaps even including summary execution for disloyalty, it would make even more difference to the moral status of someone who is participating on the side in a war that is objectively unjust.[65]

Some may argue that anything short of capital punishment for dissent should basically be omitted from this type of consideration—there is no real coercive factor at play without the risk of death, so unless someone is, quite literally, holding a gun to your head or the firing squad is a real possibility, it makes no practical difference whether one might end up in prison or not. Those who knowingly participate in an unjust war do so willingly. In none of the three case studies employed in this chapter would those raising a moral objection to participating in a particular war have faced death as a result of refusing to go to war. However, that is not to say that the cost of refusing to serve is therefore negligible in each of those cases. The ruination of one's career, the social shame of being charged and prosecuted for what many would see as cowardice, the very real risk of substantial jail time, not to mention the cost to one's family and friends cannot and should not simply be dismissed as irrelevant. Instead, the costs of exercising moral judgment should be seen as a type of sliding scale. The more onerous the sanction for those who would refuse to participate, the less culpable are the actors. Where the cost of exercising one's moral autonomy is low or even nonexistent, the culpability of those doing the wrong thing must be considered to be higher. Of course, you still don't know who would have exercised their individual moral autonomy had it been more freely available, meaning there is likely to be a range of culpability demonstrated in the military of a state that does not permit selective conscientious objection. This presumably moves the epistemic burden onto the other side in the revisionist model to determine who is more or less culpable and therefore more or less liable to defensive harm.

While this demonstrates some of the messy reality of trying to actualize this theoretical position in the real world, it also generates a much clearer moral position in certain specific cases—the moral status of soldiers who fight for states that do permit selective conscientious objection. As long as those soldiers genuinely do know they are on the "wrong side" of a conflict and freely choose to participate anyway as there is no cost to them to do otherwise, they *can* be considered morally culpable. They are all equally liable to defensive harm for their unjust actions as there is no element of compulsion in their "wrong" choice. As such, and for the purposes of the theme of this volume, it could also be assumed that the practical implications in the real world of the revisionist challenge is that soldiers from Germany or the United Kingdom who knowingly fight in an

[65] If it is, indeed, possible to make such an assessment.

unjust war are more liable to any harm they receive as a result of their participation than soldiers from the United States in the same situation.

References

"Anti-War Rally Makes Its Mark." BBC News, February 19, 2003. http://news.bbc.co.uk/1/hi/uk/2767761.stm.

"At least 1,000 UK soldiers desert." BBC News, May 28, 2006. http://news.bbc.co.uk/1/hi/uk/5024104.stm.

Augustine. "Against Faustus the Manichean." In *Augustine: Political Writings*, edited by Ernest L. Fortin and Douglas Kries, translated by Michael W. Tkacz and Douglas Kries, 220–229. Indianapolis, IN: Hackett, 1994.

Bellamy, Alex J. *Just Wars: From Cicero to Iraq*. Cambridge: Polity Press, 2006.

Bernton, Hal. "Officer at Fort Lewis calls Iraq war illegal, refuses order to go," *Seattle Times*, June 7, 2006. http://old.seattletimes.com/html/iraq/2003044627_nogo7m.html.

Brecher, Jeremy, and Brendan Smith. "The Trials of Ehren Watada." *The Nation*, June 1, 2009.

Carrick, Don, James Connolly, and Paul Robinson, eds. *Ethics Education for Irregular Warfare*. Farnham, UK: Ashgate, 2009.

Cohn, Marjorie, and Kathleen Gilberd. *Rules of Disengagement—The Politics and Honor of Military Dissent*. Sausalito, CA: PoliPointPress, 2009.

Coleman, Stephen. *Military Ethics: An Introduction with Case Studies*. New York: Oxford University Press, 2012.

Deakin, Stephen. "Conscientious Objection to Military Service in Britain." In *When Soldiers Say No: Selective Conscientious Objection in the Modern Military*, edited by Andrea Ellner, Paul Robinson, and David Whetham, 115–136. Abingdon-on-Thames, UK: Routledge, 2014.

Douglas-Home, William. *Sins of Commission*. Salisbury, MD: Michael Russell, 1985.

Ellner, Andrea. "War Resisters in the US and Britain—Supporting the Case for a Right to Selective Conscientious Objection?" In *When Soldiers Say No: Selective Conscientious Objection in the Modern Military*, edited by Andrea Ellner, Paul Robinson, and David Whetham, 213–238. Abingdon-on-Thames, UK: Routledge, 2014.

Ellner, Andrea, Paul Robinson, and David Whetham. "Sometime They'll Give a War and Nobody Will Come." In *When Soldiers Say No: Selective Conscientious Objection in the Modern Military*, edited by Andrea Ellner, Paul Robinson, and David Whetham, 1–15. Farnham, UK: Ashgate, 2014a.

Ellner, Andrea, Paul Robinson, and David Whetham. "The Practice and Philosophy of Selective Conscientious Objection." In *When Soldiers Say No: Selective Conscientious Objection in the Modern Military*, edited by Andrea Ellner, Paul Robinson, and David Whetham, 239–254. Abingdon-on-Thames, UK: Routledge, 2014b.

Gow, James. *Defending the West*. Cambridge: Polity Press, 2005.

Hayes, Denis. *Conscription Conflict*. London: Sheppard Press, 1949.

Lucas, George R. "Advice and Dissent: The Uniform Perspective." *Journal of Military Ethics* 8, no. 2 (2009): 141–161.

McMahan, Jeff. *Killing in War*. Oxford: Oxford University Press, 2009.

McMaster, H. R. *Dereliction of Duty: Johnson, McNamara, the Joint Chiefs of Staff, and the Lies that Led to Vietnam*. New York: Harper Perennial, 1998.

"Navy Afghan War Objector Michael Lyons Detained." BBC News, July 5, 2011. http://www.bbc.co.uk/news/uk-england-devon-14028167.

Norton-Taylor, Richard. "Iraq Dossier Drawn Up to Make Case for War-Intelligence Officer." *Guardian*, May 12, 2011. http://www.theguardian.com/world/2011/may/12/iraq-dossier-case-for-war.

O'Brien, Jane. "The Soldiers Who Can No Longer Fight." BBC News, March 4, 2009. http://news.bbc.co.uk/1/hi/world/americas/7900059.stm.

Orend, Brian. *The Morality of War*. Toronto, Canada: Broadview, 2006.

"Prisoner of Conscience: RAF Doctor Who Refused Iraq Service Is Jailed." *Independent*, April 14, 2006. http://www.independent.co.uk/news/uk/crime/prisoner-of-conscience-raf-doctor-who-refused-iraq-service-is-jailed-6103758.html.

Rae, John. *Conscience and Politics*. London: Oxford University Press, 1970.

"RAF Doctor Jailed Over Iraq Refusal." *Guardian*, April 13, 2006. http://www.guardian.co.uk/uk/2006/apr/13/military.iraq.

Rayment, Sean. "I Didn't Join the British Army to Conduct American Foreign Policy." *Daily Telegraph*, March 12, 2006. http://www.telegraph.co.uk/news/uknews/1512767/I-didnt-join-the-British-Army-to-conduct-American-foreign-policy.html.

Rodin, David. "Justifying Harm." *Ethics* 122 (2011): 109.

Rose, Jürgen. "Gehorsam bis zum Hindukusch?." *S&F Sicherheit und Frieden* 22, no. 3 (2004): 134–135.

Rose, Jürgen. "Aufklären, damit die anderen bomben können. Dokumentation. Antrag des \ Oberstleutnants Jürgen Rose, von allen dienstlichen Aufgaben bei einem Tornado-Einsatz in Afghanistan entbunden zu werden." *Freitag—Die Ost-West-Wochenzeitung*, March 23, 2007.

Rose, Jürgen. "Conscience in Lieu of Obedience: Cases of Selective Conscientious Objection in the German Bundeswehr." In *When Soldiers Say No: Selective Conscientious Objection in the Modern Military*, edited by Andrea Ellner, Paul Robinson, and David Whetham, 177–193. Abingdon-on-Thames, UK: Routledge, 2014.

Second Senate for Military Jurisdiction of the Federal Administration Court, Judgment June 21, 2005, BVerwG 2 WD 12.04, http://www.bverwg.de/entscheidungen/pdf/210605U2WD12.04.0.pdf.

Shue, Henry. "Do We Need a Morality of War?' In *Just and Unjust Warriors: The Moral and Legal Status of Soldiers*, edited by David Rodin and Henry Shue, 106–111. Oxford: Oxford University Press, 2010.

Vitoria. "On the Law of War." In *The Ethics of War: Classic and Contemporary Readings*, edited by Gregory M. Reichberg, Henrik Syse, and Endre Begby, 318–319. Oxford: Blackwell, 2006.

Walgrave, Stefaan, and Dieter Rucht, eds. *The World Says No to War: Demonstrations Against the War on Iraq*. Minneapolis: University of Minnesota Press, 2010.

Walzer, Michael. *Just and Unjust Wars: A Moral Argument with Historical Illustrations*. 4th ed. New York: Basic Books, 2006.

Whetham, David. "Introduction: Purpose, Content and Structure." In *Ethics, Law and Military Operations*, edited by David Whetham, 1–9. Basingstoke, UK: Palgrave Macmillan, 2010.

Whetham, David. "The Just War Tradition: A Pragmatic Compromise." In *Ethics, Law and Military Operations*, edited by David Whetham, 65–89. Basingstoke, UK: Palgrave Macmillan, 2010.

Whetham, David. "My Country, Right or Wrong: If the Cause Is Just, Is Anything Allowed?" In *Ashgate Research Companion to Military Ethics*, edited by James Turner Johnson and Eric D. Patterson, 283–294. Farnham, UK: Ashgate, 2015.

Whitman-Bradley, Buff, Sarah Lazare, and Cynthia Whitman-Bradley, eds. *About Face—Military Resisters Turn Against War*. Oakland, CA: PM Press, 2011.

Zupan, Dan. "Selective Conscientious Objection and the Just Society." In *When Soldiers Say No: Selective Conscientious Objection in the Modern Military*, edited by Andrea Ellner, Paul Robinson, and David Whetham, 89–95. Farnham, UK: Ashgate, 2014.

4

Defensive Liability

Four Common Mistakes

KAI DRAPER

This chapter is about defensive liability, the species of moral liability that is present in (among other cases) standard cases of justifiable defense.[1] I want to identify four common mistakes about defensive liability. I do not catalogue all of the instances of these mistakes in the literature, nor do I credit every theorist who manages to avoid at least some of them. Instead, I focus on pointing out their presence or absence in two recent books: Helen Frowe's *Defensive Killing*[2] and Jeff McMahan's *Killing in War*.[3] I choose these two works partly because of their excellence: I hold them in the highest regard and have learned much about both the ethics of defense and the ethics of war from them. I hope to show, however, that the authors of even these two works need to modify their respective accounts of defensive liability.

First, what is liability? Unfortunately, not every writer on the ethics of defense uses that term in precisely the same way.[4] Frowe says that "a person is morally liable to a harm if she lacks a [moral] right against having that harm inflicted upon her because she has forfeited her usual rights by behaving in a particular way" (p. 3). McMahan is somewhat more restrictive in his use of

[1] I use *defense* to refer to both self-defense and other-defense.

[2] Helen Frowe, *Defensive Killing* (Oxford: Clarendon Press, 2009).

[3] Jeff McMahan, *Killing in War* (New York: Oxford University Press, 2014).

[4] Indeed, many define liability tendentiously, begging certain substantive questions about the subject matter. I want to say, for example, that liability does not require a loss (as opposed to a lack) of rights, but it will be difficult to do so given either Frowe or McMahan's definition of liability; for if either of those definitions are accurate, then it is true by definition that liability requires a loss of rights.

the term; but, like Frowe, he uses *liability* to indicate the loss of a right by way of forfeiture. He emphasizes that in the case of *defensive* liability the right that is lost is very narrow: it is a right not to be harmed "for certain reasons, by certain persons, in certain circumstances" (p. 10). Moreover, he distinguishes forfeiture and hence liability from both waiving a right and deserving harm (pp. 8–9).

Although there are differences in how Frowe and McMahan understand the concept of *liability*, there is enough similarity for my purposes here. They both say that if someone is liable, then inflicting upon him or her the harm to which he or she is liable would not violate or even infringe upon his or her rights.[5] Thus, they agree that one necessary condition for the presence of liability and, a fortiori, defensive liability is lacking certain rights. It is this necessary condition for defensive liability that is my focus here. The basic issue I want to explore is this: in a standard case of justifiable defense, what is the source of the aggressor's lack of a right not to be subjected to defensive violence?

Frowe suggests that "only those who are morally responsible for an unjust threat can be liable to defensive harm" (p. 1). She defines "an unjust threat" as "a threat of harm to a person who has a right not to suffer that harm" (p. 10), and she argues that a person who poses an unjust threat is morally responsible for doing so "if she intentionally fails to avail herself of a reasonable opportunity to avoid posing that threat" (p. 10). (Her criteria for determining whether an opportunity is reasonable are discussed below.) Focusing on lethal threats, she also distinguishes two basic kinds of threats: one poses a *direct* threat if one's actions, movements, or presence will, in the absence of preventive measures, kill someone; one poses an *indirect* threat if one's actions, movements, or presence will, in the absence of preventive measures, contribute to someone's death but will not kill anyone (p. 22).

McMahan says that "responsibility for a wrongful threat is the criterion of liability to defensive attack," and he defines a "wrongful threat" as a "threat of wrongful harm—that is, harm to which the victim is not liable—posed by action that is objectively wrong" (p. 38). Furthermore, he argues that liability does not require posing a threat oneself. Even if one is morally responsible for someone else's posing a wrongful threat, one can be liable to defense (pp. 205–208).

[5] Unlike McMahan, I use the expression *infringe upon rights* broadly to include both justified and unjustified incursions upon rights. I use the expression *violate rights* more narrowly to refer to unjustified incursions upon rights.

Mistake 1: Failing to Recognize That Defensive Liability Requires an *Unjust* Threat

Both Frowe and McMahan have well-motivated accounts of defensive liability, and each of them avoids some of the mistakes I want to discuss here. The first of these mistakes is the failure to recognize that defensive liability requires an *unjust threat* in the sense of a threat to a right or a threat that infringes upon a right. Frowe makes it very clear that she thinks that defensive liability requires a threat to a right not to suffer a harm. Thus, she avoids the first mistake. McMahan, on the other hand, appears to deny that liability requires an unjust threat. He says that defensive liability requires a "wrongful threat," where wrongful threats are "threats of harm to which the victim is not liable, via action that is objectively unjustified" (p. 42). One might suppose that if there is a "threat of harm to which the victim is not liable," then the victim must have a right not to suffer the threatened harm, so the threat to the victim is a threat to the victim's rights. However, not being liable to a harm, or to a threat of harm, does not imply having a right not to suffer that harm. Given that I meet the relevant performance standards, I am not liable to the harm of losing my job, for example; but it does not follow that I have a right not to be laid off. Moreover, on McMahan's definition of liability, I am not liable to harm that I deserve or to harm that I have consented to suffer, but I do lack a right not to suffer those harms.

To be fair to McMahan, when he discusses cases of individuals who bear no responsibility and hence no liability for the threats they pose, he remarks that "[i]nsofar as the justification for self-defense by the victim depends on the assumption that she is thereby defending her rights against infringement, it will not extend to these cases" (p. 180). This remark suggests that McMahan does take seriously the possibility that defensive liability requires an unjust threat. Perhaps McMahan, at least at the time he is writing his book, is simply uncertain whether defensive liability requires an unjust threat.

Be that as it may, there is good reason to believe defensive liability does require an unjust threat. I may be selfish in not helping the elderly gentleman to safely cross the busy street, for example, but because he has no right to my help, I do not forfeit any of my rights by acting selfishly; and this remains true even if it turns out that, because of my selfish failure to help, the only way to save the elderly victim from being hit by a speeding truck is to toss myself in front of the truck. This is not to say that lacking or losing a natural right requires a threat to a right. One can voluntarily relinquish or waive a natural right. One can also lose a right because one loses the capacities necessary to possess the right. But if one lacks a right in virtue of posing a threat of harm to others, then I see no reason to reject Locke's view that one must either pose a threat to or have already infringed upon the rights of another. The mere fact that one has acted wrongly cannot be the basis for the lack of a right.

It might be objected that my lack of liability in the example is due not to my failure to pose a threat to a right but rather to the fact that I merely allow, as opposed to cause, a threat. Consider, then, a further example. Suppose that someone freely and knowingly consents to be struck by me. (Perhaps he wants to prove to me that he is fearless.) Then, in spite of his consent, my striking him would be morally wrong; for there is nothing of significant value to be gained by striking him, and doing so might cause him serious harm. Nevertheless, striking me to prevent me from wrongly striking him would be morally impermissible, and this is true even though I would clearly be the cause of the threat. If we say that defensive liability requires an unjust threat, we can explain this fact in a most natural way; for by consenting to be struck, he waives his right not to be struck, so preventing me from striking him would not enforce his rights.

Although defensive liability requires an unjust threat, it does not require a wrongful threat; for some unjust threats that are permissible or even justified nevertheless yield liability. Suppose that, through no fault of his own, a police officer will be killed unless he throws a punch at you. (Perhaps he is an undercover police officer who will be murdered by thugs if he does not engage in thuggish behavior to convince them that he is one of them.) Then it is justified for him to throw a punch at you. Suppose further that you know all of this, but you also know that his life depends only on throwing a punch and not on landing one. Then it seems clear to me that you can justifiably strike him if that is the only way to prevent his punch from landing. Given that liability requires an unjust threat as opposed to an unjustified threat, this can easily be explained, for the police officer's aggression in this case, although justified, nevertheless threatens your right not to be struck.

McMahan disagrees. He proposes that defensive liability is "defeasible by justification." More specifically, he suggests that contributions to a wrongful threat through actions that are objectively justified do not generate liability. His only argument in defense of that view, however, is that in criminal law and in tort law usually one can escape legal liability for an action by showing that the action was justified (p. 44). This is not surprising in the criminal law because typically none of the usual reasons to punish apply to persons who act justifiably. As for tort law, there are enough cases where justification does not defeat liability to make McMahan's appeal to the law less than compelling. Furthermore, in the case above it seems intuitively clear that self-defense is justified and that the police officer is not in a position to complain or to demand compensation from you if you strike him in self-defense. The hypothesis that he lacks a right to be struck by you in self-defense explains these intuitions. Thus, barring an adequate alternative explanation, these intuitions support that hypothesis.

Mistake 2: Failing to Recognize That Defensive Liability Requires *Posing* (or Taking Part in a Group's Posing) an Unjust Threat, as Opposed to Merely *Contributing to* an Unjust Threat

This is perhaps the most common way that the scope of liability gets distorted. Moreover, it is potentially the most dangerous of the four mistakes I want to expose in that, if applied to war, it can result in many innocent bystanders being mistakenly regarded as appropriate targets of attack. To their credit, Frowe and McMahan both have sophisticated views here—views that avoid, for example, the absurd suggestion that any contribution whatsoever to unjust aggression yields liability. Nevertheless, McMahan and, to a lesser extent, Frowe are guilty of this mistake; and that leads them to incorrectly assign liability to some who are in fact immune.

Before proceeding, I need to make clear what the distinction is that I want to draw between posing a threat of unjust harm and merely contributing to such a threat. Neither McMahan nor Frowe uses the expression "pose a threat of unjust harm" (or the abbreviated equivalent expression, "pose an unjust threat") in the way I do. In my use of this expression, an individual poses a threat of unjust harm if and only if, unless he or she is prevented from doing so, he or she will infringe upon a right with the result that interests protected by that right are damaged or at least jeopardized. For an individual to contribute to a threat of unjust harm, on the other hand, there needn't be any infringement of, or threat to, a right *against that individual.* It suffices if there is a right against some third party and some contribution by the individual in question to that third party's infringement of, or threat to, that right.

With this distinction in mind, consider one of Frowe's examples:

> *Malicious Bridge*: Victim is fleeing Murderer, who wants to kill him. Victim's only escape route is across a narrow bridge that can hold only one person at a time. Pedestrian is out for a walk on the bridge. Pedestrian could easily get off the bridge in time to allow Victim to escape Murderer. But she dislikes Victim and decides to stay where she is, realizing that this will impede Victim's escape. Only by knocking Pedestrian off the bridge, killing her, can Victim save his own life. (p. 25)

McMahan believes that in this sort of case Pedestrian does not pose a wrongful threat but is nevertheless liable due to her moral responsibility for the wrongful threat posed by Murderer. Indeed, he argues that this sort of case supports his general view that "what matters is not whether one *poses* a wrongful threat through one's one action but whether one is morally responsible for a wrongful threat" (pp. 172–173). Unconvinced by McMahan's argument, Frowe writes,

> There is something troubling about McMahan's assertion that Victim may kill Pedestrian not because Pedestrian poses a threat, but because Pedestrian is, to some degree, morally responsible for the threat that Victim faces from Murderer. How can this be? How can her intentional presence on the bridge make Victim morally responsible for Murderer's pursuit of Victim? I do not think that it can: it isn't that for which she is responsible and that grounds a permission to kill her. Rather, by intentionally staying where she is, she is responsible for the fact that she further endangers Victim by blocking his only escape route. (p. 27)

Although I disagree with her suggestion that Pedestrian cannot bear any moral responsibility for Murderer's threat to Victim, I agree with Frowe that Pedestrian's liability is grounded in the threat she poses rather than any responsibility she bears for the threat Murderer poses. Consider the following variation on the case.

> *Malicious Bridge with Tiger*: Victim is fleeing a tiger, who wants to eat him. Victim's only escape route is across a narrow bridge that can hold only one person at a time. Pedestrian is out for a walk on the bridge. Pedestrian could easily get off the bridge in time to allow Victim to escape the tiger. But she dislikes Victim and decides to stay where she is, realizing that this will impede Victim's escape. Only by knocking Pedestrian off the bridge, killing her, can Victim save his own life.

The tiger does not, of course, pose a threat of unjust harm because tigers, not being moral agents at all, cannot infringe upon rights. Nevertheless, Pedestrian is still in the same position vis-à-vis the threat to Victim as in *Malicious Bridge*, and I take it to be obvious that, first, if Pedestrian is liable in that case, then she is liable in *Malicious Bridge with Tiger* and, second, the basis of her liability is the same in each case. Thus, since the basis for Pedestrian's liability in *Malicious Bridge with Tiger* is not her responsibility for a wrongful threat, McMahan is mistaken to suppose that the basis for Pedestrian's liability in *Malicious Bridge* is her responsibility for Murderer's wrongful threat. My proposal is that in both cases, if she is liable, then her liability is a consequence of *her* posing an unjust lethal threat to Victim. Victim has a right against her that she not maliciously obstruct his escape route, and, barring preventive action, she will infringe upon that right with the result that Victim is killed.

In a well-known article, Seth Lazar also criticizes McMahan for failing to recognize that liability requires *posing* a threat:

> [B]y arguing that liability is grounded in responsibility for unjustified threats, not the fact that one poses the threat, McMahan opens the floodgates to total war. In a modern state we all make contributions, however small, to the capacity of our government to act. When our government goes to war, especially in liberal democracies, we are to some degree responsible for the threat that it poses. If this is enough to ground liability to lethal attack, then few besides children will escape liability.[6]

As formulated by Lazar, the objection fails to take into account that McMahan believes that someone whose causal contribution to an unjust threat is minimal is typically not liable to lethal defense. Thus, directly addressing Lazar's objection in a later work, McMahan explicitly appeals to the idea that the causal contribution the typical civilian makes to her nation's war effort is "small and inessential."[7] He does this not to show that the typical civilian is not liable at all but to show that the typical civilian is not liable to be killed. And in his book, he writes,

> In some unjust wars, many civilians do bear some responsibility but the degree to which most of them are responsible is very slight. Most civilians have, on their own, no capacity at all to affect the action of their government. They may pay their taxes, vote or even campaign for particular political candidates (sometimes on the basis of general sympathy with their overall positions on matters of policy but seldom because of their advocacy of war), participate in the culture from which the country's political leaders have emerged, fail to protest their country's unjust war, perhaps because they believe that to do so would be ineffective, or perhaps because they approve of the war, and so on; but none of these things, nor even all of them together, is ordinarily sufficient for the forfeiture of a person's right not to be attacked and killed. Military attack exceeds what a person may ordinarily be liable to on the basis of these comparatively trivial sources of responsibility. (p. 225)

[6] Seth Lazar, "The Responsibility Dilemma for *Killing in War*: A Review Essay," *Philosophy and Public Affairs* 38, no. 2 (2010): 188.

[7] Jeff McMahan, "Who Is Morally Liable to be Killed in War," *Analysis* 71, no. 3 (2011): 549–550.

This response to Lazar is incomplete, however, for small and inessential contributions to a threat clearly can generate liability to lethal harm in some cases. Even if someone's contribution to a threat is a mere "drop in the bucket," he or she can be fully liable. Suppose, for example, that a group of one hundred assassins each endeavors to put an individually harmless but collectively lethal drop of poison in my tea. Given that ninety drops constitutes a lethal dose, each individual assassin makes a small and inessential contribution to the threat to my life; but it is quite obvious that all of them are liable to necessary lethal defense, so a third party could justifiably, and without infringing upon anyone's rights, kill all of them if that was necessary to thwart their collective attempt at murder. (Perhaps the third party can thwart their attempt only by setting off a bomb that will unavoidably kill them all before they have a chance to poison the tea.) Thus, pointing out that most civilians in a nation engaged in unjust aggression do not make a substantial contribution to any threat does not by itself show that most civilians are not liable to lethal attacks. McMahan himself appears to recognize this point, for he rejects the idea that responsibility can ground liability only if it exceeds a certain threshold (pp. 230–231). Nevertheless, he does not fully explain in the passage quoted above why civilians who make small and inessential contributions to their nation's unjust aggression at least typically manage to avoid liability to military attack.

He has more to say about that in the later work referenced above. There he proposes that, in addition to the fact that the causal contributions that most civilians make to threats directly posed by their armed forces are small and inessential, there are three other factors in virtue of which *most* (though not all) civilians who contribute to an unjust war effort nevertheless escape liability or at least liability to lethal attack: many of their contributions are objectively justifiable; their degree of culpability for any unjustifiable contributions they make is low; and harming them is apt to be ineffective in the sense of doing little to reduce any threat to which they contribute (pp. 549–551).

I certainly agree with McMahan that many civilians cannot be liable to attack because attacking them would be ineffective. But I do not think that McMahan successfully shows that most civilians who contribute to an unjust war effort are not liable to an *effective* attack if such an attack is possible. I have already disputed McMahan's suggestion that objective justification defeats liability, and I also see no reason to suppose that a low degree of culpability is directly relevant to liability.[8] McMahan famously ascribes liability to lethal defense even to the conscientious driver who, in spite of his or her attention to safety, ends up

[8] Degree of culpability can be indirectly relevant to whether someone is liable to defense because, as discussed below, defensive liability requires being more responsible for a threat than the potential victim of that threat.

posing a threat to the life of an innocent pedestrian. What is puzzling to me is why McMahan would think that (1) low moral responsibility (as in his example of the conscientious driver) does not by itself preclude liability to lethal defense, (2) low causal responsibility (as in my example of the one hundred poisoners) does not by itself preclude liability to lethal defense, but nevertheless (3) low moral responsibility combined with low causal responsibility (as in the case of many, if not most, civilians who contribute to unjust war) somehow does preclude liability to lethal defense. Given (1) and (2), (3) appears to me to be arbitrary.

Even if McMahan's account provides adequate protection for civilians in war, it is too liberal in assigning liability. For example, his account assigns liability to lethal harm in cases like that of the individual who legally sells guns, knowing that, at least in the long run, it is not unlikely that one of them will be purchased by someone who will use it in an attempt to commit murder. Even if through some bizarre twist of fate killing such an individual is the only way to prevent one of the guns he or she sold from being used to commit murder, he or she is not liable to being killed. However, because his or her causal contribution to a threat is substantial and he or she is minimally morally responsible for the threat in question, McMahan appears to be committed to saying that, unless he or she has an objective justification for selling the gun in question, he or she is liable to lethal defense. That result strikes me as clearly mistaken. Moreover, one can explain the gun seller's lack of liability by pointing to the fact that no one has a right against the gun seller that he or she not sell guns. Thus, although he or she predictably contributes to an unjust threat, he or she does not pose an unjust threat and hence is not liable.

In my view, then, McMahan is mistaken in assigning defensive liability to persons not solely on the basis of their own disrespect for rights but also on the basis of their responsibility for someone else's disrespect for rights. A similar problem exists in Frowe's account as well. Although she requires for defensive liability being morally responsible for "posing a threat of unjust harm," she does not understand that expression in the same way I do. In her broad conception, one poses a threat of unjust harm if and only if one's action, movement, or presence contributes to a threat of harm, and the victim of the threat has a right not to suffer that harm. She says very little about the conditions under which one has a right not to suffer a harm. Instead, she focuses her attention on moral responsibility and argues that a person is morally responsible for posing an unjust threat, and hence liable to defensive harm, "if she had a reasonable opportunity to avoid posing the unjust threat and she intentionally failed to avail herself of that opportunity" (p. 73). She also identifies criteria that are supposed to guide us in assessing whether a given opportunity to avoid posing an unjust threat is a reasonable one:

> Whether or not an opportunity to avoid posing a threat is unreasonably costly is sensitive to a range of considerations: (i) the cost to the agent (and to other innocent people) of taking the opportunity; (ii) the prospective harm to Victim (and to other innocent people) if she fails to take the opportunity; (iii) whether the agent will threaten directly, indirectly, or as an indirect cause; (iv) whether the agent will be causing herself to threaten, or allowing herself to threaten.
>
> I suggest that the threshold at which an opportunity to avoid posing a threat becomes unreasonable is set lowest in the case of indirect threats who will be allowing themselves to threaten. People posing these types of threats must bear some non-trivial cost to avoid endangering Victim, but they need not bear high costs to do so. The threshold at which an opportunity becomes unreasonable is set highest with respect to direct threats who will be causing themselves to threaten. People who will be posing this type of threat ought to bear even lethal harm rather than kill Victim. The threshold is also high with respect to those whose actions will be an indirect cause of what kills Victim. (pp. 73–74)

Due to her inattention to rights, her assignment of liability begs certain questions about the scope of our rights. Consider, for example, two more of her cases:

> *Selfish Bridge*: Victim is fleeing Murderer, who wants to kill him. Victim's only escape route is across a narrow bridge that can hold only one person. Selfish Pedestrian is out for a walk on the bridge. Selfish Pedestrian could easily get off the bridge, but doing so will involve getting her feet wet and she has on her lovely new shoes. She decides, with a certain amount of regret, to stay on the bridge, realizing that her doing so impedes Victim's escape. (p. 76)
>
> *Drowning Child*: Walker passes a lake on her morning stroll. Child is drowning in the lake. Walker observes Child's predicament, and does nothing to help Child, even though she could easily save her. Child drowns. (p. 29)

In Frowe's view, Selfish Pedestrian poses a lethal, indirect threat of unjust harm to Victim; and, because she intentionally fails to take a reasonable opportunity to avoid posing that threat, she is morally responsible for posing it and so is liable to defensive harm. However, it is not obvious that Victim has a right against Selfish Pedestrian that she move off the bridge, and if she does not, I see no reason to suppose that she is liable even if she is highly culpable for endangering Victim. Moreover, if Victim does have the right in question, then it is a positive right, a right that Selfish Pedestrian perform a certain action that will save Victim's life. Whether and to what extent basic rights against others include such positive rights to be saved from harm is controversial, and Frowe would do well to address this issue before drawing conclusions about liability. Nevertheless, I do not want to make too much of this because, although somewhat shaky, my intuition is that Frowe is correct to claim that Selfish Pedestrian is liable.

I am, however, less comfortable with Frowe's analysis of *Drowning Child.* I believe that she begs the question against positive rights in that case by ruling out, in principle, the possibility of a bystander's being liable for an unjust threat. Frowe (p. 31) defines a bystander (relative to some threat to Victim) as having two characteristics: first, a bystander is a "person whose movements, actions, or presence do not contribute, and have not contributed, to the threat to Victim" and, second, a bystander is someone the harming of whom "would serve to avert or mitigate the threat to Victim." (She calls those who have the first characteristic but not the second "onlookers.") Assuming that by harming Walker we could somehow rescue the child—perhaps Walker's being shot would be observed by people on the opposite shore of the lake and the resulting attempt to rescue her would predictably lead to the discovery and rescue of Child—Walker is a bystander, for neither her actions, movements, nor presence contribute to the threat to Child. Frowe concedes that Walker culpably fails in her moral duty to rescue Child; but because neither her *actions,* movements, nor presence contribute to a threat to Child, Walker does not, according to Frowe, pose a threat of unjust harm to Child and so cannot possibly be liable to defensive harm. Walker's *omissions* do, however, contribute to a threat to Child. It is because she does not pull Child from the water that Child's life continues to be endangered. Thus, it seems to me that Frowe should recognize that if Child has a right against Walker that she not allow Child to die, then Walker does pose a threat of unjust harm by failing to respect that right, which would make Walker liable to necessary defensive harm. The relevant question for assessing whether Walker is liable, then, is not whether Walker is a bystander, as Frowe mistakenly supposes, but whether Child holds a positive right (against Walker) to be rescued by her.

This is not to say that I am unsympathetic to Frowe's suggestion that Walker is not liable to defensive harm. If we assume, however, that because Walker dislikes Child, she maliciously stands by and does nothing instead of rescuing Child, then my own intuition is that Walker does infringe upon Child's rights and is liable to necessary defense; and I suspect that I am not eccentric in that regard. Be that as it may, my main point is that the issue hinges on whether Victim has a right against Walker to positive aid and not, as Frowe supposes, on whether Walker is a bystander.

In other cases Frowe's criteria for liability commit her to assigning liability where it appears that there is no liability. Consider, for example,

> *Coercion*: Murderer is pursuing Victim with the intention of killing her. But to continue the pursuit, he needs an injection of a common pharmaceutical drug. Finding a medical office, he storms in and threatens to kill Physician if she does not provide him with the drug he needs. Physician knows that, if Murderer receives the injection, he will pose a serious threat to Victim's life; and she also knows that if he does not receive the injection, then he will faint and be arrested, and Victim will be safe. Physician has nothing against Victim, but she wants to survive, and so she administers the injection. As luck would have it, a short time later a fleeing Victim enters Physician's office, looking for a place to hide from Murderer. Physician tells Victim what happened earlier at the office. Then Murderer shows up with a gun, looking for Victim. Victim realizes that she can save herself only by pulling Physician in front of her with the result that Physicianis shot and killed instead of herself. She also knows that if she does not do that, she will be shot and killed by Murderer, but Physician will be unharmed.

By Frowe's criteria, Physician is liable to defensive harm; for, in her view, Physician poses a threat of unjust harm because Physician is an indirect cause of the threat of harm to Victim, and Victim has a right not to suffer that harm. Furthermore, Physician is morally responsible for posing that threat of unjust harm because she intentionally fails to avail herself of a reasonable opportunity to avoid posing that threat. This is because, according to Frowe, the threshold at which an opportunity to avoid posing a threat becomes unreasonable is set high for indirect causes like Physician. Because the cost to Victim of not taking the opportunity to avoid posing the relevant threat is very high (a serious threat to Victim's life) and Physician causes (as opposed to merely allows) a threat to Victim by administering the injection, Frowe is committed to the conclusion that Physician's opportunity to avoid posing the threat to Victim is a reasonable one and so Physician is liable.

My own intuition is that this is the wrong result. It seems to me that it would be unjust for Victim to defend herself at the expense of Physician's life. Moreover, the intuition makes sense. For even though Victim has a right not to be murdered by Murderer, she never had a right against Physician that she not give the injection to Murderer. Thus, Physician does *not* pose a threat of unjust harm in the sense that, in my view, is required for defensive liability. Perhaps some do not share my intuition that Victim's killing Physician would be morally wrong. I suspect that at least most of them would also not share my inclination to deny that Victim has a right against Physician that she not give the injection to Murderer. The reader can judge for herself or himself. My own tentative conclusion is that, because of her broad notion of what it means to pose an unjust threat, Frowe's standards for liability are too low.

Mistake 3: Failing to Recognize That Defensive Liability Requires Not Merely Posing an Unjust Threat But Also Being More Responsible Than the Potential Victim for the Threat One Poses

In order to determine whether an aggressor is liable, one must do more than determine whether that aggressor is morally responsible for posing a threat of unjust harm. One must compare the aggressor's degree of responsibility for the threat to the potential victim's degree of responsibility for the threat. The aggressor is liable only if his or her degree of responsibility exceeds that of the potential victim's—or so I have argued in *War and Individual Rights.*[9] Here, I will focus on one of the theoretical advantages of this view. This advantage appears when one considers cases of provoked aggression. Sometimes defense is justified in such a case. Even a mild verbal insult may provoke a serious physical assault, but self-defense is not thereby rendered impermissible. On the other hand, if the provocation is severe, and especially if it is severe relative to the seriousness of the provoked threat, then defense is apt to be unjustified. Consider, for example,

> *Bully*: Jones is a bully. Out for a drink at a bar, he decides to pick on the innocent Smith. He calls him names and gets no reaction except a "What the hell is your problem?" He then knocks Smith's glass of beer over and says, sarcastically, "Oops." Now Smith is very angry, and he warns Jones to leave him alone or suffer the consequences. Jones responds by pouring his own beer into Smith's lap and then laughing and telling others at the bar that Smith is so scared he wet himself. Smith finally loses his temper and comes at Jones, fists clenched. Jones realizes that, if he does not strike Smith, Smith will strike him. He proceeds to strike Smith in self-defense.

Here, self-defense is clearly impermissible, and it seems relevant that the potential victim is not innocent: he is partly to blame for the threat to his own rights. However, as illustrated by cases in which, although there is provocation, the provocation is slight relative to the seriousness of the threat, defense is sometimes permissible even if the defended individual is not innocent. The natural

[9] Kai Draper, *War and Individual Rights* (New York: Oxford University Press 2016), 76–81.

way to handle such cases is to suppose that, at least typically, justice permits harming the aggressor in defense of the potential victim only if the aggressor is, in the relevant sense, more responsible than the potential victim for the relevant threat. That would explain why defense in cases of provoked aggression can be permissible or impermissible, depending on the severity of the provocation relative to the seriousness of the threat. If the provocation is mild and the threat relatively serious, then the aggressor is apt to be more at fault than the potential victim and defense is justified; but if the provocation is severe and the threat is relatively unserious, then the potential victim of the aggression is apt to be the more culpable party and defense is unjustified. Because in Frowe's account of defensive liability the responsibility of the potential victim of aggression is irrelevant, her account fails to adequately address cases of provoked aggression. Her account assigns liability to the aggressor in such cases even when the victim is more to blame for the aggression than the aggressor. In *Bully*, for example, Frowe's theory of liability commits her to saying that, because Smith is morally responsible for the unjust threat he poses, he is liable to defense.

It might be objected that Jones, in virtue of his bullying of Smith, has forfeited his right not to be struck by Smith. I do not think, however, that Jones has forfeited that right. He may have forfeited his right not to have a beer poured in his lap, for example, but striking someone with a closed fist is a much more serious physical assault than the assaults on Smith by Jones; and I see no reason to think that one can forfeit a right against a serious physical assault by committing a relatively minor assault.

Frowe's failure to recognize the relevance of comparative responsibility to liability leads her to make another mistake, which is to think that defensive liability extends to unnecessary defensive harm. (She calls her view "externalism" and contrasts it with the "internalist" view that defensive liability is limited to necessary defense.) To support her view, she relies on the following case:

> *Lucky Escape*: Murderer is shooting at Victim to try to kill him because he dislikes Victim. He chases Victim to the edge of a cliff. Unbeknown to Murderer, Victim has both a gun and a parachute. He can thus save his own life by either (a) jumping to safety, using no force against Murderer, or (b) shooting and killing Murderer. (p. 88)

Frowe proposes that, although it would be impermissible for Victim to resort to shooting and killing Murderer, doing so would nevertheless not infringe upon Murderer's rights because Murderer is liable even to unnecessary harm. In support of that proposal, she suggests that if we adopt the opposite view, then we must say that, should Victim shoot at Murderer, he would be morally responsible for posing an unjust lethal threat to Murderer and hence would be liable to defensive harm. But clearly it would infringe upon Victim's rights to kill her in defense of Murderer (p. 115).

That argument is unconvincing, however. I want to say that the threat posed by Victim to Murderer if he decides to shoot Murderer would be an unjust one, and we can explain Victim's lack of liability to defense by appealing to the idea that a necessary condition of liability is being more responsible for the relevant threat than the potential victim of the threat. Thus, in my view, Victim would not be liable to defense because Murderer would be at least as responsible as Victim for Victim's attack. Murderer provokes the attack, after all, and the provocation—an unjust attempt on Victim's life—is very severe. Victim's attack on Murderer is highly blameworthy, but Murderer's provocation is even more blameworthy.[10]

Frowe argues, however, that such an explanation of Victim's lack of liability is itself implausible:

> For a start, it's not obvious that Murderer is more responsible than Victim for the current situation. Murderer did have an opportunity to ensure that neither he nor Victim need bear a cost, since he could have refrained from attacking Victim. But Victim also has such an opportunity, since he could have jumped to safety without harming Murderer. If he chooses not to, it *is* his choice. This is not a case in which someone other than Victim is solely—and therefore more—responsible for bringing it about that someone must suffer a harm. Murderer may be partly responsible—presumably Victim would not have tried to harm Murderer at all if Murderer hadn't tried to kill him. But this doesn't show that Murderer is *more* responsible than Victim for the fact that, now, one of them must bear a cost.
>
> Even if we grant that Murderer is more responsible than Victim for the unjust threat that Victim poses, I'm not sure that this is helpful to the internalist. Being morally responsible for an unjust threat usually rules out one's having defensive rights because it is a ground of liability to harm. But taking this line here is effectively a denial of the internalist view, because it means that Murderer is liable to unnecessary force. Moreover, it looks incoherent. What would make Murderer liable to harm is his moral responsibility for an unjust threat. In this case, what grounds Murderer's liability is his responsibility for the very

[10] McMahan and I both raised this objection against Frowe's position at a conference on the ethics of self-defense at Bowling Green State University in April of 2013.

> unjust threat that internalists are saying he may not fend off—the threat posed by Victim. But if he's liable to suffer the harm that Victim will inflict, in virtue of his moral responsibility for it, Victim's responding threat is no longer an *unjust* threat. And if it's not an unjust threat, how can Murderer's moral responsibility for it be the ground of liability. Something has gone wrong here. (p. 116)

In my view, Victim's liability would require his being more responsible than Murderer for attacking Murderer. Thus, even if Frowe is correct that Murderer is not more responsible, that doesn't undermine my position. Indeed, by suggesting that both Victim and Murderer had an opportunity to ensure that neither Murderer nor Victim need bear a cost, Frowe identifies a standard under which Murderer and Victim are equally responsible for the threat posed by Victim; and in my view equal responsibility does not yield liability. Nor is my view incoherent in the way that Frowe suggests. Murderer is responsible for an unjust threat to himself, but he does not *pose* an unjust threat to himself because he does not have a right against himself that he does not influence someone to create an unjust threat against himself. Thus, in my view, Murderer's responsibility for Victim's unjust threat does not make him liable to anything.

Of course, even if I am right about all of this, it does not follow that my explanation of why Victim is not liable to defense if he chooses to attack Murderer is better than Frowe's. Its superiority does emerge, however, if we consider cases of unjust aggression in which the original aggressor is barely culpable or only minimally responsible for his aggression. Suppose that we alter Lucky Escape so that, although Murderer's threat to Victim's life remains an unjust one, he reasonably though mistakenly believes that he must kill Victim to prevent Victim from unjustly killing him. Murderer knows that he might be mistaken in his belief that Victim poses a threat of unjust harm, and the evidence is rather ambiguous. Thus, Murderer is minimally responsible or just slightly to blame for posing a threat to Victim's life. Finally, suppose that Victim knows all of this (including the fact that Murderer's mistake is a reasonable one) but nevertheless chooses to defend himself by killing Murderer even though he could easily escape. I am strongly inclined to think that in this case it would be permissible for a third party to intervene on behalf of Murderer and kill Victim if that is the only way to prevent Victim from killing Murderer. The salient difference between this case and the earlier one is that now Victim is far more responsible than Murderer for the threat to Murderer's life. Because Frowe ignores the relevance of comparative responsibility, she cannot reach the correct result in this case.

Mistake 4: Thinking That Defensive Liability Requires an Objective Threat

Frowe and McMahan both require for defensive liability an objective threat of harm, although, as we shall see, McMahan appears to be inconsistent on this point. Whether an objective threat of harm exists does not depend on epistemic factors such as beliefs or available evidence. Thus, even if someone aims a gun at me and prepares to pull the trigger, and even if both the gunman and I have strong evidence that, barring self-defense, he will kill me, this does not guarantee that there is an objective threat to my life. If the gun would in fact malfunction should the trigger be pulled, leaving me alive and well, then the gunman does not pose an objective threat to my life.

Does defensive liability require an objective threat? Let us call those who answer this question in the affirmative "objectivists" and those who answer it in the negative "subjectivists." Now consider the following example:

> *Sniper*: Sniper enjoys putting the lives of others at risk, but he always does so covertly. Each and every day he hides on some rooftop and, using a six-chambered gun and a single bullet, subjects one passerby below to what amounts to a game of Russian roulette. Those who are shot and killed never see it coming, and those who are not killed (because there is no bullet in the relevant chamber when Sniper pulls the trigger) are unaware that they were exposed to a one-in-six chance of being killed. The police are aware of all of this—Sniper has sent them taunting messages describing his routine—and a police investigator has finally located Sniper. She rushes to the location and sees Sniper on the roof, taking aim at Victim. The police investigator knows that if she doesn't shoot Sniper, then there is roughly a one-in-six chance that Sniper will shoot and kill Victim. She shoots and kills Sniper in defense of Victim. She then examines Sniper's gun and learns that there was no objective threat to Victim because the bullet was not in the relevant chamber.

Objectivists will say that Sniper is not liable to defensive harm in this case because there is never any objective threat of harm to Victim. That seems to me to be a mistake. I want to say that even if shooting Sniper is objectively unnecessary and hence objectively unjustified[11] because the bullet is not in the relevant

[11] I follow others in distinguishing "evidence-relative" (or "subjective") justifications from "fact-relative" (or "objective") justifications. Thus, if I observe that someone has begun shooting his gun at what appears to be a young child, then (based on the information I have) I may have an adequate evidence-relative justification for killing the gunman in defense of his potential victim. Nevertheless,

chamber, Sniper does pose an unjust threat to Victim and so is liable to defensive harm. I want to say this partly because it strikes me as implausible to say that the police investigator infringes upon Sniper's rights by shooting him. Imagine Sniper, wounded by the police investigator, complaining to her that she violated his rights or that she demonstrated a lack of respect for his rights by acting in a way that had a five-in-six chance of violating his rights. No one would, or should, take such a complaint seriously.

There is, however, a much more compelling reason to embrace subjectivism, one that can be discovered if we compare *Sniper* with the following:

> *Sniper II*: Sniper has been sent to prison, but his son, Sniper Jr., decides to follow in his father's murderous footsteps except that, being less fond of gambling, he dispenses with his father's game of luck in favor of shooting one passerby each and every day. The police investigator locates Sniper Jr., and she and the SWAT team move in. Unfortunately, Sniper Jr. is up on the roof that is now also occupied by five SWAT team snipers. The police investigator sees a sniper on the roof looking through the scope of his rifle, but she cannot tell if the person she sees is Sniper Jr., preparing to shoot Victim, or a police sniper, merely adjusting the scope of his rifle. She realizes that there is only roughly a one-in-six chance that sees Sniper Jr. preparing to murder Victim and roughly a five-in-six chance that she sees one of the five police snipers. Nevertheless, the police investigator shoots the sniper she sees and, unfortunately, that sniper turns out to be a fellow police officer.

The investigator behaved blamelessly in *Sniper,* but she is clearly one of the villains in *Sniper II*. Her actions in defense of Victim in *Sniper* are blameless, but her actions in defense of Victim in *Sniper II* are blameworthy. The subjectivist has no difficulty accounting for this difference. For the subjectivist can say that Sniper (the sniper who is shot in *Sniper*) is liable in virtue of endeavoring to impose a one-in-six chance of death upon Victim, so the police investigator has an evidence-relative justification for shooting him in defense of Victim. But the sniper who is shot in *Sniper II* is not liable, nor does the police investigator who shoots him have good reason to believe that he is liable, so the police investigator lacks even an evidence-relative justification for shooting him. Thus, because she also lacks an exculpating excuse for her behavior, her behavior in *Sniper II* is blameworthy.

if the individual who looks like a child is actually a terrorist disguised as a child and is attempting to detonate a bomb in a crowded marketplace, then defense might well be a terrible though understandable mistake, so it is likely that I lack a fact-relative justification for killing the gunman.

The objectivist, on the other hand, cannot distinguish the cases in this way. Given objectivism, the police investigator in both cases knows that there is a five-in-six chance that the sniper she shoots is *not* liable. Thus, in both cases she has neither an evidence-relative defense justification nor an exculpating excuse for shooting him. How, then, can the objectivist account for the fact that the investigator is blameworthy in *Sniper* but not in *Sniper II*? There are two possible approaches—one implicit in Frowe's discussion of similar cases, the other implicit in remarks by McMahan—but ultimately neither of them can succeed.

Frowe's approach is to distinguish defensive liability from other sorts of liability and to suggest that whereas defensive liability requires an objective threat, other sorts of liability do not. She uses the following example of justifiably killing someone who does not pose an objective threat:

> *Apparent Murderer*: Enemy hates Victim and therefore wants to kill him. He points what he mistakenly believes to be a loaded gun at Victim. Victim, thinking that the gun is loaded, believes that only by killing Enemy can he save his life. (p. 85)

Frowe believes that Enemy is liable to being killed by Victim but that liability is not defensive liability. Her argument is that "any harm that Victim inflicts on Enemy cannot be defensive harm, because there is no threat against which Victim needs to defend himself" (p. 85). She proposes that Enemy's liability is based on his "responsibility for the fact that Victim believes that if he does not kill Enemy, Enemy will kill him" (85–86). Frowe's conceptual argument is unconvincing. We often speak of threats even when there is only a small probability of harm. In *Sniper*, for example, no one would deny that, prior to being shot, Sniper poses a threat to Victim, and that is the case even if everyone knows that the likelihood that Sniper will harm Victim if he pulls the trigger is only one-in-six. Similarly, when Victim kills Enemy in *Apparent Murderer*, she does so to prevent herself from being subjected to a high risk of being murdered. Thus, I see no conceptual reason to deny that Enemy poses a threat to Victim or that the harm that is inflicted on Enemy is defensive in nature.

Still, one might think that, given that Frowe ultimately does assign liability to Enemy, the difference between her position and my own is merely a minor, verbal dispute about whether to call the liability in question "defensive liability" or something else. The disagreement runs deeper than that, however, for if we apply Frowe's analysis of *Apparent Murderer* to *Sniper*, it does *not* provide an explanation of why it is not blameworthy for the police investigator to shoot Sniper. For in that case the police investigator does *not* believe that if she does not kill Sniper, then Sniper will kill Victim. She believes that there is only a one-in-six chance that if she does not kill Sniper, then Sniper will kill Victim.

Moreover, if Frowe tries to broaden her account and assign liability to Sniper on the grounds that he is responsible for the police investigator's believing that there is a one-in-six chance that if she does not kill Victim, Sniper will kill Victim, then the explanation has shifted from an appeal to responsibility for a false belief—in *Apparent Murderer* Victim falsely believes that Enemy will kill her if he does not kill Enemy—to an appeal to responsibility for a true belief—in *Sniper* the police investigator truly believes that, barring defensive action, Sniper will impose a one-in-six chance of death on Victim. But responsibility for a true belief hardly seems like adequate grounds for liability. Rather, it seems that what really explains the liability of Sniper is not his responsibility for the police investigator's true belief that Sniper will impose a risk of death if not shot but rather his responsibility for the fact that he will impose a risk of death if not shot.

It might be objected that if we modify *Sniper* so that when the police investigator arrives Sniper is in fact merely adjusting the scope of an unloaded gun—call this case *Sniper III*—then Sniper's liability has to be explained in terms of his responsibility for the police investigator's false belief that he must be shot to be prevented from imposing a one-in-six chance of death upon Victim. So why not unify the account of *Sniper III* and the account of *Sniper* so that responsibility for a belief explains the liability in both cases? In reply, I think that *Sniper III* is a case in which Sniper is *not* liable at all but the police investigator is subjectively justified in shooting Sniper because she has good reason to believe that Sniper is liable.

Still, it might be objected that if we deny Sniper's liability in *Sniper III,* then we cannot explain why the police investigator is quite clearly not liable for posing a threat to Sniper's life by shooting at him. For if Sniper is not liable in that case, then Sniper has a right not to be shot, so the police investigator poses an unjust threat of harm when she endeavors to shoot Sniper. To answer that objection, I need only remind the reader of the earlier point that liability requires more than merely posing an unjust threat. It also requires being more responsible than the potential victim of the unjust threat for that threat. In *Sniper III,* Sniper is clearly more to blame for the threat that the police investigator poses to him than the police investigator herself is. Thus, the police investigator is not liable.

McMahan's view on these matters is more difficult to discern. He does make it clear that he believes that liability requires "objectively unjustified action," and he distinguishes objective from subjective justification as follows:

> An act is objectively permissible or justifiable when what explains its permissibility or justifiability are facts that are independent of the agent's beliefs. By contrast, an act is subjectively permissible or justifiable when two conditions are satisfied: first, the agent acts on the basis of beliefs, or perhaps reasonable or justified beliefs, that are false, and,

> second, the act *would* be objectively permissible or justified if those beliefs were true. (p. 43)

Given these definitions, the police investigator's shooting at Sniper in *Sniper II* is neither objectively nor subjectively justified. So far so good. But given McMahan's definitions, the police investigator's shooting of Sniper in *Sniper* is also neither objectively nor subjectively justified. That action is not subjectively justified because the police investigator does not act on the basis of some false belief, let alone a false belief that, if true, would make her shooting Sniper objectively justified. Moreover, her shooting of Sniper appears to be objectively unjustified because the facts independent of her beliefs include the fact that Sniper will not harm anyone even if he is not shot. Nor can McMahan plausibly say that her action is unjustified but fully excused by her ignorance, for then by the same token he would then have to say that in *Sniper II* her clearly blameworthy action is fully excused by her ignorance.

McMahan does have a solution to the problem, though. For he introduces the notion of "objective risk" and suggests that, independently of whether such a risk is realized, someone who is morally responsible for a threat of imposing such a risk can be liable. Thus, perhaps McMahan would want to say that in *Sniper* the police investigator's shooting of Sniper is objectively justified and Sniper is liable because the risk that Sniper will impose if not shot is an objective one, so the fact that he threatens to impose that risk is independent of anyone's beliefs.

If that is McMahan's view, then he is close to the truth. Sniper is liable in part because if he is not shot, he will impose a risk of death on Victim. However, that risk is not objective in the sense of being independent of anyone's beliefs. Risk is an inherently subjective notion because it is relative to an epistemic situation. Relative to the police investigator's evidence, Sniper will, if not shot, impose a one-in-six chance of death on Victim. If, however, we allow ourselves to be fanciful enough to suppose that Superman arrives on the scene and, using his X-ray vision, discerns the precise location of the bullet in Sniper's gun, then, relative to Superman's evidence, even if Sniper is not shot, Sniper will not put Victim at risk. So it appears that McMahan ultimately arrives at the correct view, but he misidentifies it as a kind of objectivism due to a confusion about the nature of risk.

A Positive Proposal

In *War and Individual Rights*, I defend an account of defensive liability that avoids the four mistakes I have discussed here. The core of the account is the proposition that the following principle identifies the basis of an aggressor's liability in standard cases of justifiable defense (and in many other sorts of cases as well):

> *The defense liability principle*: If (1) an individual *x* poses a threat of unjust harm to a second individual *y* (i.e., *x* behaves in such a way that, barring preventive action, *x* will infringe upon *y*'s non-contractual rights and thereby jeopardize interests protected by those rights), or *x* belongs to a group that poses such a threat, and (2) *x* is more responsible than *y* for that threat, then (3) (ceteris paribus) it would not infringe upon *x*'s rights to eliminate or reduce the threat to *y* by inflicting necessary and proportionate harm on *x*. (p. 83)

Whatever weaknesses this principle might have (and no doubt there are some), it avoids the four mistakes I have discussed here. Its first condition ensures that it assigns liability only in cases where there is an unjust threat and only to individuals who pose, or take part in a group's posing, an unjust threat. Its second condition ensures that it assigns liability only to those who are more responsible for a threat than the potential victim of the threat. Finally, because the notion of an unjust threat is spelled out in a way that allows for posing an unjust threat in virtue of imposing a risk of harm, the principle also avoids the mistake of requiring for liability an objective threat of harm.

References

Draper, Kai. *War and Individual Rights*. New York: Oxford University Press, 2016.

Frowe, Helen. *Defensive Killing*. Oxford: Clarendon Press, 2009.

Lazar, Seth. "The Responsibility Dilemma for *Killing in War*: A Review Essay." *Philosophy and Public Affairs* 38, no. 2 (2010): 180–213.

McMahan, Jeff. "Who Is Morally Liable to Be Killed in War." *Analysis* 71, no. 3 (2011): 544–559.

McMahan, Jeff. *Killing in War*. New York: Oxford University Press, 2014.

5

Fighting for One's Self

MICHAEL ROBILLARD

Introduction

Imagine the following case. Country A is currently mired in a vicious and bloody civil war between an unjustified, morally oppressive regime and a small group of morally justified insurgents. Seeing what is occurring in country A, several members of the international community decide to offer military aid to the insurgent group, who are significantly outgunned and outnumbered. Despite this offer, the insurgent group, as well as the vast majority of the oppressed political community for whom they fight, refuse external assistance since they want to win the war by themselves and on their own terms. Doing otherwise, they believe, would be highly injurious to their political self-determination and to their future reputation as a sovereign state. If the international community intervenes, then the war can be ended within a week's time and with minimal casualties. However, in such a case, it will not have actually been won by members of the oppressed group. If the international community does not intervene, there will be much greater bloodshed on both sides over many months and the chance of success will be far less certain. However, if the members of the oppressed community do in fact win, then it will be *their* win and theirs alone.

In considering this case, we might ask, *What is the moral significance of allowing justified persons and/or communities to fight for themselves, even in cases where doing so will predictably result in greater overall harm and a lower likelihood of success?* In such cases, it appears that potential interveners must wrestle with two competing obligations: (1) an obligation to respect the consent of those persons on whose behalf they might fight and (2) an obligation to see that those same persons satisfy conditions of necessity were they to fight on their own. We may express these competing obligations as follows,

Consent: One must receive consent from victims before it is permissible to fight "on their behalf."

Necessity: Other things being equal, of the set of equally effective means of defense, one is morally obligated to use the means which will produce the least overall harm or to ensure that other parties do so as well.[1]

From these competing obligations, a dilemma arises for third-party interveners like the members of the international community. If the members of the international community offer defensive assistance to the insurgents but allow the insurgent group to then disavail themselves of what would then be the new most effective and least harmful means of proportionate defense (assuming they refuse such assistance), then in allowing the insurgents to continue to fight, the members of the international community would be failing in their duty to enforce necessity.[2] However, if the members of the international community attempt to satisfy conditions of necessity by intervening on behalf of the insurgents without their authorization, then they would thereby fail in their duty to respect consent. It therefore appears impossible, at first glance, for third parties to satisfy these two competing duties simultaneously in cases where victims refuse to consent to third-party assistance that will be predictably more effective and less harmful.[3]

In this chapter, I explore the peculiar dilemma arising from these competing duties with respect to fighting for one's self. In the first section, I consider the value and moral import of victims being allowed to fight for themselves, even in cases where doing so would fail to be the most effective and/or least harmful means of defense were third parties authorized to intervene on their behalf. I then explore several possible explanations as to what could possibly ground the permission to fight for one's self in such cases involving excessive use of force. And finally, borrowing largely from Mill, I consider what implications our analysis holds for interventions at the state and international levels. Here I argue that political communities may gain additional moral permissions when fighting on

[1] I would like to note that the relationship between necessity and "effectiveness" is much more nuanced in the just war literature than I am here making it out to be. Seth Lazar's "Necessity in Self-Defence and War," *Philosophy & Public Affairs* 40, no. 1 (2012): 1–42; and Joseph Bowen's "Necessity and Liability: On an Honour-Based Justification for Defensive Harming," *Journal of Practical Ethics* 4, no. 2 (2016): 79–93, for instance, both explore some of these nuances and finer distinctions. However, for the purposes of this chapter, I will restrict my formulation of necessity with respect to effectiveness to the commonly accepted definition above.

[2] This duty to enforce conditions of necessity seems to hold equally for both "externalist" and "internalist" accounts of necessity with respect to liability. For more on "enforceable duties," see Victor Tadros, *The Ends of Harm* (Oxford: Oxford University Press, 2011).

[3] For the purposes of this chapter, I use the term *victim* to broadly refer to those persons who are targets of attack, targets of wrongdoing, and/or targets of rescue.

behalf of themselves as well as on behalf of an emergent *impersonal* good over and above the community's individual members. Despite positing this additional impersonal good, I nonetheless conclude that such a move is wholly consistent with the reductive individualist project and does not commit one to a collectivism of any sort.

Fighting for One's Self

Nearly everyone is familiar with a common scene often found in film or in popular television where the protagonist, after being suddenly and unjustly attacked, promptly calls off assistance from his comrades with a hearty and confident "Stay back. I've got this." Here the protagonist signals that he is capable of handling the wrongful attacker on his own and that he does not require any assistance. More importantly though, by making such an utterance, the protagonist also stakes a claim of sorts and, in effect, asserts that this is now *his* fight to finish. Accordingly, even if it were the case that a third party could quickly intervene and subdue the attacker more effectively and with less overall harm to the attacker than could the protagonist, there is still a sense in which some injustice would be befalling the protagonist were the intervener to actually do so. There therefore appears to be some basic intuitive notion that victims of wrongdoing have a prima facie claim to defend themselves prior to anyone else doing so on their behalf, even if such defensive action would not be as effective or as minimally harmful as the defensive means of others—in other words, even if doing so would fail to meet conditions of necessity.

Indeed, when it comes to issues of desert, for instance, our justice system appears to recognize and value something quite similar when families of victims are allowed to attend the executions of their loved one's wrongdoer(s). Thus, the general sentiment in both ex ante and ex post cases is that victims, in virtue of being wronged, attain a special kind of "standing" and therefore a special right to defend themselves, if only symbolically, prior to others acting on their behalf. Consideration of such cases combined with the common view that liability and desert are symmetrical expressions of justice gives plausibility to the idea that there is at least *some* moral weight to one being given the opportunity to fight for one's self. But just how much moral weight? Consider the following scenario.

Big Brother

Bully wants to beat up Little Brother. Little Brother is capable of defending himself against Bully; however, if he does so, he will cause Bully greater

> overall harm in the process. Big Brother can intervene on Little Brother's behalf and easily defeat Bully by wrestling him into submission.

Even if the most effective and minimally harmful way to stop Bully from harming Little Brother would be for Big Brother to intervene on Little Brother's behalf each and every time, there is still a certain value, it would seem, in Big Brother opting *not* to intervene, even if it meant that Bully would suffer additional harm. To a certain threshold of harm there seems to be a strong moral reason for third parties to allow victims the opportunity to fight for themselves and to be able to be the agential cause of their own defense, even if such defensive harming was suboptimally effective and excessive with respect to harming the attacker. Were Big Brother to therefore intervene each and every time Bully attempted to harm Little Brother, Big Brother would, in effect, be denying Little Brother the value and benefits that would be achieved by fighting for himself, even if doing so meant Bully (and perhaps even Little Brother) suffered a greater harm that could have otherwise been prevented.

All that being said, there appears to be a limit to the value to be gained from allowing a victim to defend herself "on her own terms" as well as a limit to the permissions that such value might grant. Consider this next case.

Taser

> Adam is trying to murder Victoria with an axe. Fortunately, Victoria has a shotgun that she can use to defend herself. Seeing what is about to occur, Thelma intervenes between Adam and Victoria with her trusty taser and suggests to Victoria that she (Thelma) stun Adam into unconsciousness on Victoria's behalf. Victoria vetoes this plan and takes the lethal shot instead.

Given such a case, we may ask, what is the primary duty for capable third parties such as Thelma? By fulfilling her duty to offer assistance, Thelma adds to Victoria's total set of defensive options a new defensive option that is equally effective but less harmful.[4] In light of this fact, for reasons of necessity, Victoria therefore seems obligated to accept and to make use of this new least harmful/most effective means if she chooses to defend herself at all. To do otherwise and to continue to lethally defend herself with her shotgun as if this new option had not been made available to her would appear to be a clear and blatant violation of necessity. If this is the case and if necessity is in fact an

[4] Let us, for the sake of argument, stipulate that the risk to Thelma from intervening would be minimal and that she in fact does have an obligation to do so.

enforceable duty, then Thelma now appears to be under obligation *either* to ensure that Victoria let Thelma defend her with the taser (if Victoria opts to be defended at all) or to defend *Adam* against Victoria if Victoria still opts to use her shotgun.

What then is the fundamental difference between *Big Brother* and *Taser*? One obvious thought is that third-party obligations to respect a victim's withholding of consent to defensive assistance and to thereby give that victim first chance to defend herself obtain for third parties only up until a certain threshold where the foreseeable harms that would occur for the victim and/or the attacker override whatever goods would be gained from allowing the victim to be her own source of defense. It is at this point where the third party's duty to enforce necessity overtake her duty to respect the victim's withholding of consent to defensive assistance.

In the case of a simple fistfight, third-party obligations to enforce necessity can arguably be relaxed so as to fulfill the more demanding obligation to respect consent and to thereby give the victim a first chance to defend himself. In cases of life and death, however, the harms to be averted by fulfilling one's obligations to enforce necessity trump whatever goods would be achieved by continuing to respect the victim's withholding of consent. It therefore seems that in low to moderately harmful cases (in a fistfight, for instance) our prima facie duty will be to respect the victim's consent, even if it means failing to fulfill our duty to enforce necessity. Only when harms become severe enough (as in cases of life and death) does our prima facie duty to respect the victim's consent get overridden.

But just how important is the value of fighting for one's self? If it is valuable enough to sometimes justify defensive actions that are excessively harmful and to thereby obligate third parties to refrain from enforcing conditions of necessity, is it also valuable enough to sometimes obligate third parties *to refrain from rendering aid* to victims? In other words, could the value of fighting for one's self ever be so important that even if the victim's defensive actions would be excessive and even if the victim actively requested aid, a third party would nonetheless be obligated, or at the very least permitted, to deny such a request? Intuitively, I think the answer here is "yes." Consider the following case:

For Your Own Good

> Bully wants to beat up Little Brother. Little Brother is capable of (proportionately) defending himself against Bully but not as effectively as Big Brother. Little Brother requests Big Brother's assistance, but Big Brother

> denies Little Brother's request so that Little Brother learns to fight for himself.

It certainly seems that in such cases it might genuinely be in Little Brother's best interest that he learn to fight for himself rather than for Big Brother to fight for him even if it meant Little Brother sustaining some degree of physical harm. The interesting question here is how much extra harm is Bully liable to in order that Little Brother secure the intangible goods associated with sticking up for himself? It seems to me here that Bully is liable to a fair bit. Insofar as he physically threatens Little Brother's bodily integrity, Bully makes himself liable to a proportionate degree of defensive harming. Even if Big Brother intervening would be the least harmful defensive option, it still seems permissible for him to refrain from fulfilling both his duty of aid as well as his duty to enforce necessity in order for Little Brother to secure the goods of learning to fight for himself. Accordingly, it would be permissible for Little Brother to then employ *his* most effective, least harmful proportionate means of defense against Bully. If it just so happened then that Little Brother was an amateur boxer instead of a wrestler (it's a tough family), then Bully would, quite unfortunately, be liable to Little Brother's more harmful punches instead. By physically threatening Little Brother, Bully makes himself liable to be used as an opportunistic means. The *way* in which he is used as an opportunistic means in this particular case is simply a nonstandard one, wherein Big Brother uses Bully as a means for Little Brother to reap the intangible goods and benefits of learning to fight for himself.

Regardless of where one's intuitions lie for these particular cases, the main point worth re-emphasizing is that it appears that both duties (of respecting consent and enforcing necessity) cannot be simultaneously fulfilled by third parties if victims refuse to authorize defensive assistance. If Thelma's prima facie duty is to respect consent, then it appears she cannot simultaneously fulfill her duty to enforce necessity (as in *Big Brother*). If Thelma's prima facie duty is to enforce necessity, then it appears she cannot fulfill her duty to respect consent (as in *Taser*).

It is important to note that our intuitions in these individual self-defense cases may not carry over cleanly to cases involving state-level actors where additional considerations of political self-determination, mixed consent among the *demos*, and the near inevitability of collateral damage enter into the moral equation. Nonetheless, what we ultimately decide about these individual self-defense cases will likely have significant implications for the permissions and duties of state-level actors at the international level. I will return to this question of state-level actors later (see "Implications at the State Level").

Grounding Permissions

For now, let us consider what it is that could explain our valuing so highly the opportunity for one to act in one's own self-defense. What is it specifically that could explain the intuition that Big Brother would be wronging Little Brother in some way by always intervening to fight his fights for him, even if it turned out that such an option would be the most effective and least harmful means of defense against Bully? What good could there be worth securing that is so valuable that it could obligate us to neglect our duty to enforce necessity?

One explanation we might turn to is the value of future deterrence. Such an appeal to future deterrence hinges on the key assumption that Bully will likely continue to look for opportunities to prey upon Little Brother when Big Brother isn't present. However, if Little Brother can effectively stand up for himself, so it is thought, then doing so will likely serve to deter Bully from future attacks. Hence, even if Little Brother's act of fighting for himself is neither the most effective nor the least harmful defensive means in the short term, *in the long term* such defensive action actually turns out to be just that. Thus, by fighting for himself, Little Brother's defensive act would in fact satisfy conditions of necessity in the long run if it turned out that it did in fact deter Bully's future attacks.

Closely related to this idea of future deterrence, one might try to explain the value of Little Brother's act of fighting for himself in terms of the defensive act's *expressive power*. In other words, one might think that by merely standing up for himself, win or lose, Little Brother's act of self-defense is valuable because it expresses to Bully that Little Brother acknowledges himself as a being worthy of respect and that he will therefore not acquiesce to wrongdoers without a fight. What's more, not only could Little Brother's act express this important truth to Bully but it might also have the potential to express this truth to other potential victims and to potential aggressors. Such expressive power we therefore think to be valuable in its own right.

While these ancillary goods may provide us with a partial explanation as to why we think Little Brother's act of self-defense is valuable despite it failing to meet conditions of necessity, I do not think either of these goods are the primary reason guiding our basic intuitions in such cases. Rather, the primary reason we believe there to be value in Little Brother's act of fighting for himself is because in doing so he would be *defending his honor* and thereby affirming his status as a moral agent.

Building on the work of Daniel Statman, in *Defensive Killing*, Helen Frowe offers just such an honor-based justification for several problematic cases where conditions of necessity do not appear to be met. Frowe motivates her position with several key cases to include the following:

Rape

Eric is in the midst of culpably raping Fran. Eric is much bigger and stronger than Fran, and consequently there is nothing she can do to stop him from continuing to rape her. While being raped, Fran threatens to break Eric's wrist, though this will do nothing to stop the rape from occurring. The only way Eric can stop Fran breaking his wrist is to quickly break her wrist first.[5]

Here it appears that Fran's breaking of Eric's wrist is excessive insofar as it is *insufficient* to prevent Eric from continuing to rape her. In this sense, Fran's act is unnecessary. Thus, on a standard *internalist* reading of necessity, where necessity is presumed to be a constitutive component of liability and therefore must always be satisfied in order for liability to obtain, Fran's unnecessary defensive act, according to Frowe, would be unjust and therefore make her liable to a proportionate degree of counterdefense on the part of Eric. What's more, in bringing such excessive harm against Eric, Fran would also potentially make herself liable to similar counterdefensive harming by a third party's acting on Eric's behalf.[6]

This conclusion cannot possibly be right. Clearly we want to say that Eric *continues* to remain liable to some degree of defensive harming, even if that degree of defensive harming fails to be enough to effectively stop him from continuing to rape Fran. Consequently, if we want to say that Eric remains liable while nonetheless conceding that Fran's defensive actions are ineffective and therefore technically unnecessary, then, Frowe argues, we must conclude that the condition(s) of necessity is "external" to liability. In other words, unjust parties can be liable to harms that are not always necessary.

So why is Fran still permitted to harm Eric even if her defensive actions fail to meet conditions of necessity? Frowe's answer is that Fran is justified in harming Eric because in so doing she would be *defending her honor*. When someone tries to harm us, Frowe argues, he or she is not recognizing our status as moral agents worthy of dignity. Accordingly, when one makes a physical threat against us, supervening on that physical threat is also a threat to our honor. Such a threat to our honor, Frowe argues, provides us with justification to forcibly resist our attackers, even when such resistance would prove ineffective at stopping the mere *physical* threat. This account, argues Frowe, seems intuitively appealing since most of us will normally think that victims are allowed to at least

[5] Helen Frowe, "Liability and Necessity," in *Defensive Killing* (Oxford: Oxford University Press, 2014), 99. Adapted from Joanna Mary Firth and Jonathan Quong, "Necessity, Moral Liability, and Defensive Harm," *Law and Philosophy* 31 (2012): 689.

[6] Frowe, "Liability and Necessity," 99.

do *something* to resist their attackers, even if their actions prove ultimately ineffective. Indeed, any moral theory that did not allow for such defensive action, Frowe argues, quoting Statman, would demand of us, "submission to evil and passivity in the face of wickedness."[7]

In responding to Frowe, an internalist about necessity might simply try to incorporate the goods of "defending one's honor" into their pre-existing internalist framework.[8] Thus, one might say that the goods to be achieved by our defensive actions and the harms that might otherwise befall us in the absence of those defensive actions fail to be exhausted by the set of goods and harms relating to our physical bodies. Thus, while Fran's breaking of Eric's wrist would count as excessive and therefore unnecessary insofar as it would fail to effectively thwart the continued threat to Fran's *physical body*, it would *not* be excessive or unnecessary since it would succeed in allowing Fran to effectively defend her honor. Such an account would therefore not force us to have to give up on an understanding of necessity that remained internal to our notions of liability.

While Frowe later responds to this move, giving her explanation as to why the externalist account of liability still wins out over the internalist account, she nonetheless admits that the internalist can coherently help himself or herself to her honor-based justification without having to abandon any of his or her internalist commitments regarding necessity. I see no reason to think otherwise and therefore argue that an internalist reading of necessity could just as adequately accommodate the problem cases we have been investigating thus far but without having to take on some of the more controversial theoretical baggage associated with the externalist view.[9] Let us consider what that might look like.

As we see in the case of *Rape*, the victim's use of harm is *physically ineffective* though justified on account of its effectiveness in defending the victim's honor. In the case of *Big Brother*, the victim's use of harm *is* in fact physically effective but it is *excessive*. Nonetheless, it seems plausible that an appeal to honor could similarly justify an agent's physically effective, though excessive, use of force such that conditions of necessity would in fact be met.

Accordingly, what this examination shows is that honor-based justifications extend to cases that both Frowe and Statman fail to explicitly address. Indeed, not only could a victim's defense of honor justify her (apparent) failure to meet necessity due to ineffective force, but it could also explain (apparent) failures to meet necessity due to effective though excessive uses of force. Thus, whatever it is that is justifying the use of ineffective defensive force in cases like *Rape*,

[7] Frowe, "Liability and Necessity," 111. Daniel Statman, "On the Success Condition for Legitimate Self-Defense," *Ethics* 118, no. 4 (2008): 664.

[8] Frowe does not argue that they cannot.

[9] For a lengthy critique of Frowe's externalist view, see Bowen, "Necessity and Liability."

I contend, is the same essential moral feature underpinning the value of fighting for one's self by means of excessive harm (as in *Big Brother*). Just as the aforementioned cases pick out a morally salient feature that is intangible and not explainable in terms of physical harms that would befall a victim, so too do cases of fighting for one's self track this very same feature. Thus, insofar as we believe it permissible for one to defend one's honor by use of force, even in situations where success appears utterly hopeless, then, I argue, defense of one's honor by use of excessive force ought to be permissible, up to a certain threshold of harm, in those cases where success is in fact reasonably attainable but by predictably more harmful means.

Thus, one solution to the apparent dilemma between respecting consent and enforcing necessity is to incorporate the goods and benefits to be conferred upon agents by the act of fighting for one's self into the set of overall goods (and harms) considered in our proportionality calculation. That is to say that among the overall set of goods and harms to be achieved by a defensive act and the overall set of goods and harms to be prevented from a defensive act, we may include within this weighing the goods of being allowed to fight for one's self. These goods may include future deterrence value, expressive value, and the value of defending one's honor. Inclusion of these additional goods within our proportionality calculus will therefore have direct bearing on what defensive actions we ultimately deem to be necessary and what defensive actions we deem to be excessive.[10]

Let us imagine then, for the sake of argument, that to attain the goods of fighting for one's self in a common fistfight is permissible up to the generation of ten units of harm against one's attacker (say, up to the harm of a broken arm). Thus, consider a case where a victim could defend herself from an attacker but only by breaking the attacker's arm. If a third party therefore offered less harmful defensive assistance that the victim then refused, while her defensive actions would appear excessive and therefore unnecessary *in the defense of her physical body*, they would not, as it were, be excessive or unnecessary for the securing of the aforementioned intangible goods (defense of honor, expressive value, and future deterrence). Accordingly, after having offered his less harmful assistance to the victim, the third party could still fulfill his duty to respect the victim's choice to refuse such assistance *and* he could fulfill his duty to enforce necessity (since conditions of necessity would already be met). If, however, the victim refused the third party's less harmful assistance so that she could defend her honor with a defensive action that exceeded ten units of harm (say, by blinding her attacker), we would not think that her defensive actions met conditions of necessity even

[10] I thank Joseph Bowen for the development of this point.

after taking into account the goods that would be achieved by her fighting for herself.

Thus, on an internalist reading of necessity, one that incorporated the goods of fighting for one's self into the set of proportionality considerations, Little Brother's act of fighting for himself would satisfy conditions of necessity since his actions would in fact be effective in defending these particular goods (both tangible and intangible). And since conditions of necessity would technically be met, Big Brother would have no remaining duty of necessity left to enforce and could thereby fulfill his duty to honor Little Brother's consent by remaining on the sidelines. Such an internalist reading of necessity, I argue, could thereby incorporate Frowe's honor-based justification for harm to explain cases of fighting for one's self with excessive force but without taking on the conceptual baggage associated with the externalist view.

Implications at the State Level

Certainly there are many key differences between individual intervention cases and intervention cases involving political communities and state-level actors within the international forum. Additional factors such as the likelihood of collateral damage, mixed consent among the *demos* of the intervened upon community, radical uncertainty with respect to predicting future political and military consequences, and the value of political self-determination stand out as some of the most noteworthy. This is to say nothing of the weighty epistemic difficulties third-party actors often face in terms of accurately determining a political community's consent to be intervened upon at all.[11] That being said, in considering the addition of these particular factors and added complexities, we still must determine whether typical intervention cases at the state and international levels are more like the case of *Big Brother* or more like the case of *Taser*. Central to this determination are two main questions: How does the good of being allowed to fight for one's self by less effective and more harmful means weigh against other associated goods and harms? And how does the moral weight of fighting for one's self change, if at all, when considered at the state and international levels?

If we think that typical intervention cases at the state and international levels are more like the case of *Big Brother*, then this would mean that we would be putting a moral premium on a community's right to political self-determination.

[11] See Allen Buchanan, "The Ethics of Revolution and Its Implications for the Ethics of Intervention," *Philosophy & Public Affairs* 41, no. 4 (2013): 291–323, for an in-depth analysis of how a political community's *conditional* consent muddies the epistemic waters even further when it comes to interventions at the state level.

Giving a burgeoning political community the chance to "fight its own fight" would, in a sense, be a way of recognizing it as a self-reliant political entity as well as respecting its collective autonomy. Intervening too early, one might think, could seriously jeopardize the legitimacy of that newly forming political community and could likewise injure its reputation on the international stage. This would then mean that a state's prima facie duty would be to *refrain* from rendering aid to victim groups and to let the conflict play out. If we think however, that intervention cases at the state and international levels are more like *Taser,* then we would be putting a premium on the mitigation of the ravages of war. This would then mean that a state's prima facie duty would be to ensure that the demands of necessity were met, even if that meant failing in its duty to respect a community's authorization and thereby forcing aid upon it.

Despite reductive individualist accounts that conceive of war as being nothing more than a collection of many individual acts and moments of individual self-defense, the full set of *goods* achieved by a political community fighting for itself intuitively appears somewhat resistant to such a reduction. In other words, were we to aggregate all of the personal goods that would be gained by each individual member of a political community through that political community's collective act of fighting for itself, the sum total of those goods would, for many philosophers, still seem to fall short in explaining the *total* good of that particular collective defensive act. Indeed, there appears to be a noticeable disparity in the domestic analogy when going from the micro-individual level to the macro-state level. In individual cases, if a victim desired to fight for himself by using lethal force in a case involving a violation of his property rights, for instance, we typically would not think the goods that would be achieved from such an act would be weighty enough so as to obligate third parties to refrain from intervening. On the collective level, however, we typically do think that something like unjust taxation, as in the case of the American war for independence, could serve as adequate justification for the use of lethal force by members of that political community in order to achieve the goods of fighting for themselves. Furthermore, we typically think that such goods could serve to obligate third-party actors to refrain from intervening to any significant degree.[12] Both Mill as well as Walzer echo this strong anti-interventionist sentiment.

In, "Liberty, Statehood, and Sovereignty: Walzer on Mill on Non-intervention," Endre Begby critiques Michael Walzer's interpretation of Mill's strong noninterventionist leanings. Begby points out that for reasons of respect for a community's political autonomy and self-determination, Mill concludes

[12] Obviously, France's assistance to the colonists would constitute a certain degree of intervention. However, I do not think the degree of France's external contributions was enough to undermine the political self-determination of the burgeoning American state.

that states ought to adopt a general presumption against intervention. Begby explains here how Mill's general attitude is that a sovereign state that cannot fight its own wars or police its own people is fundamentally not worthy of being regarded as a sovereign state. Hence, if we want to give burgeoning political communities the chance to be regarded as a sovereign political entity at all, we must thereby also give that community a chance to fight its own fights. Citing Walzer, Begby captures the fundamental problem that then faces third-party actors:

> Walzer draws the conclusion for us—that the problem with intervention is not merely that it may have no legal backing; rather, it is strategically askew from the start: "[Mill] doesn't believe that intervention fails more often than not to serve the purposes of liberty; he believes that, given what liberty is, it *necessarily* fails."[13]

Walzer's articulation of the main problem with interventions seems strikingly similar to one horn of the dilemma that we have here been discussing. That is, that a state cannot simultaneously fulfill its duties of aid *and* its duty to respect political autonomy without the fulfillment of one duty logically undercutting its capacity to fulfill the other. In this chapter, I have argued that the problem with intervention is even *more* complex than Walzer makes it out to be, by introducing a third duty of enforcing necessity that third-party states have to fulfill. Thus, we see that not only does the strength of our duty to allow agents to fight for themselves logically cancel out our duty to render aid in typical cases but it also logically cancels out our duty to enforce conditions of necessity while victims are given the chance to attain the good of fighting for themselves. As noted, at the state and international levels, there seems to be even *more* reason for us to prioritize the goods of a community fighting for itself over the fulfillment of the duty to enforce conditions of necessity. But why exactly? What could possibly be grounding this intuition that seems to so strongly fly in the face of the reductive individualist view?

The answer, I contend, is that over and above the set of personal goods achieved by each individual of a political community fighting for themselves exists an *impersonal* good that gives additional moral weight to our duty of nonintervention at the collective level, even when excessive force will be used. Indeed, this notion of an impersonal good does not appear to be a wholly foreign concept as we already seem to give some weight to this notion (if only tacitly) in other, closely related areas of moral discourse. Consider, for instance, the unique

[13] Endre Begby, "Liberty, Statehood and Sovereignty: Walzer on Mill on Non-intervention." *Journal of Military Ethics* 2 (2010): 48.

wrongness of acts like genocide, ethnic cleansing, or atrocity. The fact that we give special attention and special language to such acts seems to strongly speak to the fact that we recognize these acts as exhibiting a unique *kind* of wrong, one that appears to exceed the sum total of the personal wrongs of the individual members of the affected group. Indeed, the wrongness of the Holocaust, for instance, seems to resist explanation *merely* in terms of the sum of individual wrongs done to each affected Jewish person. Rather, the mere fact that the target of extermination in this particle case *was an entire culture* seems to carry with it, an additional *impersonal* wrong-making feature of its own. In the same way, we often think that the extinction of an animal species, for instance, could simply be bad *for the world*; barring certain exceptions, it seems like something similar can be said about the (human-made) extinction of pre-existing cultures.[14]

When a culture or people, one with a unique heritage and history, is wiped from existence by human hands, the world itself seems somehow diminished in a way that can't be accounted for merely in terms of the absence of the individual members who once made up that culture. *That a culture was exterminated* seems to constitute an additional impersonal wrong, one that exceeds the mere loss of the culture's individual members. This impersonal good, the good of pre-existing cultures, I therefore argue, is what gives the value of fighting for one's self greater moral weight and moral significance at the state and international levels and thereby generates, in some cases, greater moral permissions on the battlefield.

To be clear, though, positing such an impersonal good over and above the individual members of a political community *does not* entail at all that we must therefore accept any of the metaphysical baggage of the collectivist view (group agents, group minds, group intentions, etc.). Indeed, other goods, such as the goods of art, natural beauties like the Grand Canyon, and impersonally better future worlds, also seem to be goods that are of an "impersonal" nature that the reductive individualist can likewise endorse. Thus, by accepting the notion that an impersonal good can exist over and above a group of individuals, the reductive individualist is not therefore committed to having to accept collectivism. While collective goods are a subset of the set of impersonal goods, impersonal goods are not a subset of the set of collective goods.[15]

[14] Certainly, though, we do not think the extinction of *all* cultures is always a bad thing. Clearly, an end to the cultures of Nazi Germany, apartheid South Africa, and Taliban-controlled Afghanistan is unquestionably good rather than bad as a development in human history. In general, though, my claim is that unique and diverse cultures are intrinsic and impersonal goods.

[15] I should note that other philosophers have also recognized the value of these impersonal goods and their relevance to just war. In "Towards a Non-Reductivist National Defence," Jeremy Davis (unpublished manuscript, date consulted, September 1, 2014. Microsoft Word file.) acknowledges the additional impersonal value of distinct political groups. However, I believe he goes a bit too far in moving from commitments to impersonal goods to the entailment that we must therefore adopt

Conclusion

In this chapter, we have looked at two seemingly inconsistent obligations that face third-party actors when it comes to the question of intervention, namely, the obligation to respect a victim's consent to defensive assistance and the obligation to enforce conditions of necessity. As we have seen, which of these duties we ultimately ought to uphold and which of these duties we ought to neglect will largely hinge on the amount of overall expected harm associated with their prioritization under certain conditions. All things being equal, however, our prima facie duty appears to be our duty to respect a victim's consent, up to a certain threshold of harm, primarily for reasons of autonomy. What's more, we have considered various candidates for grounding this permission to fight for one's self according to both internalist and externalist formulations of necessity primarily involving "defense of one's honor." Lastly, we have considered how the goods of fighting for one's self appear to be of greater moral importance at the collective level than at the individual level, and we have explained this difference by appealing to an additional *impersonal* good associated with political and cultural groups. Such a commitment to impersonal goods, we have also seen, does not commit one to having to adopt collectivism. Indeed, such a move is wholly compatible with the reductive individualist project.

In considering the value of fighting for one's self at both the individual and state levels, we are reminded of a simple yet important truth: that some of the most important goods worth defending and some of the greatest harms worth defending against, for both the individual as well as the group, are often not at all of a tangible sort. Accordingly, any account of our duties and permissions with respect to the prevention of *physical* harms without robust consideration for these other important intangibles will be drastically and indeed dangerously incomplete.

References

Begby, Endre. "Liberty, Statehood and Sovereignty: Walzer on Mill on Non-intervention." *Journal of Military Ethics* 2, no. 1 (2010): 46–62.

Bowen, Joseph. "Necessity and Liability: On an Honour-Based Justification for Defensive Harming." *Journal of Practical Ethics* 4, no. 2 (2016): 79–93.

Buchanan, Allen. "The Ethics of Revolution and Its Implications for the Ethics of Intervention." *Philosophy & Public Affairs* 41, no. 4 (2013): 291–323.

collectivism. As stated above, while collectivist goods are a subset of impersonal goods, impersonal goods are not a subset of collective goods.

Davis, Jeremy. "Towards a Non-Reductivist National Defence." Unpublished manuscript, Date Consulted September 1, 2014. Microsoft Word file.

Firth, Joanna Mary, and Jonathan Quong. "Necessity, Moral Liability, and Defensive Harm." *Law and Philosophy* 31 (2012): 673–701.

Frowe, Helen. *Defensive Killing*. Oxford: Oxford University Press, 2014.

Lazar, Seth. "Necessity in Self-Defence and War." *Philosophy & Public Affairs* 40, no. 1 (2012): 1–42.

Statman, Daniel. "On the Success Condition for Legitimate Self-Defense." *Ethics* 118, no. 4 (2008): 659–686.

Tadros, Victor. *The Ends of Harm*. Oxford: Oxford University Press, 2011.

6

An Axiomatic Theory of Just War

Forfeiture Theory

STEPHEN KERSHNAR

Thesis

In this chapter, I defend the following thesis.

Thesis: Forfeiture Theory. Forfeiture theory best explains just war.

Specifically, it explains when a war satisfies justice. Examples include when justice allows agents to kill people and break their things. This approach applies to both individual self-defense and war in the same way because the morality of war reduces to individual self-defense cases.

This theory has strong implications for who is liable to be killed. In particular, except in the case where killing is necessary to avoid a catastrophe, only those who forfeit their rights are liable to be killed in wartime. Hence, at the heart of the theory is an account of when people forfeit their rights in general and in the particular context of wartime. This theory also has implications for which, if any, of the commonly cited restrictions on wartime killing (imminence, necessity, proportionality, and discrimination) are relevant.

The second part of this article provides an account of how forfeiture works. In this theory, a person who is an unjust threat to a second person forfeits his or her right against defensive violence with regard to the second. The third part provides the argument for this position. The argument is that forfeiture theory explains when individual and state violence is justified better than other theories. Specifically, it provides a better account of a series of issues such as who has rights, the content of rights, when a right is lost or defeated, and when a right is forfeited. The fourth part discusses some implications of the theory. The fifth part summarizes the theory and argument. This last part also notes that this theory explains just war in the context of cyberwar, moral restrictions on wartime violence, legal restrictions on wartime violence, and various puzzle cases, such as justified threats to third parties.

How Forfeiture Works

Here is a brief account of how forfeiture works. First, I provide the relevant concepts. Second, I argue that forfeiture is needed to account for when defensive violence is justified.

A person loses a right if and only if he or she waives it or forfeits it.[1] A person waives a right if and only if he or she consents to waive it. A person forfeits a right if and only if he or she loses a right and does not waive it. In particular, a person forfeits a right when he or she is an unjust threat. This is true whether the right is one against defensive violence, punishment, or compensation.[2] This is also true in the context of individual self-defense and wartime violence. In law, there are other ways to forfeit rights (for example, one's right to appeal might be forfeited by failure to file the appropriate paperwork in time), but this is not true for morality.

There is an issue as to what counts as an unjust threat. Consider, for example, preemption, overdetermination, and omission that threatens unjust harm. Consider, also, the agency types that might make someone or his or her action an unjust threat (for example, complicity, omission, group membership, being the recipient of a benefit from an unjust cause, and impossible attempts). In this chapter, my account is neutral on the issue. My view, though, is that only individual causal contribution of the right sort (specifically, right-infringing) makes someone an unjust threat.

[1] A forfeiture theory of just war killing can be seen in David Rodin, *War & Self-Defense* (New York: Oxford University Press, 2002), 70–77. People who assert that a criminal forfeits some moral rights include Stephen Kershnar, "The Structure of Rights Forfeiture in the Context of Culpable Wrongdoing," *Philosophia* 29 (2002b): 57–88; A. John Simmons, "Locke and the Right to Punish," in *Punishment*, ed. A. John Simmons, Marshall Cohen, Joshua Cohen, and Charles R. Beitz (Princeton, NJ: Princeton University Press, 1995), 219–260; Judith Jarvis Thomson, *The Realm of Rights* (Cambridge, MA: Harvard University Press, 1990), 365–366; Vinit Haksar, "Excuses and Voluntary Conduct," *Ethics* 96 (1986): 317–329; Murray Rothbard, *The Ethics of Liberty* (Atlantic Highlands, NJ: Humanities Press, 1982); Alan Goldman, "The Paradox of Punishment," *Philosophy and Public Affairs* 9 (1979): 30–46; Roger Pilon, Criminal Remedies: Restitution, Punishment, or Both? *Ethics* 88 (1978): 348–357. These theories differ with regard to whether right forfeiture is a fundamental feature of rights or explained by a more fundamental principle.

[2] Some of the details of the theory can be seen in Kershnar, "Structure of Rights Forfeiture."

One person is an unjust threat if and only if he or she infringes a right or, on an alternative account, is likely to infringe a right.[3] This includes rights against risk. The right forfeited expands what the respondent may do in terms of defensive violence subject to certain limits on defensive violence. The limits might include factors such as necessity, proportionality, and imminence.

A right is defeated if and only if it is overridden. A defeated right retains its normative force, it is just overcome by a weightier moral consideration. This is analogous to how, in physics, a vector force can be overpowered by an opposite and more powerful vector force. This is different from forfeiture where a right ceases to have normative force. By analogy, the vector force ceases to exist. The stringency of a right is not equal to the value of what is protected (for example, the value of autonomy the right protects) or rights would likely do no work. Nevertheless, if the ground (for example, autonomy or interest) is to explain a right, there must be some proportionality in terms of defensive violence permitted and the unjust threat to which the violence responds.

To see the argument for forfeiture, consider the following.

Case 1: Prevention in the State of Nature

> In the state of nature, Al batters, rapes, and sodomizes Betty. When Al attacks a second time, she strikes him, thereby intentionally causing him to suffer temporarily and preventing the attack. Her strike causes temporary pain but no lasting suffering, disability, or harm. Al does not intend or know that Betty will strike him or otherwise cause him to suffer, nor is he reckless with regard to the fact that she might do so.

Intuitively, Betty's act is just. Just acts are ones that do not infringe on anyone's moral rights. Here the underlying assumption is that people have a natural property to their body (and perhaps rights to it) and non-natural rights to property. Other rights are derived from these rights. If Betty's act is just (that is, consistent with justice), then there are four candidate explanations as to what happens to Al's right.

[3] An infringement is an act that fails to satisfy a right. A violation is a wrongful infringement. An infringement is sufficient to make someone an unjust threat. An unjust threat might have an all-things-considered justification for doing something that fails to satisfy someone's right (for example, torturing the child of a terrorist who has planted a ticking time bomb, though relative to the child he or she is an unjust threat). Because a right infringement is necessarily an other-things-being-equal wrong, there is a sense in which all right infringements are wrong.

First, Betty's act might not infringe on Al's right because his right to his body is complex, having something like the following content: *Betty-and-others-have-a-duty-not-to-touch-Al's-body-unless-it-is-necessary-for-just-defense-or-just-punishment-etc.* This content will result in a right that is indistinguishable from forfeiture theory because it has the same implications for just defense. They are indistinguishable in that the two theories would generate identical conclusions in terms of what is just and permissible. However, this theory is unhelpful because the just-defense condition cannot be explained in terms of the right to one's body because the latter includes the former as part of its content. On this account, then, we cannot explain why Betty's violence is okay in terms of Al's rights. That is, we want a right to explain what may justly be done to Al rather than what may justly be done to Al explaining the content of his right.[4]

Second, Betty's act might permissibly trump Al's right. A reason (or an act done from a reason) trumps a right if it infringes on a right and the agent is justified in doing so.[5] However, if Al's right is infringed, whether trumped or not, then Al is owed compensation or at least some other residue duty, for example, an apology. Intuitively, Al is not owed either. The residue duty exists because Al's right exists and exerts normative force on Betty and when the normative force is overpowered by another moral entity, the result is a residue duty.[6] This can be intuitively seen in the classic Joel Feinberg case when a desperate hiker breaks into another person's cabin and burns his furniture in order to stay alive. Although the hiker's action is just, he still owes compensation to the cabin owner because he infringed on the owner's right.[7]

Third, Al might voluntarily lose or suspend his right. This might occur via consent or promise.[8] A person does something voluntarily only if he or she does it intentionally (that is, with purpose, knowledge, or recklessness), and this

[4] In addition, the conjunction Al has a right that Betty-not-harm-his-body-unless-he-is-an-unjust-threat-or-warrants-punishment-or-must-pay-compensation and Al is an unjust threat has an unclear structure. This structure is less clear than the notion that Al has a right to his body (against Betty) unless he is an unjust threat to her and he is an unjust threat to her. See Jeremy Waldron, *The Right to Private Property* (Oxford: Clarendon Press, 1991), ch. 3.

[5] If rights cannot conflict, then it follows that if A lacks or loses his or her right against B that B not X, then A does not have a claim against B not X. If A does not have a claim against B, then B does not have a duty regarding A not to X. If B does not have a duty regarding A not to X, then B is permitted to X. This permission might be overridden if there are duties that are free-floating (not owed to anyone) or if there can be conflicting rights.

[6] See Kershnar, "Structure of Rights Forfeiture."

[7] See Joel Feinberg, "Voluntary Euthanasia and the Inalienable Right to Life," *Philosophy and Public Affairs* 7 (1978): 93–123.

[8] The consent theory of punishment is defended in C. S. Nino, "A Consensual Theory of Punishment," *Philosophy and Public Affairs* 12, no. 4 (1983): 289–306, "Does Consent Override

is not true here. Hence, Al does not voluntarily suspend or lose his right. The underlying assumption here is that actual consent, but not hypothetical consent, is morally transformative, so hypothetical consent is not relevant.

Fourth, given the failure of the above three theories, Al's right must be forfeited. This is the *forfeiture theory*. On this account, this forfeiture is a primitive feature of how rights work.[9] That is, forfeiture does not depend on a more fundamental theory of rights or morality. Table 6.1 summarizes these results.

If in the state of nature the right to defense were not held by the victim alone and if a third party acts on his or her own and attacks a bad person (who has launched an unjust attack) in defense of another, then either the victim would not be able to justly defend against the bad person or there would be no proportionality limit on just defense. Both intuitively seem incorrect.[10]

In addition, the right forfeited is either the right in question or an equivalent right. This is in part because otherwise defense would be impossible in some cases. For example, a blind man who tries to blind another could not be prevented from doing so. Nor could anyone defend against a man who does not own a car and tries to steal one from another. In these cases, the unjust attacker's right not to be blinded or not to have his or her car taken is not infringed because he or she has no (working) eyes or car. If defensive violence against him or her is just, then he or she forfeits an equivalent right. This equivalent right is relevant in explaining that the defensive violence is just and proportionate. Note whether the right that is lost has a limited scope in time or whether the right is only temporarily lost is a distinction without a difference because both descriptions are equivalent and there is no reason to prefer one over the other. On this account, the forfeited right acts as the ceiling on the amount of violence that can be used in just defense.[11]

Proportionality?" *Philosophy and Public Affairs* 15, no. 2 (1986): 183–187, and *The Ethics of Human Rights* (Oxford: Clarendon Press, 1991).

[9] Forfeiture or one of the other theories of rights could be justified not as a primitive but rather as a result of fair-and-rational choosing conditions applied to issues of economic justice. See John Rawls, *A Theory of Justice* (Cambridge, MA: Belknap Press, 1971). An account of self-defense derived from distributive justice can be seen in Michael Moore, "Torture and the Balance of Evils," *Israel Law Review* 23 (1989): 280–344; and Philip Montague, *Self-Defense as Societal Defense* (Boston: Rowman & Littlefield, 1995).

[10] On this account, forfeiture occurs only with regard to the would-be victim. Again, this is a primitive feature of rights. The victim's agents may act on his or her behalf, but he or she alone has the right to defend himself or herself. An exception occurs when he or she transfers it to someone else. In the state of nature, it is hard to see how when one person attacks a second, this changes the rights of third parties. Just as the property rights of third parties are not affected by transactions involving others, the same intuitively seems to be true with regard to defense.

[11] The right to defend oneself is a liberty against an unjust attacker to use violence. This is an absence of a duty owed to him or her not to use defensive violence. It is also accompanied by a claim

Table 6.1. **For Forfeiture**

Theory	*Assertion*	*Objection(s)*
Narrow scope	Justified defensive violence does not infringe on the attacker's right because it is part of the content of the right.	1. The right cannot explain what a defender may and may not do. 2. The theory is extensionally equivalent to forfeiture theory.[a]
Override	Justified defensive violence overrides the attacker's right.	If this were true, then the just defender would have a residue duty (to compensate or apologize to him or her) and he or she has no such duty.
Consent	Justified defensive violence does not infringe the attacker's right because he or she has consented to the defender's violence.	Many attackers do not consent.
Forfeiture	Justified defensive violence does not infringe the attacker's right because he or she has lost it.	

[a] It is equivalent in terms of the duties and permissions it generates but not the explanation it provides for those permissions or duties.

One objection here is that some people do not share the intuition that Betty's act is just. The objector might claim that intuitively Betty's act is unjust. On this account, our intuition is explained by the fact that Betty's act is a case of blameless wrongdoing. This position is that of an absolute pacifist because it makes all defensive violence a type of wrongdoing, whether blameless or not.

My intuitions do not align with the objector and nor do the majority of people who were asked the same question in a recent public lecture. I see no reason in terms of either frequency of intuition or coherence with other plausible intuitions to reject the intuition that Betty acts justly.[12]

In addition, one can imagine cases where Betty meets the conditions of responsibility; and hence, it is hard to see why, if her act were wrong, she would

to noninterference against the victimizer. This right is usually, if not always, accompanied by a power over the claim. A power is the moral standing to eliminate, modify, or leave in place this duty. It also includes an immunity over the other elements, which is a lack of power in the other party.

[12] If, however, intuitions in general or in the context of applied ethics are unreliable, then my argument is unsound.

be blameless. For example, it is possible that she is rational, meets the metaphysical condition or conditions for freedom (she has libertarian freedom, is reasons-responsive, has second-order volitions with which she identifies, etc.), and lacks an excuse (for example, provocation or duress).

Forfeiture theories vary in terms of whether in order to forfeit a right, an attacker must be blameworthy for an attack or morally responsible for putting another at risk.[13] This is particularly relevant to war because many soldiers were, and perhaps still are, uninformed or misinformed and thus, arguably, blameless. If blame is required for forfeiture, then soldiers who were an integral part of an unjust aggressive campaign did not forfeit their rights and thus may not have been justly killed. On my account, forfeiture does not require blame or responsibility. Consider the following case.

Case 2: Psychotic Aggressor

> A woman's companion in an elevator goes berserk and attacks her with a knife. There is no escape: the only way for her to avoid serious bodily harm or even death is to kill him with her gun. The assailant acts purposely in the sense that he means to further his aggressive end. He does act in a frenzy or in a fit, yet it is clear that his conduct is non-responsible. If he were brought to trial for his attack, he would have a valid defense of insanity.[14]

Intuitively, it seems that the woman may defend herself even though the attacker is neither blameworthy for the attack nor responsible for imposing a relevant risk on the woman.[15] The reason for thinking the woman is not merely excused from defending herself is that intuitively there is no residue duty (duty to compensate or apologize) owed to the attacker. The woman's permission to use defensive violence is relative to the attacker because of the two-person nature of moral rights. The explanation for why these responsibility-related conditions are irrelevant is that moral rights protect an individual's autonomy and forfeiture is part of this function. A victim's autonomy can be set back by acts for which another is not morally responsible as well as ones for which he or she is responsible.

[13] See Jeff McMahan, *Killing in War* (Oxford: Clarendon Press, 2009), 51–60, "On the Moral Equality of Combatants," *Journal of Political Philosophy* 14 (2006): 377–393, and "The Basis of Moral Liability to Defensive Killing," *Philosophical Issues* 15 (2005): 386–405.

[14] See George Fletcher, "Proportionality and the Psychotic Aggressor: A Vignette in Comparative Criminal Theory," *Israel Law Review* 8 (1973): 367–390, esp. 371.

[15] For a similar conclusion, see a defense of the notion that culpability, responsibility, and agency are not necessary for liability to defensive violence in Judith Jarvis Thomson, "Self-Defense," *Philosophy and Public Affairs* 20 (1991): 283–310, and "Self-Defense and Rights," in Rights, Restitution, and Risk, ed. William Parent, 33–48 (Cambridge, MA: Harvard University Press, 1986).

For example, the woman loses her life and thus her autonomy in the above case whether the attacker is responsible or not. If moral rights rest on the autonomy of the right-holder and forfeiture reflects that justification, then forfeiture can occur regardless of whether the attacker is morally responsible.

Some theorists (for example, Jeff McMahan) argue that this allows forfeiture on the basis of a feature of someone who is wholly outside of his or her scope of responsibility or control. This is an implication of the woman being permitted to defend herself against the psychotic attacker because he is as innocent as she is. Here I am assuming the attacker has not forgotten to take his medication or done some other blameworthy thing. This implication also rests on the lack of correlation between the minor degree of blame some attackers have (for example, if the psychotic attacker did not seek out mental health services soon enough) and the major moral transformation (the loss of his right to life).

If the attacker doesn't have rights in virtue of not being morally responsible, whether temporarily or permanently, then forfeiture does not make defensive violence against him permissible.[16] One can't lose what one doesn't have. In such a case, the defender has options similar to what happens when the attacker forfeits his rights. That is, the attacker lacks a claim against violence against him and, hence, a potential defender has no duty not to use defensive violence.

Others argue that when the attacker does not act at all, he is not a moral subject and hence cannot infringe on an endangered person's rights.[17] Such a case might occur when you are at the bottom of your own well and a bad guy throws an innocent man down the well at you and the only way to avoid being killed is to disintegrate him with your ray gun.[18] Given that both you and the innocent man are people with moral rights, it is hard to see why this account is correct. The innocent may have an excuse for endangering you and, perhaps, he doesn't forfeit his right. Still, the endangerment either does or does not result in forfeiture. If he does forfeit his right, then being a moral subject or having agency in a particular instance is not necessary for forfeiture. If he does not forfeit, then defensive violence is not justified in either the falling-man or the elevator case because the threats are (we may assume) as innocent and as valuable as the people they endanger.

The falling man's lack of agency intuitively seems to be relevant only in so far as it relates to his being blameless. Whether his being blameless leaves his rights

[16] Forfeiture never justifies defensive violence in that it makes it obligatory or provides a reason to do it. Rather, it merely eliminates a claim against such violence, thereby making it permissible.

[17] See Michael Otsuka, "Killing the Innocent in Self-Defense," *Philosophy and Public Affairs* 23 (1994): 74–94; and Rodin, *War & Self-Defense*, 86.

[18] This example comes from Robert Nozick, *Anarchy, State, and Utopia* (New York: Basic Books, 1974).

intact depends on the way in which autonomy justifies rights. This might depend on whether the threat to the body of the person at the bottom of the well is due to the falling innocent man or to the combination of the falling innocent man and the person at the bottom of the well.[19] Alternatively, it might depend on how autonomy links up to property rights.[20]

In any case, though, my overall theory is compatible with blame- and responsibility-based accounts of forfeiture; and thus, for the purposes of this chapter, nothing rests on this issue.

Consider objections to forfeiture theory. First, there are issues regarding how rights can be forfeited when what justifies them (for example, the right-holder's autonomy or interest) is still present. Second, forfeiture has to explain a lot. Specifically, it has to explain why military violence is limited by requirements, including, depending on the account, necessity, imminence, proportionality, and discrimination.[21] This is a lot of explanatory work.

Third, there are discrimination issues. It intuitively seems that many civilians, such as legislators who intentionally cause the military to unjustly attack others, are unjust threats and thus forfeit their rights. Yet they are often considered inappropriate targets. If intention to contribute to an unjust attack is not necessary for forfeiture, then it is unclear why military support staff (for example, truckers, cooks, and construction workers) forfeit rights against attack, whereas nonmilitary support workers (for example, farmers) do not.

Fourth, forfeiture theory asserts that forfeiture occurs following an attempted attack, rather than a completed one; but it is unclear why an attempt by itself is an injustice at all, let alone one that warrants lethal violence. By itself, an attempt need not trespass on another's body or property. If any of these problems are fatal, then we need another account of permissible wartime killing.

Fifth, there are puzzle cases that forfeiture has trouble handling, such as the issue of what happens to the rights of two qualitatively identical people who simultaneously launch unprovoked attacks against the other. In that case, you have an unstable scenario similar to a liar paradox. Each person either has or lacks the right to defend against the other. If one attacker has the right, then the other does not and vice versa. Yet the two are qualitatively identical, so it is

[19] The notion that the cause of the harm is the combination of the two men can be found in Ronald Coase, "The Problem of Social Cost," *The Journal of Law and Economics* 3 (1960): 1–44.

[20] See Stephen Kershnar, "Private Property Rights and Autonomy," *Public Affairs Quarterly* 16 (2002a): 231–258.

[21] Forfeiture provides a unified account of these constraints, perhaps as primitive features of how forfeiture works. For a discussion of these constraints independent of forfeiture, see Brian Orend, *The Morality of War* (Orchard Park, NY: Broadview, 2006), ch. 4.

impossible for one to have the right if the other does not.[22] Note that both cannot forfeit the right to self-defense because if one, A, forfeits his or her right, then he or she is an unjust threat to the other, B, and because B is responding to an unjust threat with proportional force, he or she does not forfeit his or her right.

Another rival theory, threshold deontology, asserts that consequentialist reasons can justify wartime killing and destruction. A consequentialist override occurs when action is justified because it brings about very good results and the value of these results trumps a nonconsequentialist side-constraint. Even if this is correct, the results must be very good for it to override stringent side-constraints against killing and destruction.[23] In addition, if someone's right is overridden, compensatory justice requires that the person whose right is overridden be given an apology, if not compensation. However, unjust wartime aggressors intuitively seem to be owed neither. Thus, there is reason to doubt that wartime killing is justified by an overriding of military members' rights.

The Achilles heel of forfeiture theory is that it depends on an attacker acting unjustly when he imposes an increased risk of a right-infringement (beyond a certain threshold) or imposes a risk that is a right-infringement. The former account (increased risk of a right-infringement) is problematic in that posing a risk of right-infringement is not itself a right-infringement. Hence, it is not enough to make the attacker's action unjust. The latter account (increased risk is itself a right-infringement) is better but still problematic.

First, it is not clear how to understand risk. Understood as an increased probability (perhaps a significant increase), this notion conflicts with libertarian freedom because human freedom is arguably incompatible with a specific change in probabilities. It also conflicts with determinism because the latter is incompatible with agents increasing the chance an injustice or harm will occur. This might, however, be a reason to reject libertarian and determinist theories of events rather than drop the notion of risk from an account of what justifies self-defense.

Second, the threshold of risk that justifies defensive violence is arbitrary. Our acts frequently impose risks on others, and it is intuitively implausible that there is a specific increase in risk above which a risk-imposition justifies defensive

[22] Older versions of this paradox can be seen in Otsuka, "Killing the Innocent," 74–94; Stephen Kershnar, "Consent-Based Permission to Kill People and Break Their Things," *Reason Papers* 37 (2015a): 34–53, and "Fetuses Are Like Rapists: A Judith-Jarvis-Thomson-Inspired Argument on Abortion," *Reason Papers* 37 (2015b): 88–109.

[23] Given that standard trolley and surgeon's harvest cases indicate that a net saving of five lives is not weighty enough to do so and that many wartime killings do not generate a benefit worth more than five lives, the consequentialist override will not justify many instances of wartime killing. See Judith Jarvis Thomson, "The Trolley Problem," *The Yale Law Journal* 94 (1985): 1395–1415; and Phillipa Foot, "The Problem of Abortion and the Doctrine of the Double Effect," *Oxford Review* 5 (1967): 5–15.

violence and below which it does not. In addition, there is often little correlation between an attacker's blameworthiness and the degree to which he or she imposes harm on an innocent party.

Third, if there were a determinate threshold, it would likely rest on consequentialist considerations such as the (probability-adjusted) benefit to the individual who imposes a risk and the (probability-adjusted) harm to the one put at risk. For example, consider whether a diseased person who takes a public bus infringes on another passenger's right by risking his or her health. Imagine that the sick man has Ebola. This depends on what the sick man gains and what the healthy rider loses if the sick man takes the bus. The balance of costs and benefits might also involve third parties. Consider, for example, what is true of the population of bus riders. The problem is that rights do not rest on such consequentialist considerations, especially if rights trump consequences.[24]

Fourth, the account generates an infinite regress. Forfeiture based on increased risk depends on two claims. (1) *There is a right against unjust risk.* This is true because just defenders may impose very severe risks on an attacker. It is an unjust risk, rather than any risk, that justifies defensive violence. (2) *A risk is unjust in case it infringes on a right.* This is because an injustice is a right-infringement. But the right in question is itself a right against risk. If a defender successfully prevents an attack, then other rights (for example, rights to property or body) are sometimes not infringed. When we combine (1) and (2), *the right against an unjust risk* becomes *the right against risk of an unjust risk,* which in turn becomes the *right against a risk of a risk of an unjust risk,* and so on.

One could escape this by viewing defensive violence as justified only if it succeeds in lessoning or preventing an attack, but then ineffective defensive violence is wrong. This is implausible as, on this account, a woman who strikes a rapist to make him stop would act wrongly if her strike accomplishes nothing. This is hard to believe.[25]

In summary, then, forfeiture theory appears to a better account of individual defense than competitor theories, such as narrow-scope theory, permissible infringement, and consent theory. On this account, forfeiture is a primitive feature of how rights work and only affects the right-related relations (claim, liberty, power, and immunity) between the one who attacks and the one who defends.

[24] Ronald Dworkin, "Rights as Trumps," in *Theories of Rights,* ed. Jeremy Waldron (Oxford: Oxford University Press, 1984), 153–167; and Alan Gewirth, "Are There any Absolute Rights?" in *Theories of Rights,* 81–109. See, also, Hillel Steiner, *An Essay on Rights* (Oxford: Blackwell, 1994a).

[25] A forfeiture theorist can argue that narrow-scope theory faces the same issue because it is part of the boundary for the relevant right (for example, the right against violence). The consent theory escapes this objection but faces the fatal problem that unjust attackers don't consent to allow those whom they target to defend themselves. For now, let us consider whether forfeiture theory, aside from the difficulty with risk, is the best account of wartime killing.

Argument

Here is the argument for the thesis.

(P1) If forfeiture theory explains when individual and state violence is justified better than other theories, then forfeiture theory best explains just war.
(P2) Forfeiture theory explains when individual and state violence is justified better than other theories.
(C1) Hence, forfeiture theory best explains just war. [(P1), (P2)]

Premise (P1) is trivially true.

Premise (P2) rests on the above argument and the following assumptions. The above argument argues for forfeiture theory in the case of individual self-defense. The below assumptions apply it to state violence. I will assume there are no consequential overrides and then revisit this assumption later.

Assumption 1: Rights. Individuals alone have rights and are owed duties.

Underlying this assumption is the idea that a right is grounded by autonomy or an interest and that individuals alone have autonomy or an interest.[26]

Assumption 2: Wrongness of Individual Killing to Duty-Infringement. Outside of war, if one individual wrongly kills a second, then the first fails to satisfy a duty he or she owes to someone.

If one person acts wrongly, then he or she wrongs someone. That is, there are no free-floating, nonconsequentialist wrongs.[27] If one person wrongs someone, then he or she fails to satisfy a duty he or she owes to that individual.

[26] The autonomy-based theory of rights is called the "will theory of rights." This theory asserts that rights function to protect choices. As such, they always include a Hohfeldian power plus the other Hohfeldian elements over which the power ranges. See, e.g., H. L. A. Hart, *Essays on Bentham: Studies in Jurisprudence and Political Theory* (Oxford: Clarendon Press, 1982); Carl Wellman, *A Theory of Rights* (Totowa, NJ: Rowman and Allenheld, 1985); and Steiner, *Essay on Rights*. I should mention that on my version of the will theory, rights are constituted by claims, although these claims are often accompanied by powers. In contrast, the interest theory asserts that rights function to protect interests. As such, they are constituted by a claim. See, e.g., David Lyons, *Rights, Welfare and Mill's Moral Theory* (New York: Oxford University Press, 1994); Neil MacCormick, "Rights in Legislation," in *Law, Morality and Society: Essays in Honour of H. L. A. Hart*, ed. P. Hacker and J. Raz (Oxford: Oxford University Press, 1977), 189–209; Joseph Raz, *The Morality of Freedom* (Oxford: Oxford University Press, 1986); and Matthew Kramer, "Rights Without Trimmings," in *A Debate over Rights*, ed. Matthew Kramer, N. E. Simmons, and Hillel Steiner (New York: Oxford University Press, 1998), 7–111.

[27] There are other theories that argue against this, such as consequentialist theories, motive-based theories, and nonidentity theories of wrongness. If these theories are true as well as a rights-based

Assumption 3: Duty-Infringement to Right-Infringement. If one person fails to satisfy a duty owed the second, then the first infringes on the second's right.

This assumption rests on the Hohfeldian notion that a right is a claim and a claim is to be owed a duty.

Assumption 4: Wrongness of State Killing. State killing is morally similar to individuals' killings outside of war.

The fact that the state does the killing does not by itself change the relation between a wrong act and a moral right. Also, the fact that the state does the killing does not change what rights individuals have (specifically, their content, distribution, or stringency). To see this, consider the following cases.

Case 3: Mob

A mob of mothers from a particular region of Sudan burn down a house containing a renter. They have just watched a news show that mistakenly identified the renter having Ebola. They kill him because they want to protect their children. The mob's members have spontaneously got together and have not made any promises to each other. Nor have they consented to anything involving the others.

Case 4: Partnership

A collection of mothers from a region of Sudan form a partnership to promote and protect their children. The partnership pays someone to burn down a house containing a renter. The partners have just watched a news show that mistakenly identified the renter as having Ebola. They kill him because they want to protect their children.

Case 5: Government

A collection of mothers from a particular region of Sudan occupies the lion's share of the Somali government (legislature, executive, and judiciary). Their priority is to promote and protect Somali children. Following Democratic procedure, they pass a law declaring war on biological

account of morality also being true, then my theory merely establishes the case for just defensive violence and other-things-equal permission for defensive violence. If these theories are false, then my theory address just defensive violence and all-things-considered permission for defensive violence. I do not think there is motive-grounded or non-identity-grounded wrongness, although a defense of this is beyond the scope of this discussion. See, for example, David Boonin, *The Non-Identity Problem and the Ethics of Future People* (New York: Oxford University Press, 2014).

threats. Following the passage of this law and a presidential order, the army burns down a house containing a renter; the house is in Ethiopia on a property adjacent to Sudan. The leaders have just watched a news show that mistakenly identified the renter as having Ebola. They kill him because they want to protect their children.

Wartime killing is a type of state killing. The underlying reasoning here is that there is no morally relevant difference between the spontaneously formed mob of mothers in Case 3 and the partnership in Case 4. The presence or absence of a partnership cannot affect the rights of third parties. Similarly, there is no morally relevant difference between the partnership in Case 4 and long-standing institution in Case 5. Again, the difference between a partnership and a state institution cannot affect the rights of third parties.

Assumption 5: Assumption to Forfeiture Theory. If the first four assumptions are true, then the best theory of just war focuses on when rights are lost or defeated. Forfeiture theory alone focuses on when rights are lost or defeated.

Note that if there is a consequential override of rights, then acts that would otherwise be permissible are wrong or vice versa. The forfeiture account is compatible with such overrides. In fact, I think that not only can such overrides occur, but they sometimes do occur during wartime.

The forfeiture theory of wartime killing has several advantages. First, it coheres with the notion that individuals alone have rights. Because this is a plausible notion given that the standard justifications of rights in terms of autonomy and interests because individuals alone have autonomy and interests, it nicely dovetails with an account of who has rights.[28] The background picture is that people have natural rights that are almost all, if not all, negative.[29] Non-natural rights are all derived from these natural rights. As a result, every right is had by an individual.

Second, it coheres with what happens to the rights of the attacker in a standard case of self-defense. As argued above, forfeiture is the most plausible account of why a just defender does not wrong an unjust attacker. This is a significant

[28] For the interest theory, see Matthew Kramer, "Some Doubts About Alternatives to the Interest Theory of Rights," *Ethics* 123 (2013): 245–263, "Refining the Interest Theory of Rights," *American Journal of Jurisprudence* 55 (2010): 31–39, and "Rights Without Trimmings." For the will theory, see Hillel Steiner, "Directed Duties and Inalienable Rights," *Ethics* 123 (2013): 230–244, and "Working Rights," in *A Debate over Rights*, ed. Matthew Kramer, N. E. Simmons, and Hillel Steiner (Oxford: Blackwell, 1994b), 239–247.

[29] See Nozick, *Anarchy, State, and Utopia.*

advantage in that it is hard to see how war could change the distribution and operation of rights from what occurs in ordinary self-defense. The mere fact that people coordinate their efforts or join voluntary groups, such as nations, does not intuitively seem capable of changing these facts. In general, the analogy here is to the principle of the conservation of mass—namely, in a closed system, mass is neither created nor destroyed, although it is rearranged. When people enter or leave groups, their rights are neither created nor destroyed, although they can be rearranged via waiver and forfeiture.

This approach might be consistent with traditional just war theory if forfeiture writ large contains the same conditions as just war theory with people being subject to them via valid consent on joining the military and the military being subject (perhaps via international law) to just war criteria. My theory is better viewed as revisionist in so far as forfeiture in the aggregate (even when linked via consent) likely does not support some of the criteria. Consider, for example, the following criteria: last resort, right intention, and probability of success. None of these intuitively applies to forfeiture or just self-defense in individual cases. Thus, it is likely that it does not apply to self-defense for an aggregation of people unless put in place by some agreed-upon law.

Third, the theory views war as merely a collection of violent acts in which individuals' rights govern what one individual may do to another. In understanding and evaluating war, it need not posit additional metaphysical or moral complexities. In particular, it need not posit a group as a metaphysical entity distinct from the collection of individuals who are its parts. Nor need it posit a new moral relation that emerges when a collection of individuals interact in a complex manner. For example, it need not posit group rights that are morally distinct from an aggregation of individual rights. Nor need it assume that acts are made right or wrong by something other than moral rights. It is thus compatible with the view that desert, fairness, equality, exploitation, virtue, and so on either do not make acts right or wrong or ground rights. There is independent reason to think this correct.[30]

Fourth, the theory fits cleanly with theories of punishment and just compensation that apply to the state of nature and to criminal and tort law. This is

[30] For theories of desert that view it as addressing the good and not the right, see Fred Feldman, "Adjusting Utility for Justice: A Consequentialist Reply to the Objection from Justice," *Philosophy and Phenomenological Research* 55 (1995): 567–585; Shelly Kagan, "Equality and Desert," in *What Do We Deserve?* ed. Louis P. Pojman and Owen McLeod (New York: Oxford University Press, 1999), 298–314; Thomas Hurka, "The Common Structure of Virtue and Desert," *Ethics* 112 (2001a): 6–31, *Virtue, Vice, and Value* (New York: Oxford University Press, 2001b); and Neil Feit and Stephen Kershnar, "Explaining the Geometry of Desert," *Public Affairs Quarterly* 18 (2004): 273–298. For the notion that exploitation is not wrong, see Stephen Kershnar, *Pedophilia and Adult–Child Sex: A Philosophical Defense* (Lanham, MD: Lexington Books, 2015c), ch. 5.

not true for theories that make self-defense, punishment, or just compensation depend on the state for either metaphysical or moral reasons.

Table 6.2 summarizes the theory so far.

There are several objections that might be raised against the overall theory. The ones I find most challenging are those discussed above regarding forfeiture. Here I focus on two other powerful objections.

One objection is to the above account of rights. The objector might deny that individuals alone have rights. Alternatively, he or she might think that what nations may do during wartime is not solely a function of rights. David Rodin argues that individualism about the ethics of war is incorrect because permissible national defense allows for war-fighting options not available to a collection of individuals. Specifically, he argues, nations are allowed to attack unarmed members of the enemy's army, use pre-emptive attacks (for example, mines) to prevent future enemy attacks, and have less, if any, of a duty to retreat.[31] Rodin's theory conflicts with the metaphysical theory adopted above because, on the above theory, individuals alone have rights and because the justice of war (and, perhaps, the morality of it) is solely a function of rights.

Henry Shue argues that an individualist account of war cannot handle the moral basis for the laws of war. In particular, he argues, if such an account were true, then all combatants who are part of an unjust campaign would be subject to punishment for violating international law.[32]

Michael Walzer rejects the individualist account because war is a relation between political entities, not individuals. As such, he argues, the moral duties and permissions apply to the political entities and not to individuals, at least not directly. Also, he argues, war is so different from what is found in civilian life in a functioning peaceful society that it has its own moral norms.[33]

Noam Zohar argues that war is permissible even when self-defense cannot justify it. This is because, he claims, the self-defense justification requires guilt, fault, or aggression on behalf of the attacker and many combatants do not have these features. Instead, he argues, soldiers are treated as embodying a nation's agency rather than their own.[34]

The objections all fail if nonconsequentialist right and wrong are a function of, and only of, rights and if rights rest on autonomy or interests. The former

[31] See Rodin, *War & Self-Defense*, chs. 5–7.

[32] See Henry Shue, "Do We Need a 'Morality of War'?" in *Just and Unjust Warriors*, ed. David Rodin and Henry Shue (Oxford: Oxford University Press, 2008), 87–111.

[33] See Michael Walzer, *Just and Unjust Wars* (New York: Basic Books, 1977), 127, and "Response to McMahan's Paper," *Philosophia* 34 (2006): 43–45.

[34] See Noam Zohar, "Innocence and Complex Threats: Upholding the War Ethic and the Condemnation of Terrorism," *Ethics* 114 (2004): 734–751.

Table 6.2. **Specific Forfeiture Account**

Name	*Issue*	*General Theory*	*Specific Theory*
Holder	Who has rights?	Individual people	Autonomous beings alone have rights.
Content	What rights do parties have?	All rights are **natural rights** or **rights derived from them**.	1. **Natural rights** are negative rights to one's body. 2. **Non-natural rights** are derived from natural rights. They are rights to property (and, perhaps, compensation).
Protection	When is a right lost or defeated?	1. A right is **lost** if and only if it is waived or forfeited. 2. A right is **defeated** if and only if another moral consideration overrides it.	1. A right is **waived** via consent. 2. A person **forfeits** a right if and only if he or she is an unjust threat. Whether he or she is an unjust threat does not depend on respondent's mental state. 3. A right is **overridden** if and only if a consequentialist consideration is opposed to and more stringent than the right-based one.
Closure	Is an act wrong if it infringes on a right and the right is not lost or defeated?	Yes	Same as left.
Forfeiture	When is a right forfeited?	A person forfeits a right if he or she is an unjust threat.	A person is an unjust threat if he or she imposes an unjust risk on someone.

assumption is plausible because it is intuitively difficult to come up with a plausible case when a wrong act does not wrong someone and when one person wrongs a second without infringing a duty owed to him or her. Standard examples such as exploitation, non-identity duties, and imperfect duties are unconvincing and in any case likely involve a covert duty-infringement, albeit a disjunctive one in the case of an imperfect duty.

The latter assumption rests on the notion that rights function to protect something valuable and autonomy and interests are the most plausible valuable things warranting such protection. That autonomy is had by, and only by, an individual can be seen in that almost every theory of responsibility focuses a feature of an individual that requires consciousness (for example, reason-responsiveness, aligned desires, capacity for self-revision, knowledge of the true and good, and agent causation).[35] Individuals alone are conscious. The same is true for theories of well-being, almost all of which focus on, whether in part or in whole, pleasure, desire-fulfillment, or knowledge; and each of these requires consciousness.

The first objection does raise an interesting issue with regard to the consent of members of the military. It might be objected that, for many countries, members of the military consent to be killed in virtue of their consenting to governments that in turn have consented to international laws that set forth various rules about when and how nations may go to war. They have thus consented to rules about killing in the case of international conflict as part of their consent to their government's authority. Consider, for example, the rules of war found in the Hague and Geneva Conventions. This is analogous to the way in which, on some theories, offenders consent to be punished in virtue of their having consented to a government that contains either a particular penalty system or a more fundamental procedure by which a penalty system is chosen and implemented.[36]

This assumes that government authority is justified by consent. I think this is correct, although it should be noted that many theorists deny this. They argue that citizens don't consent and that if they did, it would be invalid because it was done involuntarily or without adequate knowledge. In addition, A. John Simmons argues that consent cannot justify government because the government's proposed deal (for a given territory, an individual and government trade consent for government-dependent benefits) presupposes that the government

[35] For the first model, see John Martin Fischer and Mark Ravizza, *Responsibility and Control: A Theory of Moral Responsibility* (New York: Cambridge University Press, 1998). For the second model, see Harry Frankfurt, "Freedom of the Will and the Concept of a Person," *Journal of Philosophy* 68 (1971): 5–20; and Gary Watson, "Free Agency," *Journal of Philosophy* 72 (1975): 205–220. For the third and fourth models, see Susan Wolf, *Freedom Within Reason* (New York: Oxford University Press, 1990).

[36] The consent theory of punishment is defended in Nino, "A Consensual Theory of Punishment," "Does Consent Override Proportionality?" and *Ethics of Human Rights*.

already has legitimate authority over the territory and thus may offer such a deal.[37] This, Simmons argues, pushes the issue of government authority one step back.

There is a further problem with consent theory in that, on some accounts, asking people to consent to certain arrangements is wrong, even if the consent is informed and free. For example, it seems wrong to ask women to consent to marriages that permit marital rape even if this is made clear to them and they are not coerced into marrying. That is, on some accounts, valid consent is not sufficient for a just agreement, even if it is necessary. It might be impossible to consent to marital rape if rape is nonconsensual sex. If so, the problem should focus on sex that is against a woman's will. The idea is that we cannot bulk-consent to future actions that we might will against or strongly disagree with later.

Assuming the problems with consent legitimating governments can be overcome, and I think they can, the issue is whether the international warfighting conventions are binding on citizens, especially members of the military. A concern is that a person's consent is effective only if what he or she consents to is reasonable, fair, or nonexploitative. Because members of the military consent to conditions that are unreasonable, unfair, or exploitive, their consent is morally ineffective. I do not think these are side-constraints at all; rather, they are covert appeals to rights or desert and usually mistaken ones. In any case, if the consent argument goes through, it is compatible with forfeiture theory.

A second objection might be that morality applies to the actions of a nation as a group. On this account, the nation as a group is distinct from the collection of individuals who compose it because the group might have been composed of a different collection of individuals from those who actually composed it.[38] The objector might claim that this is also true for a military unit (for example, an

[37] See A. John Simmons, "Political Obligation and Consent," in *The Ethics of Consent: Theory and Practice*, ed. Franklin Miller and Alan Wertheimer (New York: Oxford University Press, 2010), 305–328.

[38] For a similar argument that a group is compatible with different sets of members, see David Cooper, "Collective Responsibility," *Philosophy* 43 (1968): 258–268, esp. 260. A different argument in support of collective responsibility is that group actions are not reducible to individual actions because the relations between individuals are essential to the action. See Larry May, *The Morality of Groups* (Notre Dame, IN: University of Notre Dame Press, 1987), 55. On some theories of persons, they consist of both matter and form. On this account, then, a person is not reducible to his or her parts. For a contemporary version of this, see William Jaworski, *Philosophy of Mind: A Comprehensive Introduction* (New York: Wiley-Blackwell, 2011). Perhaps a similar argument could be given with regard to groups.

army) that serves a nation. The objector concludes that the individualist forfeiture theory fails because it incorrectly reduces the status of a military campaign to a collection of individual relationships.

This objection is problematic for several reasons. First, the objection assumes that a thing is distinct from its parts either in general or with regard to groups of people, and this is controversial. Second, even if the group is distinct from its parts, it is unclear how it can be a moral patient, that is, the type of thing that can be owed duties. To be owed duties, a thing must be capable of having different levels of well-being, and to have different levels of well-being a thing must be conscious.[39] It is unclear how a group can be conscious given that it does not have a mind.[40] Third, to do acts that warrant praise or blame, a thing must be morally responsible or a moral agent, and a group is neither.[41] If one thinks that right-infringements require moral responsibility or agency, then a group can't infringe someone's right. Fourth, even if an organization is distinct from its parts, can be owed duties, and is a moral agent, it is not clear what would be the basis for its acting wrongly or infringing on another's rights. If the objector asserts that this is true because individuals attacked others, this focuses on what individuals did and we are back to considering what is owed by or to individuals.

A third objection is that the metaphysical reduction of war to a collection of individual acts of aggression is mistaken. If the second objection fails, then so does the third. If the relevant entities for the purpose of deontic status are individuals and their actions, then whether war is an aggregation of individuals' acts is irrelevant. It might not be, although I have a hard time seeing why; but if so, this is irrelevant to the morality of war.

[39] Alastair Norcross argues that animals can be moral patients even if they are not moral agents. He appears to base this claim on the notion that animals can suffer. This focus on suffering involves levels of well-being. See Alastair Norcross, "Puppies, Pigs, and People: Eating Meat and Marginal Cases," *Philosophical Perspectives* 18 (2004): 229–245.

[40] For the notion that groups do not have minds in a nonderivative manner, see David Sosa, "What Is It Like to Be a Group?" *Social Philosophy and Policy* 26 (2009): 212–226, esp. 215. For similar arguments that groups do not have minds, make choices, hold beliefs, or form intentions, see Jan Narveson, "Collective Responsibility," *Journal of Ethics* 6 (2002): 179–198; J. Angelo Corlett, "Collective Moral Responsibility," *Journal of Social Philosophy* 32 (2001): 573–584; and Stephen Sverdlik, "Collective Responsibility," *Philosophical Studies* 51 (1987): 61–76.

[41] For an argument that groups cannot be morally responsible, see R. S. Downie, "Collective Responsibility," *Philosophy* 44 (1969): 66–69, esp. 67. For the notion that only individuals can have moral agency, see Narveson, "Collective Responsibility," 179. For arguments to the contrary, see Cooper, "Collective Responsibility," 258–268; Deborah Tollefsen, "The Rationality of Collective Guilt," *Midwest Studies in Philosophy*, 30 (2006): 222–239; and Larry May, "State Aggression, Collective Liability, and Individual Mens Rea," *Midwest Studies in Philosophy*, 30 (2006): 309–324.

Implications

The theory has implications for when countries can kill people and break their things. First, consider cyberwar. If a cyberattack justifies defensive war, then (1) it is an unjust threat and (2) the sum of the right- and consequentialist-based permissions has greater stringency than any opposing claims, if there are any. This is useful because it tells us what the criterion is for when cyberwar justifies violence.

Second, consider moral restrictions on wartime violence. If violence against an unjust threat is morally wrong, then either the threat has not forfeited his or her right against an attack of a specific type or magnitude or he or she has but consequentialist considerations override the forfeiture-based permission.

Third, consider legal restrictions on wartime violence. If violence against an unjust threat is morally wrong because it is legally wrong, then just combatants have waived their right against an attack of a specific type or magnitude. On this view, some restrictions on wartime violence are similar to restrictions in boxing or wrestling in that at least some of the boundaries of wrongness are set via consent. So, for example, it might be wrong to use poison gas because of international law even if it would not be wrong but for such law.

Fourth, the theory handles various puzzle cases. Specifically, violence in puzzle cases needs to be analyzed by reference to right forfeiture. Consider this case.

Case 6: Pilots

> A group of pilots, whose country is fighting a just war of defense, need to blow up a factory. To do so, they will need to drop multiple bombs that will also incidentally kill several innocent civilians who live across the border in a neutral country. These deaths are proportionate to the good that destroying the factory will produce, and the pilots are thus objectively justified in dropping the bombs. The civilians have an anti-aircraft gun that they can use to shoot the pilots in self-defense.[42]

This case and ones like it can be handled by considering that there are paired rights issues between each pilot and each factory worker and between each pilot and each civilian from the neutral country. The permission of one member of the pair relative to the other depends on whether forfeiture occurs. Thus, the case can be boiled down to issues of whether each individual forfeits a right had against another individual.

[42] This example comes from McMahan, "Basis of Moral Liability," 388.

It is worth noting here that the pilot and civilians have a moral symmetry from an evidence-relative standpoint and not a fact-relative standpoint. In this case, the civilians may, as a matter of justice, use the anti-aircraft gun. The pilots are not permitted, as a matter of justice, to bomb the factory because, in relation to the civilians, they would be unjust attackers.

Conclusion

In this chapter, I argued that forfeiture theory best explains just war. My argument rested on the claim that forfeiture theory explains when individual and state violence is justified better than other theories. My argument rested on a number of assumptions. First, individuals alone have rights and are owed duties. Second, outside of war, if one individual wrongly kills a second, then the first fails to satisfy a duty he or she owes to someone. Third, if one person fails to satisfy a duty owed the second, then the first infringes on the second's right. Fourth, state killing is morally similar to individuals' killings outside of war. Fifth, if the first four assumptions are true, then the best theory of just war focuses on when rights are lost or defeated. Forfeiture theory alone focuses on when rights are lost or defeated. I then considered objections to the individualist theory of rights and briefly mentioned some of the theory's implications.[43]

References

Boonin, David. *The Non-Identity Problem and the Ethics of Future People*. New York: Oxford University Press, 2014.

Coase, Ronald. "The Problem of Social Cost." *Journal of Law and Economics* 3 (1960): 1–44.

Cooper, David. "Collective Responsibility." *Philosophy* 43 (1968): 258–268.

Corlett, J. Angelo. "Collective Moral Responsibility." *Journal of Social Philosophy* 32 (2001): 573–584.

Downie, R. S. "Collective Responsibility." *Philosophy* 44 (1969): 66–69.

Dworkin, Ronald. "Rights as Trumps." In *Theories of Rights*, edited by Jeremy Waldron, 153–167. Oxford: Oxford University Press, 1984.

Feinberg, Joel. "Voluntary Euthanasia and the Inalienable Right to Life." *Philosophy and Public Affairs* 7 (1978): 93–123.

Feit, Neil, and Stephen Kershnar. "Explaining the Geometry of Desert." *Public Affairs Quarterly* 18 (2004): 273–298.

Feldman, Fred. "Adjusting Utility for Justice: A Consequentialist Reply to the Objection from Justice." *Philosophy and Phenomenological Research* 55 (1995): 567–585.

[43] I am grateful to Col. David Barnes, Rebecca Chan, Randy Dipert, Neil Feit, David Hershenov, Ryan Jenkins, Duncan Purves, Mike Robillard, Bradley Strawser, and participants in the 2014 meeting of the International Society for Military Ethics for their extremely helpful comments and criticisms of this chapter and a related presentation.

Fischer, John Martin, and Mark Ravizza. *Responsibility and Control: A Theory of Moral Responsibility*. New York: Cambridge University Press, 1998.
Fletcher, George. "Proportionality and the Psychotic Aggressor: A Vignette in Comparative Criminal Theory." *Israel Law Review* 8 (1973): 367–390.
Foot, Philippa. "The Problem of Abortion and the Doctrine of the Double Effect." *Oxford Review* 5 (1967): 5–15.
Frankfurt, Harry. "Freedom of the Will and the Concept of a Person." *Journal of Philosophy* 68 (1971): 5–20.
Gewirth, Alan. "Are There Any Absolute Rights?" In *Theories of Rights*, edited by Jeremy Waldron, 81–109. Oxford: Oxford University Press, 1984.
Goldman, Alan. "The Paradox of Punishment." *Philosophy and Public Affairs* 9 (1979): 30–46.
Hart, H. L. A. *Essays on Bentham: Studies in Jurisprudence and Political Theory*. Oxford: Clarendon Press, 1982.
Haksar, Vinit. "Excuses and Voluntary Conduct." *Ethics* 96 (1986): 317–329.
Hurka, Thomas. "The Common Structure of Virtue and Desert." *Ethics* 112 (2001a): 6–31.
Hurka, Thomas. *Virtue, Vice, and Value*. New York: Oxford University Press, 2001b.
Jaworski, William. *Philosophy of Mind: A Comprehensive Introduction*. New York: Wiley-Blackwell, 2011.
Kagan, Shelly. "Equality and Desert." In *What Do We Deserve?*, edited by Louis P. Pojman and Owen McLeod, 298–314. New York: Oxford University Press, 1999.
Kershnar, Stephen. "Private Property Rights and Autonomy." *Public Affairs Quarterly* 16 (2002a): 231–258.
Kershnar, Stephen. "The Structure of Rights Forfeiture in the Context of Culpable Wrongdoing." *Philosophia* 29 (2002b): 57–88.
Kershnar, Stephen. "Consent-Based Permission to Kill People and Break Their Things." *Reason Papers* 37 (2015a): 34–53.
Kershnar, Stephen. "Fetuses Are Like Rapists: A Judith-Jarvis-Thomson-Inspired Argument on Abortion." *Reason Papers* 37 (2015b): 88–109.
Kershnar, Stephen. *Pedophilia and Adult–Child Sex: A Philosophical Defense*. Lanham, MD: Lexington Books, 2015c.
Kramer, Matthew. "Rights Without Trimmings." In *A Debate Over Rights*, edited by Matthew Kramer, N. E. Simmons, and Hillel Steiner, 7–111. New York: Oxford University Press, 1998.
Kramer, Matthew. "Refining the Interest Theory of Rights." *American Journal of Jurisprudence* 55 (2010): 31–39.
Kramer, Matthew. "Some Doubts About Alternatives to the Interest Theory of Rights." *Ethics* 123 (2013): 245–263.
Lyons, David. *Rights, Welfare and Mill's Moral Theory*. New York: Oxford University Press, 1994.
MacCormick, Neil. "Rights in Legislation." In *Law, Morality and Society: Essays in Honour of H. L. A. Hart*, edited by P. Hacker and J. Raz, 189–209. Oxford: Oxford University Press, 1977.
May, Larry. *The Morality of Groups*. Notre Dame, IN: University of Notre Dame Press, 1987.
May, Larry. "State Aggression, Collective Liability, and Individual Mens Rea." *Midwest Studies in Philosophy* 30 (2006): 309–324.
McMahan, Jeff. "The Basis of Moral Liability to Defensive Killing." *Philosophical Issues* 15 (2005): 386–405.
McMahan, Jeff. "On the Moral Equality of Combatants." *Journal of Political Philosophy* 14 (2006): 377–393.
McMahan, Jeff. *Killing in War*. Oxford: Clarendon Press, 2009.
Montague, Philip. *Self-Defense as Societal Defense*. Boston: Rowman & Littlefield, 1995.
Moore, Michael. "Torture and the Balance of Evils." *Israel Law Review* 23 (1989): 280–344.
Narveson, Jan. "Collective Responsibility." *Journal of Ethics* 6 (2002): 179–198.
Nino, C. S. "A Consensual "Theory of Punishment." *Philosophy and Public Affairs* 12, no. 4 (1983): 289–306.

Nino, C. S. "Does Consent Override Proportionality?" *Philosophy and Public Affairs* 15, no. 2 (1986): 183–187.

Nino, C. S. *The Ethics of Human Rights*. Oxford: Clarendon Press, 1991.

Norcross, Alastair. "Puppies, Pigs, and People: Eating Meat and Marginal Cases." *Philosophical Perspectives* 18 (2004): 229–245.

Nozick, Robert. *Anarchy, State, and Utopia*. New York: Basic Books, 1974.

Orend, Brian. *The Morality of War*. Orchard Park, NY: Broadview, 2006.

Otsuka, Michael. "Killing the Innocent in Self-Defense." *Philosophy and Public Affairs* 23 (1994): 74–94.

Pilon, Roger. "Criminal Remedies: Restitution, Punishment, or Both?" *Ethics* 88 (1978): 348–357.

Rawls, John. *A Theory of Justice*. Cambridge, MA: Belknap Press, 1971.

Raz, Joseph. *The Morality of Freedom*. Oxford: Oxford University Press, 1986.

Rodin, David. *War & Self-Defense*. New York: Oxford University Press, 2002.

Rothbard, Murray. *The Ethics of Liberty*. Atlantic Highlands, NJ: Humanities Press, 1982.

Shue, Henry. "Do We Need a 'Morality of War'?" In *Just and Unjust Warriors*, edited by David Rodin and Henry Shue, 87–111. Oxford: Oxford University Press, 2008.

Simmons, A. John. "Locke and the Right to Punish." In *Punishment*, edited by A. John Simmons, Marshall Cohen, Joshua Cohen, and Charles R. Beitz, 219–260. Princeton, NJ: Princeton University Press, 1995.

Simmons, A. John. "Political Obligation and Consent." In *The Ethics of Consent: Theory and Practice*, edited by Franklin Miller and Alan Wertheimer, 305–328. New York: Oxford University Press, 2010.

Sosa, David. "What Is It Like to Be a Group?" *Social Philosophy and Policy* 26 (2009): 212–226.

Steiner, Hillel. *An Essay on Rights*. Oxford: Blackwell, 1994a.

Steiner, Hillel. "Working Rights." In *A Debate over Rights*, edited by Matthew Kramer, N. E. Simmons, and Hillel Steiner, 239–247. Oxford: Blackwell, 1994b.

Steiner, Hillel. "Directed Duties and Inalienable Rights." *Ethics* 123 (2013): 230–244.

Sverdlik, Stephen. "Collective Responsibility," *Philosophical Studies* 51 (1987): 61–76.

Thomson, Judith Jarvis. "The Trolley Problem." *Yale Law Journal* 94 (1985): 1395–1415.

Thomson, Judith Jarvis. "Self-Defense and Rights." In *Rights, Restitution, and Risk*, edited by William Parent, 33–48. Cambridge, MA: Harvard University Press, 1986.

Thomson, Judith Jarvis. *The Realm of Rights*. Cambridge, MA: Harvard University Press, 1990.

Thomson, Judith Jarvis. "Self-Defense." *Philosophy and Public Affairs* 20 (1991): 283–310.

Tollefsen, Deborah. "The Rationality of Collective Guilt." *Midwest Studies in Philosophy* 30 (2006): 222–239.

Waldron, Jeremy. *The Right to Private Property*. Oxford: Clarendon Press, 1991.

Walzer, Michael. *Just and Unjust Wars*. New York: Basic Books, 1977.

Walzer, Michael. "Response to McMahan's Paper." *Philosophia* 34 (2006): 43–45.

Watson, Gary. "Free Agency." *Journal of Philosophy* 72 (1975): 205–220.

Wellman, Carl. *A Theory of Rights*. Totowa, NJ: Rowman and Allenheld, 1985.

Wolf, Susan. *Freedom Within Reason*. New York: Oxford University Press, 1990.

Zohar, Noam. "Innocence and Complex Threats: Upholding the War Ethic and the Condemnation of Terrorism." *Ethics* 114 (2004): 734–751.

7

Dignity, Self-Respect, and Bloodless Invasions

SABA BAZARGAN-FORWARD

The Problem of Bloodless Invasions

A so-called bloodless invasion is a hypothetical form of military aggression in which the aggressing party imposes the following sort of conditional threat: they will resort to maiming and killing only if their victims resist the purely political aims of the aggressing party. The political control the aggressors seek is unauthorized and unjust—achieving it would violate the political rights of their victims. So the victims are, in effect, given this choice: accede to the violation of their political rights or engage in a kinetic war.

Crucial to the concept of a bloodless invasion is that the victims' *vital* interests—viz., their lives and their bodily integrity—are conditionally threatened as a means to undermining their *nonvital* interests—viz., their political rights. If the victims of the aggressing party choose to resist the bloodless invasion, the result will be all the attendant horrors of war, including, we can assume, massive civilian casualties.

Some theorists have cast doubt on the moral permissibility of resisting bloodless invasions on the grounds that such resistance is likely to violate the constraint of proportionality which states that the harms inflicted cannot be too great relative to the wrongful harms thereby averted.[1] Since resisting a bloodless invasion averts threats to nonvital interests by maiming and killing, it seems that such resistance is likely to be unjust, on the grounds that it violates the constraint of proportionality. This is a problematic outcome insofar as a defensive war against an aggressor aiming at imposing unjust political dominion is supposed

[1] See David Rodin, "Justifying Harm," *Ethics* 122, no. 1 (2012): 74–110, for a discussion of some of the factors relevant to proportionality.

to be paradigmatic of a just war. If post-Walzerian reductive individualism about the morality of war is correct insofar as it analyzes war as a relation between individuals rather than between states, then it seems we are forced to concede that defense against bloodless invaders is likely unjust. This means we can only fight a defensive war against aggressors who maim and kill (or violate equally stringent vital interests) for its own sake rather than as a means to or a side effect of establishing political control over territory. The only just defensive wars, then, would be those against genocidal aggression or mass enslavement. Such wars are comparatively rare. The upshot, then, is that if defensive wars against otherwise bloodless invasions are unjust, we are forced into adopting a version of contingent pacifism.[2]

Some theorists regard this conclusion as evidence against the plausibility of reductive individualism[3]; others regard a version of contingent pacifism as a welcomed consequence[4]; still others argue that reductive individualism has the resources to avoid the conclusion that resisting bloodless invasions is unjust.[5] I will call the problem of how to respond to the possibility of bloodless invasions, the *dilemma of bloodless invasions*. This states that we either have to deny that defensive wars against bloodless invasions are morally permissible or must deny reductive individualism. The first option seems to many excessively pacifistic, while the second option is unpalatable to those sympathetic to reductive individualism.

There are at least two versions of the dilemma's first horn. Both conclude that defensive wars against otherwise bloodless invasions violate the proportionality constraint. The first version argues that such wars violate the *narrow* proportionality constraint, which states that harms imposed on parties *morally liable to be harmed* cannot be too great relative to the wrongful harms thereby averted. So,

[2] For a discussion of different versions of contingent pacifism, see Saba Bazargan, "Varieties of Contingent Pacifism," In *How We Fight*, ed. Helen Frower and Gerald Lang (Oxford: Oxford University Press, 2015), 1–17.

[3] See, for example, Seth Lazar, "National Defence, Self-Defence, and the Problem of Political Aggression," in *The Morality of Defensive War*, ed. Cécile Fabre and Seth Lazar (Oxford: Oxford University Press, 2014), 11–39.

[4] See especially Richard Norman, *Ethics, Killing, and War* (Cambridge: Cambridge University Press, 1995), 133, 135; and David Rodin, *War & Self-Defense* (New York: Oxford University Press, 2002), 43–48. In David Rodin, "The Myth of National Self-Defence," in *The Morality of Defensive War*, ed. Cécile Fabre and Seth Lazar (Oxford: Oxford University Press, 2014), 89, he argues that "a self-help regime centered on presumptive rights of self-defense" against political aggression is morally unjustified.

[5] See, for example, Cécile Fabre, "Cosmopolitanism and Wars of Self-Defence," in *The Morality of Defensive War*, ed. Cécile Fabre and Seth Lazar (Oxford: Oxford University Press, 2014), 90–114; and Jeff McMahan, "What Rights May Be Defended by Means of War?" in *The Morality of Defensive War*, 115–156.

for example, it is presumably wrongful to defensively kill someone attempting to painfully pinch you unjustly even if that is the only way to avoid the pinch. This constraint on defensive violence falls under the aegis of the narrow proportionality constraint because the unjust pincher is morally liable to some degree of defensive harm necessary to stop him or her. He or she is not, however, liable to be killed. Defense against bloodless invasions is sometimes likewise construed as a violation of narrow proportionality insofar as it is argued that an individual who is only conditionally threatening your vital interests in order to exact concessions undermining your nonvital interests is morally liable only to the amount of defensive violence necessary to avert the threat to your nonvital interests. That is, the degree of harm that the violation of your nonvital interests consists in sets the baseline by which the proportionality of your defensive harm is measured. So the maximum amount of defensive harm you can permissibly inflict to stop a mugger who threatens to kill you if you do not hand over the money in your wallet is determined by the moral value of that money, rather than the moral value of your life.[6] Likewise for bloodless invasions: the maximum amount of defensive harm the victims can permissibly inflict on the invaders is determined by the moral value of the nonvital interests they unconditionally threaten—the victims' political rights—rather than the vital interests that they conditionally threaten—the victims' lives. Accordingly, the aggressors might not be morally liable to lethal defensive violence.

This argument operates by "scaling up" from a case in which a single individual is wrongly prevented from exercising his or her political rights by a wrongful aggressor. Suppose a villain threatens to kill you if you vote in a particular political election. The villain points a pistol at you—the only way to preserve your own life is to shoot the villain first (which you are able to do) or to accede to his or her demands. It is probably a violation of the narrow proportionality constraint to defensively kill the villain even if doing so is necessary in order to vote.

If it is a violation of proportionality to kill one unjust aggressor preventing you from exercising your political rights by conditionally threatening your life, it follows that it is a violation of proportionality to kill many unjust aggressors who are similarly preventing their victims from exercising their political rights by conditionally threatening their lives; this describes a bloodless invasion (or so it is argued).

There are problems, though, with this version of the argument. The most pressing one, in my view, is this: each invader is complicitously liable for what his or her comrades do because each combatant has the formal function of assisting

[6] Norman, *Ethics, Killing, and War*, 130. =

one another in furtherance of the war's aims.[7] As a result, each invader will be morally responsible for violations of the political rights of millions. These individual violations might aggregate in a way making each invader morally liable to be killed if necessary to stop the bloodless invasion.

A more compelling version of the dilemma of bloodless invasions adverts to the *wide* proportionality constraint which states that harms imposed on parties who are *not* morally liable to be harmed cannot be too great relative to the wrongful harms thereby averted. Wars typically kill many civilians, the vast majority of whom are not morally liable to be killed. If the violation of nonvital, political rights determines the threshold of the wide proportionality constraint, then killing many civilians as a side effect of protecting those nonvital interests will likely violate that constraint. The duties of care owed toward our own citizens who would be killed by the enemy compound the wrongfulness of the harms resulting from resisting the bloodless invasion—or so it is argued.[8]

To recap, the dilemma of bloodless invasions is that we must either accept that resisting bloodless invasions is impermissible or reject reductive individualism. The first horn of the dilemma has two versions. The first version adverts to the narrow proportionality constraint, whereas the second adverts to the wide proportionality constraint. Since the latter is the more compelling version of the dilemma's first horn, that is the version I will target.

The bloodless invasion dilemma assumes that the political rights the invaders violate are nonvital, in that they are not the sorts of rights that we can defend at the cost of innocent lives. But bloodless invasions typically violate not just political rights but our interests in retaining the capability of living recognizably meaningful lives. And these are indeed vital—or so I will argue. The focus on political rights has had a distorting effect on discussions of the bloodless invasions dilemma. Appreciating the interests we have in regarding our own practical identities as worthwhile will reveal that many bloodless invasions can indeed be resisted by way of war. This will not completely dissolve the bloodless invasion dilemma since there remains the conceptual possibility of a bloodless invasion violating only political rights without undermining our interests in retaining the capability of living meaningful lives. But my goal here is not to dissolve the dilemma but to complicate it by showing that there are some rights aside from those pertaining to life and limb that we can kill to protect—namely, the right to self-respect.

[7] I argue for this view in Saba Bazargan, "Complicitous Liability in War," *Philosophical Studies* 165, no. 1 (2013): 177–195.

[8] See Rodin, "Myth of National Self-Defence," 84.

Dignity and Respect

To understand what self-respect is and the role it plays in the dilemma of bloodless invasions, it is necessary to analyze respect simpliciter. And to do that, we need to look at the concept *dignity* since it is the grounds of our entitlement to be treated with respect. *Dignity* is used in various ways by ethicists. One of the most important disambiguations is between dignity as the grounds of rights and dignity as the content of those rights. That is, the concept might be used to refer to the source of the claim that we have that others treat us in certain ways; or it might be used to characterize that very treatment.[9] So when we say that particular conduct—such as a violation of my autonomy—violates my dignity, we might be saying, for example, that it is in virtue of my inherent dignity as a person that I have a right not to have my autonomy violated. Or we might be saying that it is because of my status as a person that I have a right to be treated with dignity, which includes a right not to have my autonomy violated. I will use *dignity* in the former sense to refer to the moral status persons have in virtue of which we have rights.[10]

This analysis of dignity finds its origins most famously in Immanuel Kant. He used *wërde*—commonly translated as "dignity"—to refer to a type of intrinsic worth inhering in rational agents. The worth is intrinsic in that it does not confer value by promoting an end but rather has value in itself. It is our nature as rational agents which grounds our dignity. Rational agents possess dignity in virtue of their autonomy, which is the power to legislate moral laws and to act in accordance with them without influence from heteronomous inclinations. We connote this special status by calling the beings possessing it "persons." The required response to dignity is *achtung*—"respect"—which requires we treat persons as ends in themselves. Because dignity is absolute and noncomparable and because dignity is grounded in features that all persons possess, the intrinsic worth of all person is equal, on Kant's account. Hence each person, in virtue of his or her autonomous nature, is owed respect regardless of personal achievements, social rank, or moral conduct.

More modern writers also ground rights in dignity-as-status. James Griffin, inspired by the fifteenth-century writer Pico della Mirandola, develops the idea that dignity is the human capacity "to . . . be that which he wills." Beings possessing this capacity are what Griffin calls "normative agents."[11] Possessing this

[9] Jeremy Waldron, *Dignity, Rank, and Rights* (New York: Oxford University Press, 2012), 17.

[10] For example, the International Covenant of Civil and Political Rights seems to conceptualize dignity in this way when it states in the preamble that rights "derive from the inherent dignity of the human person." See http://www.ohchr.org/EN/ProfessionalInterest/Pages/CCPR.aspx.

[11] James Griffin, *On Human Rights* (Oxford: Oxford University Press, 2009), 31.

capacity is "a highly prized status"—one which grounds "[t]he sort of dignity relevant to human rights."[12] It grounds our rights in that protecting them—for example, by respecting our autonomy—upholds our normative agency.

Joel Feinberg and Jan Narveson also propound the view that dignity-as-status grounds rights. On their account, to have a legal right is to possess the dignity of a "recognized claimant"—someone entitled to demand that his or her case be considered. They suggest that human dignity consists in the status of possessing "the recognizable capacity to assert claims."[13] Similarly, Stephen Darwall states that dignity consists in "the second-personal standing" each individual has which authorizes every individual "to make claims and demands on one another as free and rational agents"—claims and demands that others must respect.[14]

On all these views, dignity-as-status grounds a right to what has come to be called *(moral) recognition-respect.* Recognition-respect is an attitude consisting in giving appropriate consideration to some (morally relevant) features of the object of respect in the course of deliberation. To say that a person qua person is entitled to recognition-respect is to say that he or she is entitled to have others, in their deliberations, take seriously and weigh appropriately the fact that he or she is a person. What qualifies as "taking seriously" and "weighing appropriately" will depend on the specific account of what recognition-respect requires.[15] But regardless of how the details work out, recognition-respect requires that the relevant features of its object factor into our deliberations about how to treat that object. Crucially, the restrictions and requirements on our actions deriving from recognition-respect are not incidental but instead arise from the relevant features demanding recognition-respect—such as rational agency or the ability to feel pain.

Whereas the appraisal of individual excellences will and ought to vary from person to person according to his or her character and abilities, the recognition-respect to which individuals are entitled will be the same for everyone, insofar as such respect is grounded in the dignity-as-status which each individual shares in common. Whether the dignity grounding recognition-respect derives from our status as autonomous agents (as Kant thinks) or our status as normative agents (as Griffin thinks) or our second-personal standing as free and rational agents (as Darwall thinks) or our recognizable capacity to assert claims (as Feinberg and Narveson think), the fact remains that everyone who has the relevant status

[12] Griffin, *On Human Rights*, 152.

[13] Joel Feinberg and Jan Narveson, "The Nature and Value of Rights," *Journal of Value Inquiry* 4, no. 4 (1970): 252.

[14] Stephen Darwall, "Respect and the Second Person Standpoint," *Proceedings and Addresses of the American Philosophical Association* 78, no. 2 (2004): 43–44.

[15] Stephen L. Darwall, "Two Kinds of Respect," *Ethics* 88, no. 1 (1977): 38.

has it to the same degree and in the same way, thereby demanding the same basic treatment: the recognition-respect of our fundamental dignity as persons.

Expressivist Accounts

Some have tried to ground the claim that we are permitted to resist otherwise bloodless invasions by appealing to the claim that oppressive regimes systemically violate the recognition-respect we are owed.[16] When we harm someone in a way that violates the recognition-respect owed in virtue of his or her dignity, we are acting wrongfully. Insofar as oppressive regimes not only violate political rights but systemically deny the recognition-respect the population is owed, the wrong that they commit is compounded in a way that permits violent resistance—or so it might be argued. The challenge is to specify the way that denying recognition-respect wrongs its victims.

When we commit a wrong, we do not always thereby deny the victim fundamental recognition-respect since not all rights-violations suggest that the wrongdoer thinks that the victim is less than a full-fledged person. For example, an assassin might murder a target despite knowing that what he or she is doing is morally verboten; he or she knows that the victim has a legitimate moral claim against him or her, grounded in his or her status as a person, that the assassin refrain from ending his or her life. But he or she does so anyway because he or she is not properly or sufficiently motivated by what he or she knows to be true.

Perhaps, though, the assassin's conduct belies the claim that he or she believes that the victim is a full-fledged person with all the attendant rights. We can nonetheless usefully distinguish the assassin from a wrongdoer for whom the victim's status plays an explicit motivational role in explaining why the wrongdoer committed the harm. A racist who kills partly because he or she believes that the victim is not a full-fledged person is an example. This partly explains why we might think that rights-violations motivated by abject forms of racism, sexism, or other forms of bigotry are especially wrongful. The wrong of a racist assault

[16] See Mattias Iser, "Beyond the Paradigm of Self-Defense? On Revolutionary Violence," in *The Ethics of War*, ed. Saba Bazargan and Samuel Rickless (New York: Oxford University Press, 2016), 207–226. Whereas he argues that averting violations of recognition-respect is itself sufficient grounds for resisting otherwise bloodless invasions, I will argue that the effects such violations have on the self-respect of its victims are what provides such grounds. The practical difference is this: on Iser's account, virtually all bloodless invasions can be permissibly resisted as a last resort since such regimes by imposing unauthorized laws eo ipso violate the recognition-respect the people are owed. On my account, however, we can only resist bloodless invasions that will otherwise impose norms that undercut our ability to live recognizably meaningful lives (see later, "Undermining Subjective Self-Respect" and "Undermining Objective Self-Respect").

violates the right that the victim has against being physically harmed, but this wrong is aggravated by the fact that it was motivated by a belief that the victim bears a fundamental moral status less exalted than that of the wrongdoer's preferred race. So the wrongdoer here commits a double wrong (or perhaps a morally aggravated wrong). He or she fails to abide by the rights in question and violates the recognition-respect of the victim at least partly out of the belief that the victim lacks the fundamental dignity-as-status grounding a moral protection against such rights-violations.

So wrongs motivated in part by the belief that the victim is not a full-fledged person seem morally worse. One might attempt to explain this by appealing to expressivist accounts of wrongdoing. According to such theories, what individuals express in their actions matters morally in that such expressions play a substantial role in explaining or grounding the wrongfulness of certain kinds of immoral conduct.[17] When a harm we commit is motivated or otherwise explained by a wrongful attitude—such as the belief that the victim lacks fundamental moral worth—the manifestation of that attitude in our action makes the act especially wrongful.[18] This is an expressive wrong. Expressivism is not a theory of normative ethics, on par with consequentialism or Kantianism. It does not specify substantive, independent, content-laden grounds for moral content. Rather, it makes a claim about how attitudes are manifest in action and the way doing so is relevant to the moral assessment of action: *expressive* wrongs are wrongs over and above the object-level violation of a right not to be attacked, deceived, and so on.

Importantly, expression is not the same as communication. An actor expresses an attitude simply by adverting to particular reasons for action. "To ascribe attitudes to an agent coherently," write Elizabeth Anderson and Richard Pildes, "we need only be able to sensibly interpret the agent's actions as resulting from reasons—that is, as taking particular goals or purposes as reasons for particular actions."[19] Acting on the reasons in question manifests the expressive content of the action. Communication, on the other hand, requires (on a Gricean account) that the communicator intends to induce certain attitudes in an audience where the audience reasons its way to those attitudes via its recognition of the communicator's intention to induce those very attitudes. Accordingly, communicative acts represent a small subset of expressive acts.

Expression should not be confused with profession either. Linguistic utterances fail to carry the same social meaning as expressive actions, in that "there

[17] Elizabeth Anderson and Richard H. Pildes, "Expressivism: A General Restatement," *University of Pennsylvania Law Review* 148 (2000): 1570.

[18] Anderson and Pildes, "Expressivism," 1509.

[19] Anderson and Pildes, "Expressivism," 1520.

are some things we can express only with deeds because words alone cannot adequately convey our attitudes."[20] On this view, the wrongfulness of an expressive wrong is not limited to what it reveals about the wrongdoer's attitudes. The reification and manifestation of that attitude via action constitute part of the wrong. The medium, as it were, is an ineluctable part of what is expressed. When a wrongdoer is motivated to commit a rights-violation out of the belief that the victim is not entitled to the recognition-respect to which full-fledged persons are entitled and when this belief is expressed in actions thereby revealing to the victim that the wrongdoer has this belief, the victim is thereby harmed over and above whatever harm the rights-violation itself consists in.

This version of expressivism has the resources, I believe, to explain why we are permitted to resist certain bloodless invasions. In what follows I argue that systematically denying recognition-respect by imposing oppressive social and legal norms can inflict expressive harms which undercut the victim's self-respect to an extent that makes it difficult to live a recognizably meaningful life. It is, ultimately, to prevent this sort of outcome that we can resist bloodless invasions.

On Self-Respect

Systemically denying the recognition-respect a victim is owed in virtue of his or her dignity-as-status can result in a harm over and above each individual harm in which that denial consists. Specifically, systemically denying recognition-respect to a victim can do violence to the victim's sense of self-respect.

John Rawls famously wrote that "perhaps the most important primary good is that of self-respect."[21] Laurence Thomas identifies securing the self-respect of blacks as *the* goal of the civil rights movement.[22] Modern philosophical accounts vary greatly, though, in what self-respect fundamentally is. Some conceptualize

[20] Anderson and Pildes, "Expressivism," 1568.

[21] John Rawls, *A Theory of Justice* (Cambridge, MA: Harvard University Press, 1971), 386. I will return to Rawls's account of self-respect. For criticism of the view that self-respect is *the most important* primary social good, see Stephen J. Massey, "Is Self-Respect a Moral or a Psychological Concept?" *Ethics* 93, no. 2 (1983): 259. Other have argued that Rawls equivocates between two different notions of self-respect. See Gerald Doppelt, "The Place of Self-Respect in a Theory of Justice," *Inquiry* 52 (2009): 127–154; Nir Eyal, "'Perhaps the Most Important Primary Social Good': Self-Respect and Rawls's Principles of Justice," *Politics, Philosophy and Economics* 4 (2009): 195–219; and Jeffrey Moriarty, "Rawls, Self-Respect and the Opportunity for Meaningful Work," *Social Theory and Practice* 35 (2009): 441–459. But see also Cynthia A. Stark, "Rawlsian Self-Respect," in *Oxford Studies of Normative Ethics*, vol. 2, ed. Mark Timmons, 238–261 (Oxford: Oxford University Press, 2011).

[22] Laurence Thomas, "Self-Respect: Theory and Practice," in *Philosophy Born of Struggle: Anthology of Afro-American Philosophy from 1917*, ed. Leonard Harris (Dubuque, IA: Kendall Hunt, 1983), 174–189.

self-respect as fundamentally a *belief* about one's self.[23] Some take it to be fundamentally a disposition.[24] Others regard it as fundamentally interpersonal in that it includes expectations about how others will respond to one's own actions.[25] Some argue in favor of an "objective" account in which you have self-respect only if such self-respect is warranted. Others argue in favor of a subjective account.[26] But, as Robin Miller points out, all of these accounts share in common the view that self-respect involves "a sense of self-worth."[27]

The sense of worth implicit in *self*-respect can be divided into the kind of worth that individuals earn—merit, which can be gained or lost—and the kind of worth inhering in our fundamental status as persons—dignity, which is inalienable, unearned, and invariable. I will focus on the latter kind of self-respect. In the same way that respecting others means appreciating their fundamental status as persons, bearing self-respect means appreciating one's own fundamental moral status as a person. To have self-respect, then, "is to understand oneself to be a person with the same intrinsic value and standing in the moral community as every other person and unconditionally owed the equal recognition respect of all persons."[28]

Diminished self-respect threatens to undermine what Robin Dillon calls "basal" self-respect, which establishes at the most basic level our sense of whether our practical identity is of any worth. "The heart of basal self-respect," she says, "is our most profound valuing of ourselves."[29] Diminished self-respect threatens basal self-respect in the following way. A person will believe that his or her practical identity imparts a life worth living only if he or she believes that he or she is constitutionally capable of possessing a life worth living in the first place. If his

[23] See Rawls, *Theory of Justice*, 386–391; Thomas, "Self-Respect"; and Michele M. Moody-Adams, "Race, Class, and the Social Construction of Self-Respect," *Philosophical Forum* 24, no. 1–3 (1993): 251–266.

[24] See Elizabeth Telfer, "Self-Respect," *Philosophical Quarterly* 18, no. 71 (1968): 114–121; Darwall, "Two Kinds of Respect"; and David Sachs, "How to Distinguish Self-Respect from Self-Esteem." *Philosophy and Public Affairs* 10, no. 4 (1981): 346–360.

[25] See Gabrielle Taylor, *Pride, Shame, and Guilt: Emotions of Self-Assessment* (Oxford: Oxford University Press, 1985).

[26] See Massey, "Is Self-Respect a Moral or a Psychological Concept?"

[27] Robin S. Dillon, "Introduction," in *Dignity, Character, and Self-Respect*, ed. Robin S. Dillon (London: Routledge, 1995), 20

[28] Robin S. Dillon, "Toward a Feminist Conception of Self-Respect," *Hypatia* 7, no. 1 (1992): 55.

[29] Robin S. Dillon, "Self-Respect: Moral, Emotional, Political," *Ethics* 107, no. 2 (1997): 242. As Daniel Statman notes (in addition to Dillon herself), the psychological literature bears out Dillon's notion of basal self-respect. He cites empirical work distinguishing between "contingent" and "true" self-esteem, where the former esteem results from satisfying one's one special criteria of excellence, whereas the latter is grounded in "a solid sense of self" largely independent of meeting meritorious criteria. See Daniel Statman, "Humiliation, Dignity, and Self-Respect," *Philosophical Psychology* 13, no. 4 (2000): 538.

or her recognition self-respect is damaged, then he or she by definition does not think of himself or herself as a person with the same intrinsic value as everyone else. This means no matter what practical identity he or she has or adopts—no matter how he or she chooses to live her life—there is a ceiling on the value of who he or she is. If the absence of recognition that self-respect is thoroughgoing, he or she believes that *no* practical identity of substantial worth is available to him or her. And this is just to say that he or she lacks basal self-respect.

Self-respect, as I have discussed it so far, is chiefly a psychological concept.[30] It refers to favorable self-regarding evaluative beliefs and feelings. To possess this sort of self-respect, it is not necessary that the beliefs be correct or that the feelings be warranted. The only criteria relevant to determining whether an agent is worthy of the favorable self-regarding evaluative beliefs and feelings are the agent's own. That is, there are no independent standards he or she must meet in order to have this sort of "subjective" self-respect.

In contrast, an individual possesses *objective* self-respect only if the favorable self-regarding evaluative beliefs and feelings satisfy objective criteria. Thus, an individual possesses objective self-respect only if he or she *correctly* recognizes and values his or her moral status as a person with equal basic rights. And a person possesses objective appraisal self-respect only if his or her achievements actually warrant the positive evaluation he or she gives them. On this view, self-respect is not just a matter of valuing yourself but of doing so properly. This means that sometimes individuals might possess subjective self-respect but not objective self-respective, or vice versa. This happens in cases where a person's own basis for self-respect comes apart from what the appropriate bases are. We might accordingly say that such an individual possess too much or too little subjective self-respect, in that his or her behavior and attitudes fail to match independent standards of evaluative worth.

Perhaps the most famous subjective account of self-respect in modern philosophy belongs to John Rawls. In *A Theory of Justice*, he defines self-respect as including "a person's sense of his own value, his secure conviction that his conception of the good, his plan of life, is worth carrying out."[31] In *Political Liberalism*, he characterizes self-respect as "rooted in our self-confidence as a fully cooperating member of society capable of pursuing a worthwhile conception of the good over a complete life."[32] In what follows I describe the sorts of psychological harms that wrongfully undermining this sort of subjective self-respect can cause. After, I explain how undermining objective self-respect can be harmful even if it doesn't cause those psychological harms.

[30] Massey, "Is Self-Respect a Moral or a Psychological Concept?"

[31] Rawls, *Theory of Justice*, 440.

[32] John Rawls, *Political Liberalism*, 2nd ed. (New York: Columbia University Press, 2005), 318.

Undermining Subjective Self-Respect

Diminished subjective self-respect, to the extent that it undermines basal self-respect, infects every aspect of the victim's life. When our basal self-respect is damaged, we are unable to justify who we are and what we do to ourselves or to others. The result, as Dillon puts it, is that

> the abiding flavor of our life is shame, self-contempt, or self-hatred, or anxiety, despair, or apathy about our worth . . . we experience a profound and pervasive sense of ourselves as inconsequential, inadequate, worthless, not as comparatively valuable, or not as worthy as they of the good things in life . . . our lives seem meaningless, our activities of little value, our capabilities minimal, our character base . . . when living is like this living well is impossible.[33]

For this reason, among others, having a secure sense of self-respect is morally important. A powerful political regime is capable of undermining the self-respect of entire populations, thereby plunging their lives into the kind of purgatory Dillon describes. This is because self-respect is in part socially constructed; it is determined in part by and reflects the norms of social life.[34] Every society, by way of its cultural, political, and economic practices and institutions, develops norms establishing criteria of self-worth; societies consequently provide the framework in which individuals may seek self-respect. In a society discriminating on the basis of race, class, or gender, the norms establishing the criteria for self-respect devalue those people. The result is that members of the disfavored groups have difficulty establishing and maintaining self-respect. To the extent that a political regime is able to influence or determine the cultural, political, and economic practices and institutions of a country, it is capable of profoundly influencing the self-respect of large swaths of the population.

When an oppressive regime undermines the self-respect of a population by instituting oppressive social and legal norms, the downstream effects can be devastating. Dillon notes for example that,

> it is impossible to address the crisis concerning the African American community, especially in America's inner cities—increasing racial discord and violence . . . the tragically high death rate of young Black

[33] Dillon, "Introduction," 34.

[34] For further discussion of the sociopolitical determinants of self-respect, see Dillon, "Self-Respect."

> men; the failure of educational systems to meet even minimal needs of African American children; chronic underemployment and welfare dependency; the wasted lives, thwarted talents and hopeless rage that characterizes the Black underclass—without some attention to the self-hatred and crippled self-worth that fuels and is fueled by these conditions.[35]

Social scientists have explained how diminished self-respect can take root and spread easily in a society with oppressive social and legal norms. For example, Robert Merton has described a phenomenon which he calls the "self-fulfilling prophecy" in which an individual is prompted to engage in behavior harmful to the self or others precisely because he or she knows that he or she is expected by others to behave as such.[36] For example, suppose an instructor does not expect superior or even adequate academic performance from her black pupils. These pupils, knowing that their efforts won't be taken seriously, refrain from putting forth that effort. The result is that these students do poorly, which seems to confirm the instructor's prediction—not only for the instructor but, crucially, for the students as well.[37] Gordon Allport describes a related social phenomenon, which he dubs the "reciprocal conduct of human beings in interaction."[38] He notes that negative expectations about behavior and the subsequent behavior exhibited will tend to converge. For example, a policy of racial exclusion and animosity toward a minority group might be motivated by the racist belief that members of that minority are violent. This policy will tend to elicit anger and bitterness in the victims, sometimes expressed through violence, which seemingly confirms the soundness of the racist policy, thereby reinforcing it.

Because social institutions have these sorts of profound effects on subjective self-respect and because undermining self-respect undermines our ability to live recognizably worthwhile lives, Thomas (in accordance with Rawls) argues that we should evaluate social institutions primarily according to whether it is conducive to the self-respect of the individuals in that society.[39] And one factor determining whether a social institution is conductive to self-respect is whether that institution recognizes equal rights by enshrining them in law. As Diana Meyers points out, such legal rights "promote self-respect by creating a

[35] Dillon, "Introduction," 36.

[36] Robert K. Merton, "The Self-Fulfilling Prophecy." *Antioch Review* 8, no. 2 (1948): 193–210.

[37] Kenneth Einar Himma, "Discrimination and Disidentification: The Fair-Start Defense of Affirmative Action," *Journal of Business Ethics*, 30 (April 2001): 277–289.

[38] Gerald W. Alport, *The Nature of Prejudice* (New York: Perseus Books, 1979).

[39] Thomas, "Self-Respect."

social environment conducive to the autonomous creation and pursuit of life plans."[40] Denying such legal recognition is wrong not just because the victims have the right to such legal recognition but because doing so has debilitating psychological effects, of the sort described.[41] We are in a position, then, to characterize the sort of expressive harms that bigoted oppressive regimes cause: the oppressive norms that the regimes impose diminish self-respect in that the victims come to believe that they are not worthy of the ends closed off to them.

Acceding to a bloodless invasion aiming to demote all or a portion of the population to second-class status—socially, legally, and culturally—does not thereby undermine that group's vital interests. But it does risk preventing them from living meaningful lives by imposing norms undermining their subjective self-respect, without which they are incapable of seeing themselves as possessing the sort of value that makes our ends worth pursuing. I submit, then, that the moral permission to prevent the sorts of psychological harms precluding the possibility of living a recognizably meaningful life is as stringent or nearly as stringent as the moral permission to protect life and limb. So if killing innocents as a side effect of preventing unjust aggressors from killing us can satisfy the wide proportionality constraint, then killing innocents as a side effect of preventing unjust aggressors from depriving us of the ability to live meaningful lives can satisfy the wide proportionality constraint as well.

This seems to show that we can permissibly respond to an otherwise bloodless invasion with warfare even if absent that response our vital interests would not have been threatened—provided that the aggressors, left unopposed, would have reduced the population or part of the population to second-class status by depriving them of their basic civil rights (though presumably the wronged population must be sizeable enough for violent resistance to satisfy the proportionality constraint—this goes for resisting violent aggression as well). Bloodless invaders often target a particular ethnicity, race, gender, nationality, religion, culture for second-class treatment. But the aggressor might deny or deprive basic civil rights to a population that meets other criteria—from geographic location to political affiliation. These groups would also be entitled to violent resistance, all things being equal, for the same reasons. In addition, there needn't be

[40] Diana T. Meyers, "The Politics of Self-Respect: A Feminist Perspective," *Hypatia* 1, no. 1 (1986): 87.

[41] It is still each individual's responsibility to ensure that the bases of his or her subjective self-respect are not overly demanding of others. Suppose my sense of self-respect demands that others grovel before me. I cannot permissibly force them to abide by this requirement even if their failure to do so will plunge me into depression. This is because *objective* self-respect places an upper limit on the permissible bases of *subjective* self-respect.

a privileged group bearing full civil rights for those deprived of their basic civil rights to violently resist permissibly.

A proponent of the view that we ought to accede to bloodless invasions might argue that this conclusion is too quick. The debilitating downstream psychological effects of instituting bigoted social and legal norms—that is, the effects of the regime's expressive harms—do not occur immediately. It might take years or decades for the new, oppressive norms to undermine the self-respect of the victimized population to the point that they are no longer capable of leading recognizably meaningful lives. In the meantime, there remains the possibility of nonviolent resistance as a means of either overthrowing the ruling regime or pressuring it to recognize the civil rights of the aggrieved population. Of course, passive resistance is not always successful—but neither is the relevant alternative, which is war with its attendant devastation. The upshot is that a contingent pacifist who argues that we should accede to bloodless invasions can acknowledge the debilitating downstream psychological effects of imposing oppressive social and legal norms, while consistently maintaining that we should nonetheless accede, provided that passive resistance remains a live possibility.

The problem with this view, though, is that it ignores the fact that over time the victims internalize the oppressive norms of the regime in ways that prevent them from recognizing the reasons they have to resist. To understand this problem, it is necessary to move from a discussion of *subjective* self-respect to *objective* self-respect.

Undermining Objective Self-Respect

As we have seen, systemic failures to give an individual the recognition-respect to which he or she is entitled as a person can undermine the victim's self-respect in profound ways. But many of the negative downstream psychological effects of forcing members of a population to see themselves as inferior are absent in cases where the victims internalize the oppressive norms by not only coming to see themselves as less worthy than others but also *failing to see this as morally problematic.* Recall that subjective self-respect is based on standards of personhood endorsed by that individual. If an individual accepts standards permitting him or her to debase or degrade himself or herself before others, the result will be that he or she possesses self-respect where it is actually unwarranted. This is a case where subjective self-respect is a force for the oppressive status quo in the form of servility. Such individuals come to accept, and even thrive in their allotted, circumscribed social roles. Take for example an "Uncle Tom"—a black man deferential to the authority of whites—which Thomas Hill described:

> He always steps aside for white men; he does not complain when less qualified whites take over his job; he gratefully accepts whatever benefits his all-white government and employers allot him, and he would not think of protesting its insufficiency. He displays the symbols of deference to whites, and of contempt towards blacks: he faces the former with bowed stance and a ready "sir" and "Ma'am"; he reserves his strongest obscenities for the latter.[42]

The Uncle Tom is not a cunning manipulator who shrewdly avoids reprisals to himself or to his family by maintaining good terms with those in power while privately disdaining their authority and disavowing his expressions of fealty. Rather, he accepts without question that as a black individual, "what he values, aspires for, and can demand is of less importance than what whites value, aspire for, and can demand."[43]

Here is another potential example of how internalizing oppressive norms can result in servility. In 1944, just after the Great Bengal Famine, 45.6% of widowers surveyed ranked their health as either "ill" or "indifferent." Only 2.5% of widows ranked themselves the same way. Yet all the other evidence indicated that the widows were either as badly off as or worse off than the widowers. In effect, masses of starving women claimed not to be ill. Amartya Sen argued that the Bengali women believed that, given the scarcity of food, they should not consume what little there was.[44] They believed this as a result of having internalized prevalent sexist norms that discounted the interests of women. As a result, they did not recognize that they had a reason to complain about their own starvation.

We can see, then, why responding to a bloodless invasion by acceding to it, and then bidding its victims to passively resist for decades to come in the hopes of overturning the oppressive social and legal norms, is problematic. A passive, intergenerational conflict against an oppressive regime will abate if the victimized population comes to internalize the oppressive norms. By doing so they fail to see these norms as morally problematic; consequently, they will not fight against them, even passively. Indeed, the challenges that many civil rights movements face are not limited to resisting the overwhelming political, military, and juridical power of a racist regime; a more basic problem is unseating the recalcitrant attitude among the oppressed that the status quo is unproblematic.

[42] Thomas E. Hill Jr., "Self-Respect Reconsidered," *Tulane Studies in Philosophy* 31 (1982): 88.

[43] Hill, "Self-Respect Reconsidered," 88.

[44] Amartya Sen, *Resources, Values, and Development* (Oxford: Blackwell, 1984), and "Gender Inequality and Theories of Justice," in *Women, Culture, and Development: A Study of Human Capabilities*, ed. Martha Nussbaum and Jonathan Glover (New York: Oxford University Press, 1995), 259–274.

As Dillon points out, one of the themes of Martin Luther King's "Letter from Birmingham Jail" is the inability of blacks to "see the intolerable as intolerable" as a result of generations of oppression.[45] Given this tendency, the suggestion by contingent pacifists that we respond to bloodless invasion by engaging in passive, intergenerational resistance risks entrenching the oppressive regime by eliminating the source of opposition—that is, the victims who are not yet in the grip of internalized oppression. In short, the prospects of effective passive resistance will likely dim as time passes.

Against this, however, one might note that those who internalize oppressive norms are often largely content with their lives, precisely because they have internalized those norms. Consider again the case of the Bengali women and that of the Uncle Tom. There is a sense in which these victims fail to respect themselves in that they do not take seriously their own moral status and rights. Yet it is perfectly possible for the victims to see themselves as acting with self-respect. For example, Stephen Massey asks us to imagine that the Uncle Tom is honest, trustworthy, and deeply concerned for the happiness of his kith and kin. "He may not regard his values and the fulfillment of his desires as having an importance equal to his master's, but he thinks they have some importance and respects himself for meeting what he regards as his obligations."[46] We can also easily imagine that the Bengali women respect themselves for recognizing and responding to the perceived self-abnegating duties. In these cases, the victims would not regard themselves as lacking self-respect. The result is that many of the debilitating psychological effects of lacking *subjective* self-respect are absent in these cases.

One might reiterate that the victims in these cases lack objective self-respect, but the challenge is to explain why we should believe that this state of affairs is particularly bad. After all, by hypothesis, the victims do not see themselves as victimized. Nor are they (we can assume) particularly unhappy or unsatisfied. To the extent that we have difficulty explaining what is so bad about this state of affairs, we have difficulty explaining how bloodless invasions leading to this state of affairs can be permissibly resisted at the cost of innocent lives. That is, though the victims of a bloodless invasion who internalize the oppressive norms of the regime might thereby come to lack objective self-respect, this seems to be no basis for resorting to war so long as they do not suffer psychologically debilitating harms. The upshot is that the contingent pacifist can admit that over time the prospect of effective passive resistance will diminish in accordance with the propensity for the population to internalize the regime's oppressive norms; but

[45] Dillon, "Introduction," 38.

[46] Massey, "Is Self-Respect a Moral or a Psychological Concept?" 252.

this is a self-correcting problem in that as the population comes to internalize those norms, the need for revolution diminishes.

The problem with this response, though, is that it understates what is wrong with the sort of servility concomitant with the absence of objective self-respect. In the *Groundwork of the Metaphysics of Morals* Kant argued that our dignity as rational beings demands not only that others respect us qua persons but that we respect ourselves qua persons—that is, as ends in ourselves. We accordingly are enjoined to refrain from acting in ways that debase, degrade, or disavow our status as rational beings. We might say, then, that we have a duty of objective self-respect. In *The Metaphysics of Morals* Kant claimed that this duty of self-respect is the most important moral duty, partly because it is a precondition for recognizing and acting upon all other moral duties. Servility, then, is contrary to a perfect nonjuridical duty to oneself. The duty is perfect in that the circumstances in which it applies are fully determinate and not subject to our own volitional preferences—we can't "pick and choose" when to abide by the duty. And the duty is nonjuridical in that a person cannot be permissibly coerced to abide by the duty.

But this account of what is wrong with servility is unconvincing because we tend to think that what morality obligates us to do can be characterized in part as claims that others have against us, whether these claims are second-personal or third-personal. This means that a moral duty that I have to respect my own status as a rational being amounts to a claim that I have against myself. But it is unclear how to make sense of first-personal claims. Some have argued, in Kantian fashion, that the object of the claim is "morality itself," rather than other individuals. Morality accordingly enjoins us not to disavow our moral status.[47]

A more promising approach—one more congenial to the view that internalized oppression is a self-inflicted harm and not necessarily a self-inflicted wrong—focuses on how internalized oppression damages our rational capacities. Carol Hay explores several ways in which internalized oppression can damage our rational capacities so thoroughly that our ability to act rationally is severely, and sometimes permanently, compromised.[48] For example, internalized oppression causes self-deception insofar as the oppressive social system creates incentives for the oppressed people to believe certain falsehoods about themselves, contrary to the available evidence. This, in turn, impinges upon our autonomy; because we are acting under substantial falsehoods inculcated by the dominant class about who we are and what we are capable of, our resulting decisions while in the grip of internalized oppression cannot be regarded as

[47] The most influential modern account of this sort belongs to Hill, "Self-Respect Reconsidered."

[48] Carol Hays, "The Obligation to Resist Oppression," *Journal of Social Philosophy* 42, no. 1 (2011): 21–45.

fully autonomous. In addition, internalized oppression can damage our capacity for rational deliberation. Servile individuals have less deliberative control over which goals they pursue and the means by which they pursue them. This impairs their deliberative capacities insofar as they are left unexercised and uncultivated (which in turn reinforces the belief that the victims are constitutionally incapable of exercising deliberative independence).

Given this account of what makes internalized oppression harmful, we can better understand why it is wrongful to oppress a people, even if they come to adapt to that oppression by internalizing its morally pernicious norms. By doing so, they maintain some degree of subjective self-respect, thereby insulating themselves from the debilitating psychological effects of coming to believe that their practical identities are without worth. But internalizing oppressive norms also has the effect of damaging their most fundamental rational capacities.

Can we go to war to protect these capacities? More to the point, is it permissible to kill innocents as a side effect of protecting our autonomy and fundamental rational capacities? It is difficult to weigh the value of protecting these capacities against the disvalue of lost innocent life. But it is not my purpose to demonstrate definitively that violently resisting bloodless invasions will typically be permissible. Rather, my goal is to show that when doing the proportionality calculation to determine whether we are morally required to surrender, we ought to include more than has been properly appreciated. In calculating the moral costs of surrendering, we obviously include the setback to our political interests resulting from surrendering our rights of political autonomy and political self-determination. But we also ought to include the moral costs of suffering from violations of recognition-respect. Specifically, systematically denying recognition-respect by imposing oppressive social and legal norms can inflict expressive harms which undercut the victim's self-respect to an extent that in severe cases makes it difficult to live a recognizably meaningful life. And if the victimized population will ultimately internalize the oppressive norms, we ought to include the moral costs of undermined objective self-respect. These costs will include diminished rational capacities and diminished autonomy. Once we grasp these debilitating moral harms and include them in the proportionality calculation, the claim that we typically must accept them rather than kill to prevent them becomes that much more difficult to accept.

Conclusion

Recall that in the dilemma of bloodless invasions, the maximum amount of defensive harm the victims can permissibly inflict on invaders is determined by the moral value of the nonvital interests they unconditionally threaten. If this is limited to the victims' political rights, then it is hard to justify a defensive war. But if what I've argued is correct, the harms the invaders will unconditionally commit are not limited to undermining our political rights when they do so by imposing oppressive social and legal norms. This is because the expressive harms caused by imposing such norms undercut the subjective self-respect among members of the oppressed population who retain the capability of recognizing that they are victims of the new social order; and they undercut the objective self-respect of those who internalize the oppressive social norms of that regime. Inasmuch, the maximum amount of harms we can inflict in such a case is determined not solely by the value of retaining legal rights to political representation but by the value of living a recognizably worthwhile life and the value of protecting our rational agency. I suggest that the aim of averting the debilitating psychological effects of diminished subjective self-respect among members of the oppressed group can satisfy the wide-proportionality constraint for war—likewise for the aim of averting the damage to deliberative capacities among members of the oppressed group who have internalized the norms of the oppressors (thereby manifesting a lack of objective self-respect).

The upshot is that we can indeed, at least in principle, go to war against an otherwise bloodless invader intent on imposing oppressive social and legal norms. This does not vindicate the view that defensive wars against *all* otherwise bloodless invasion are permissible—but I do not think that such a conclusion is one we should seek to defend.

References

Alport, Gordon W. *The Nature of Prejudice*. New York: Perseus Books, 1979.

Anderson, Elizabeth, and Richard H. Pildes. "Expressivism: A General Restatement." *University of Pennsylvania Law Review* 148 (2000): 1503–1575.

Bazargan, Saba. "Complicitous Liability in War." *Philosophical Studies* 165, no. 1 (2013): 177–195.

Bazargan, Saba. "Varieties of Contingent Pacifism." In *How We Fight*, edited by Helen Frower and Gerald Lang, 1–17. Oxford: Oxford University Press, 2015.

Darwall, Stephen L. "Two Kinds of Respect." *Ethics* 88, no. 1 (1977): 36–49.

Darwall, Stephen. "Respect and the Second Person Standpoint." *Proceedings and Addresses of the American Philosophical Association* 78, no. 2 (2004): 43–59.

Dillon, Robin S. "Toward a Feminist Conception of Self-Respect." *Hypatia* 7, no. 1 (1992): 52–69.

Dillon, Robin S. "Introduction." In *Dignity, Character, and Self-Respect*, edited by Robin S. Dillon, 1–51. London: Routledge, 1995.

Dillon, Robin S. "Self-Respect: Moral, Emotional, Political." *Ethics* 107, no. 2 (1997): 226–249.

Doppelt, Gerald. "The Place of Self-Respect in a Theory of Justice." *Inquiry* 52 (2009): 127–154.

Eyal, Nir. "'Perhaps the Most Important Primary Social Good': Self-Respect and Rawls's Principles of Justice." *Politics, Philosophy and Economics* 4 (2009): 195–219.

Fabre, Cécile. "Cosmopolitanism and Wars of Self-Defence." In *The Morality of Defensive War*, edited by Cécile Fabre and Seth Lazar, 90–114. Oxford: Oxford University Press, 2014.

Feinberg, Joel, and Jan Narveson. "The Nature and Value of Rights." *Journal of Value Inquiry* 4, no. 4 (1970): 243–260.

Griffin, James. *On Human Rights*. Oxford: Oxford University Press, 2009.

Hays, Carol. "The Obligation to Resist Oppression." *Journal of Social Philosophy* 42, no. 1 (2011): 21–45.

Hill, Thomas E., Jr. "Self-Respect Reconsidered." *Tulane Studies in Philosophy* 31 (1982): 129–137.

Himma, Kenneth Einar. "Discrimination and Disidentification: The Fair-Start Defense of Affirmative Action." *Journal of Business Ethics* 30 (April 2001): 277–289.

Iser, Mattias. "Beyond the Paradigm of Self-Defense? On Revolutionary Violence." In *The Ethics of War*, edited by Saba Bazargan and Samuel Rickless, 207–226. New York: Oxford University Press, 2016.

Lazar, Seth. "National Defence, Self-Defence, and the Problem of Political Aggression." In *The Morality of Defensive War*, edited by Cécile Fabre and Seth Lazar, 11–39. Oxford: Oxford University Press, 2014.

Massey, Stephen J. "Is Self-Respect a Moral or a Psychological Concept?" *Ethics* 93, no. 2 (1983): 246–261.

McMahan, Jeff. "What Rights May Be Defended by Means of War?" In *The Morality of Defensive War*, edited by Cécile Fabre and Seth Lazar, 115–156. Oxford: Oxford University Press, 2014.

Merton, Robert K. "The Self-Fulfilling Prophecy." *Antioch Review* 8, no. 2 (1948): 193–210.

Meyers, Diana T. "The Politics of Self-Respect: A Feminist Perspective." *Hypatia* 1, no. 1 (1986): 83–100.

Moody-Adams, Michele M. "Race, Class, and the Social Construction of Self-Respect." *Philosophical Forum* 24, no. 1–3 (1993): 251–266.

Moriarty, Jeffrey. "Rawls, Self-Respect and the Opportunity for Meaningful Work." *Social Theory and Practice* 35 (2009): 441–459.

Norman, Richard. *Ethics, Killing, and War*. Cambridge: Cambridge University Press, 1995.

Rawls, John. *A Theory of Justice*. Cambridge, MA: Harvard University Press, 1971.

Rawls, John. *Political Liberalism*. 2nd ed. New York: Columbia University Press, 2005.

Rodin, David. *War & Self-Defense*. New York: Oxford University Press, 2002.

Rodin, David. "Justifying Harm." *Ethics* 122, no. 1 (2012): 74–110.

Rodin, David. "The Myth of National Self-Defence." In *The Morality of Defensive War*, edited by C. Fabre and S. Lazar, 69–89. Oxford: Oxford University Press, 2014.

Sachs, David. "How to Distinguish Self-Respect from Self-Esteem." *Philosophy and Public Affairs* 10, no. 4 (1981): 346–360.

Sen, Amartya. *Resources, Values, and Development*. Oxford: Blackwell, 1984.

Sen, Amartya. "Gender Inequality and Theories of Justice." In *Women, Culture, and Development: A Study of Human Capabilities*, edited by Martha Nussbaum and Jonathan Glover, 259–274. New York: Oxford University Press, 1995.

Stark, Cynthia A. "Rawlsian Self-Respect." In *Oxford Studies of Normative Ethics*, vol. 2, edited by Mark Timmons, 238–261. Oxford: Oxford University Press, 2011.

Statman, Daniel. "Humiliation, Dignity, and Self-Respect." *Philosophical Psychology* 13, no. 4 (2000): 523–549.

Taylor, Gabrielle. *Pride, Shame, and Guilt: Emotions of Self-Assessment*. Oxford: Oxford University Press, 1985.

Telfer, Elizabeth. "Self-Respect." *Philosophical Quarterly* 18, no. 71 (1968): 114–121.

Thomas, Laurence. "Self-Respect: Theory and Practice." In *Philosophy Born of Struggle: Anthology of Afro-American Philosophy from 1917*, edited by Leonard Harris, 174–189. Dubuque, IA: Kendall Hunt, 1983.

Waldron, Jeremy. *Dignity, Rank, and Rights*. New York: Oxford University Press, 2012.

8

What Is the Moral Problem with Killer Robots?

SUSANNE BURRI

Introduction

An autonomous weapon system (AWS) is a weapon system that, "once activated, can select and engage targets without further intervention by a human operator."[1] Militaries around the world are intrigued by the potential that autonomous weapons technology offers, and they are investing substantial amounts of money and effort into the development of increasingly sophisticated AWS. But the technology has its vocal opponents, too. Thousands of artificial intelligence and robotics researchers have recently called for a ban on the further development of "offensive autonomous weapons beyond meaningful human control."[2] The researchers' demand is backed not only by a multitude of nongovernmental organizations[3] but—empirical research suggests—by a majority of the general public as well.[4] A fair number of philosophers, political scientists, and legal scholars have shown themselves critical of AWS also.[5]

[1] US Department of Defense. *Directive Number 3000.09 on Autonomy in Weapon Systems.* November 21, 2012. http://www.dtic.mil/whs/directives/corres/pdf/300009p.pdf.

[2] See http://futureoflife.org/open-letter-autonomous-weapons/.

[3] The Campaign to Stop Killer Robots is an international coalition of currently 61 nongovernmental organizations that are calling for a pre-emptive ban on fully autonomous weapons. See www.stopkillerrobots.org.

[4] In an international opinion poll, 67% of respondents felt that "all types of LAWS [lethal autonomous weapon systems] should be internationally banned." Open Roboethics Initiative, *The Ethics and Governance of Lethal Autonomous Weapons Systems: An International Public Opinion Poll,* November 9, 2015, http://www.openroboethics.org/category/survey/analysis/analysis-military/, 2. See also www.openroboethics.org/laws_survey_released/.

[5] See, for example, Robert Sparrow, "Killer Robots," *Journal of Applied Philosophy* 24, no. 1 (2007): 62–772, and "Robots and Respect: Assessing the Case Against Autonomous Weapon

To some extent, people feel uneasy about AWS because they think that the technology comes with a huge potential for abuse. Unlike nuclear weapons, so the thought goes, AWS would one day be widely available if the technology were developed further. It would therefore be only a matter of time before some crazy or evil person obtained autonomous weapons and used them to wreak havoc.

But people worry about AWS not only because the technology could easily be abused. An often-voiced concern is that even if autonomous weapons were to remain exclusively in the hands of well-intentioned individuals, the technology might still malfunction in unexpected and possibly disastrous ways. In a recent paper, Robert Sparrow defines an autonomous weapon as a weapon that, among other things, "is sufficiently complex such that, even when it is functioning perfectly, there remains some uncertainty about which objects and/or persons it will attack and why." This definition has the risk of malfunction built right into it.[6]

I believe that worries about the abuse of AWS and about their risk of malfunction are well grounded and, accordingly, deserve to be taken seriously. When thinking about what regulatory framework we should implement with respect to the further development and use of AWS, this means that we should carefully consider how optimally to respond to these worries.

But there is also a third type of AWS-related worry that appears to me less founded and that seems to draw attention away from the morally genuinely important issues that AWS give rise to. According to this third type of worry, a final targeting decision made by an AWS is always morally flawed in at least one respect, simply because it is a targeting decision made by an AWS as opposed to a human being. Those who are moved by this type of worry are wary of AWS

Systems," *Ethics & International Affairs* 30, no. 1 (2016): 93–116; Heather M. Roff, "Killing in War: Responsibility, Liability and Lethal Autonomous Robots," in *Routledge Handbook of Ethics and War: Just War Theory in the Twenty-First Century*, ed. Fritz Allhoff, Nicholas G. Evans, and Adam Henschke (New York: Routledge, 2013), 352–364; Mary Ellen O'Connell, "Banning Autonomous Killing: The Legal and Ethical Requirement That Humans Make Near-Time Lethal Decisions," in *The American Way of Bombing: Changing Ethical and Legal Norms from Flying Fortresses to Drones*, ed. Matthew Evangelista and Henry Shue (Ithaca, NY: Cornell University Press, 2014), 224–235; and Duncan Purves, Ryan Jenkins, and Bradley J. Strawser, "Autonomous Machines, Moral Judgment, and Acting for the Right Reasons," *Ethical Theory and Moral Practice* 18 (2015): 851–872. This is not to say that there aren't any positive voices. For a robotics researcher well disposed toward AWS, see Ronald Arkin, "The Case for Ethical Autonomy in Unmanned Systems," *Journal of Military Ethics* 9, no. 4 (2010): 332–341; for a philosopher, see Daniel Statman, "Drones and Robots: On the Changing Practice of Warfare," in *The Oxford Handbook of Ethics and War*, ed. Seth Lazar and Helen Frowe (Oxford: Oxford University Press, 2015), available at: http://www.oxfordhandbooks.com/view/10.1093/oxfordhb/9780199943418.001.0001/oxfordhb-9780199943418-e-9

[6] Sparrow, "Robots and Respect," 95. See also Armin Krishnan, *Killer Robots: Legality and Ethicality of Autonomous Weapons* (Farnham, UK: Ashgate, 2009, p. 53).

because they feel that "allowing life or death decisions to be made by machines crosses a fundamental moral line."[7]

In this chapter, I argue against the idea that allowing life-or-death decisions to be made by machines is necessarily morally problematic in at least one respect. More specifically, I scrutinize four prima facie powerful arguments in favor of this idea, and I argue that none of them is ultimately convincing. I also present an argument in favor of developing autonomous weapons technology further. Importantly, the aim of this chapter is not to present a defense of autonomous weapons but simply to show that a particular type of worry about AWS is misguided and to point out that at least some moral considerations speak in favor of developing the technology further. In this way, I hope to help sharpen the philosophical discussion of the moral issues that AWS give rise to.

The remainder of this chapter proceeds as follows. In the following section, I clarify important concepts and terminology. Then, I critically evaluate four defenses of the claim that a final targeting decision made by an AWS is always morally problematic in at least one respect, and I argue that they all lack force. Finally, I explain how the duty to protect just combatants speaks in favor of developing autonomous weapons technology further.

Terminology

Autonomous Weapon Systems

International humanitarian law currently lacks a definition of AWS. In a 2012 directive, the US Department of Defense defines the term as follows:

> Autonomous weapon system. A weapon system that, once activated, can select and engage targets without further intervention by a human operator. This includes human-supervised autonomous weapon systems that are designed to allow human operators to override operation of the weapon system, but can select and engage targets without further human input after activation.[8]

Two things are noteworthy about this definition. First, the "autonomy" that an AWS necessarily possesses is technical in nature and very narrow: a weapon system[9] counts as autonomous as soon as it has the ability—once it has been

[7] This is how the Campaign to Stop Killer Robots explains the problem with AWS. See www.stopkillerrobots.org/the-problem/.

[8] US Department of Defense, 13.

[9] It is appropriate to talk about an autonomous weapon system and not merely about an autonomous weapon because an AWS consists not only of munition but typically also numerous other

activated—to perform the two tasks of selecting and engaging a target without human intervention. Second, the definition's focus is clearly on the system's technical capacity to run in autonomous mode. Whether the system is intended to run autonomously by default is irrelevant to its status as an AWS.

The difference between autonomous and other weapon systems can also be described in terms of the role that a human operator of the system has with respect to final targeting decisions.[10] An operator can be in the loop, in which case it is necessarily the operator who decides which specific targets are to be engaged: no target can or will be engaged unless the operator directs the system to do so. Weapon systems with a human operator in the loop are not autonomous.

If a human operator is in the loop with respect to final targeting decisions, then the operator does not decide which specific targets are to be engaged but can monitor the weapon system's performance and intervene to prevent it from engaging a target if he or she does not agree with the target the machine has selected. Lastly, a human controller is out of the loop if he or she does not get to decide which specific targets should be engaged or if he or she can neither continuously monitor the system's performance nor halt it at will. Weapon systems where a human operator is either in the loop or out of the loop are autonomous in nature.

In some sense, AWSs are not a thing of the future. Landmines have been in use for centuries, and at least in a crude sense, they select and engage their own targets once a human operator has activated them. There are also other, much more sophisticated AWSs that are already operational. Consider the Israeli Harpy.[11] The Harpy is a wide-area loitering cruise missile that targets enemy radars. Deployed without a specific target in mind, it flies a search pattern over a wide area, looking for enemy radars. If it detects an object that it identifies as an enemy radar, it dive-bombs into the object with the goal of destroying it.

Landmines and weapon systems such as the Harpy are not the kind of AWS that those lobbying for a pre-emptive ban on the further development of the technology are particularly worried about. Whereas landmines seem technically too simplistic to give rise to the particular issues that advanced AWSs are thought to give rise to, the Harpy is not an especially worrisome AWS because it is purely antimachinery: it does not target human beings. The vaguely expressed concern of AWS critics is that no machine should be tasked with life-and-death

elements such as a launching platform, sensors, and software that steers the targeting process. The different elements may moreover be "distributed across multiple physical platforms." Michael Horowitz and Paul Scharre, *An Introduction to Autonomy in Weapon Systems*, February 13, 2015, 3, fn. 3, https://www.cnas.org/publications/reports/an-introduction-to-autonomy-in-weapon-systems.

[10] Horowitz and Scharre, *An Introduction to Autonomy*, 8.

[11] Horowitz and Scharre, *An Introduction to Autonomy*, 13–14; Krishnan, *Killer Robots*, 65.

decisions.[12] I take it that AWS critics are therefore primarily opposed to (1) technically sophisticated AWSs that (2) target human beings.

Lethal Autonomous Robots

Lethal autonomous robots (LARs), or killer robots, are a proper subset of AWSs. They are technically sophisticated AWSs that are also robots and that are able to lethally target human beings. As AWS critics are first and foremost worried about LARs, my primary concern in this chapter will be with LARs also.

A robot is a programmable machine that is equipped with sensors that allow it to form a representation of its environment.[13] At least to some extent, a robot has to be able to interact with or manipulate its environment without human intervention. An LAR, or killer robot, is a robot that, once it has been activated, can select and lethally engage human targets without the intervention of a human operator.

Importantly, drones as they are in use today are not killer robots as they are all remotely piloted (hence their alternative name of remotely piloted aircraft). It seems that no killer robots are currently in use anywhere.

Machine Learning

Robots run on computer programs. A computer program is a set of instructions that a computer can process and that allows it to perform certain tasks. In the case of robots, this includes processing sensory input and reacting to it in line with predefined objectives.

Algorithms form a key part of any computer program. An algorithm is a set of rules. Standard or nonlearning algorithms spell out how to perform a certain task in a stepwise manner. If I tell you to (1) wait in front of the next zebra crossing you find, (2) look left and look right, (3) cross the street if, and only if, you see no oncoming traffic from either side, I am providing you with a simple algorithm for safely crossing a street. All robots rely on nonlearning algorithms, but some rely on machine learning algorithms as well. If a robot relies entirely on nonlearning algorithms, it performs its core tasks—playing chess, assembling car parts, or selecting and engaging a target—according to a fixed procedure that was written out for it by human programmer.

[12] See, for example, Bonnie Docherty, *Losing Humanity: The Case Against Killer Robots.* Human Rights Watch, November 19, 2012, 42, https://www.hrw.org/report/2012/11/19/losing-humanity/case-against-killer-robots; O'Connell, "Banning Autonomous Killing," 232.

[13] Krishnan, *Killer Robots,* 9–10.

A robot that partly relies on learning algorithms has the ability to use data to modify the procedure by which it performs its core tasks. Depending on the degree of sophistication, learning algorithms enable a machine to sort through potentially very large, unstructured data sets and to extract from these data sets information that allows it to improve the rules it follows to perform its core tasks.

As an example, consider image recognition software, where learning algorithms have recently been put to use with considerable success. In this case, researchers improved the image recognition capabilities of their learning machine by presenting it with picture after picture, as well as with a description of what each picture displayed. The machine sorted through all of these data to extract patterns, distinctive elements, and the like. It then used this information to overhaul its basic classification mechanism.

On the plus side, learning robots have the potential to become much more skilled and flexible at performing their core tasks than their rigidly programmed nonlearning counterparts.[14] The rapid progress in artificial intelligence that we have witnessed over the past few years, and continue to witness today, is largely driven by the powerful and versatile methods of machine learning. But the potential of machine learning comes at a cost. Some of the information that learning machines extract from the data they are fed tends to bear on their core procedures in ways that we can't fully grasp. To put the same point differently, once a learning machine has been exposed to a sufficient amount of data, there is a good chance that it will perform its core tasks based on modified rules that we are no longer able to completely comprehend. Once this is the case, there is always the risk that the machine does something undesirable that takes us by surprise.[15] The popular science writer David Berreby puts the point as follows:

> [N]eural nets[16] sometimes come out with answers that are downright weird: not right, but also not wrong in a way that people can grasp. Instead, the answers sound like something an extraterrestrial might come up with. These oddball results are rare. But they aren't just random glitches . . . . [This] can be a troubling thought, even if you aren't yet depending on neural nets to run your home and drive you around. After all, the more we rely on artificial intelligence, the more we need it to be predictable, especially in failure. Not knowing how or why a

[14] Boer Deng, "Machine Ethics: The Robot's Dilemma." *Nature* 523 (2015): 26.

[15] See, for example, Eliezer Yudkowsky, "Artificial Intelligence as a Positive and Negative Factor in Global Risk," in *Global Catastrophic Risks*, ed. Nick Bostrom and Milan M. Cirkovic (Oxford: Oxford University Press, 2008), 308–345.

[16] A neural net is a set of learning algorithms modeled loosely after the human brain.

machine did something strange leaves us unable to make sure it doesn't happen again.[17]

This quote illustrates that, insofar as we are talking about learning LARs, worries that they might malfunction in unpredictable ways are well grounded.

A First Argument Against LARs: The Anti-Codifiability Thesis

A first argument in favor of the view that a killing performed by an LAR is always morally problematic in at least one respect is brought forward by Duncan Purves, Ryan Jenkins, and Bradley J. Strawser. They claim that proper moral deliberation requires Aristotelian judgment or that correctly applying a moral principle to a specific situation can never be done purely mechanically; it always requires interpretation. They call this the *anti-codifiability thesis.*[18]

Consider the *in bello* principle of necessity,[19] which states that you are morally required to minimize the harm that you inflict in order to achieve a morally worthy aim. As a commanding officer who is considering whether ordering a particular mission would satisfy the principle of necessity, you need to carefully think through all of your options for action. Once you have a good grasp of the expected effects of the mission in question, you still need to compare these effects to the expected effects of whatever alternatives are as a matter of fact available to you. This requires situational knowledge, knowledge about the means available to you, foresight, imagination, and creativity. Quite plausibly, it is not something you can do by unthinkingly running through a set of predefined steps. Purves et al.'s argument then is the following: LARs run on algorithms, which means that they unthinkingly run through a set of predefined steps. It follows that they are incapable of proper moral deliberation and that they are therefore always at risk of making significant moral mistakes.[20] It is morally objectionable to deploy LARs if they are at risk of making significant moral mistakes.

[17] David Berreby, "Artificial Intelligence Is Already Weirdly Inhuman," *Nautilus* 27 (2015). http://nautil.us/issue/27/dark-matter/_artificial-intelligence-is-already-weirdly-inhuman (original emphasis).

[18] Purves et al., "Autonomous Machines," 855.

[19] In bello principles are rules about the morally permissible infliction of harm in the context of war.

[20] Purves et al., "Autonomous Machines," 859, distinguish between empirical, moral, and practical mistakes. An LAR commits an empirical mistake if it makes a mistake in "discovering and identifying the empirical facts that are relevant" to its targeting decision; it commits a moral mistake if it comes to "the wrong normative answer about a moral problem, even given full information about the

Even if the anti-codifiability thesis is true and even if it is true that robots will therefore never be capable of full-blown moral deliberation, it does not follow that there would always be something morally objectionable about their deployment. In short, LARs don't have to be morally sophisticated deliberators to almost exclusively inflict only permissible harm. It suffices, instead, that a conscientious human commanding officer deploys them only in contexts where they are able to identify sufficient conditions for the morally permissible infliction of lethal harm. For LARs to be usefully and permissibly employable, they don't have to be able to replace human soldiers across all possible circumstances, nor do they have to be able to strategize and reason about entire missions the way higher-ranking military personnel have to.

The following two examples illustrate how LARs could usefully and permissibly be employable even with limited deliberative capacities. Following Ronald C. Arkin,[21] the general idea is that robots could be programmed conservatively: as they lack a drive for self-preservation, they could effectively be instructed to desist from selecting and engaging human targets in all but the morally most clear-cut cases. First, a robot could be programmed to engage a human target if, and only if, (1) the target has been shooting at our own combatants at some time during, say, the past ten seconds and (2) our own combatants have not indicated to the robot to refrain from firing. As enemy combatants are generally liable to be killed if we are fighting for a just cause,[22] responsibly deployed LARs that are programmed in this way should be able to highly reliably engage only in permissible killings. Second, a robot could be programmed to engage a human target if, and only if, its advanced facial recognition algorithms allow it to predict with near certainty that the human target in question is on a "kill list." On the assumption that the kill list is drawn up by morally responsible human beings, an LAR that is programmed in this way should again be able to highly reliably perform only permissible killings.

Against this, it could be argued that even if LARs are deployed only in limited contexts, there is nevertheless an ineliminable risk that they will unexpectedly display undesirable behavior,[23] at least if we are dealing with learning LARs. This seems to me correct. But the same risk is present when we are dealing with human soldiers also; their being capable of engaging in full-blown moral deliberation does not guard against this risk. Hence, what makes it permissible to

descriptive facts"; finally, it commits a practical mistake if it executes a correct decision in a flawed way, such as "by reacting a moment too slowly."

[21] Arkin, "The Case for Ethical Autonomy," 333.

[22] Child soldiers might provide an exception.

[23] By this, I mean that an LAR might always commit, in the terminology of Purves et al., "Autonomous Machines," an empirical, moral, or practical mistake. See fn. 9.

deploy learning LARs on a just mission would seem to be the same thing that makes it permissible to deploy human soldiers also: roughly, that due care has been taken to ensure that the risk in question is sufficiently small.[24]

Purves et al.[25] also argue that if the anti-codifiability thesis is true, an LAR would never be able to "resist an immoral order in the way that a human soldier might." If we take this as an argument in favor of the idea that there is always something morally problematic about deploying an LAR, the thought would seem to be that it is always better to deploy a human soldier instead as only human soldiers are able to recognize and resist immoral orders. But this argument is flawed in several respects. First, a robot doesn't have to be capable of moral deliberation to be able to resist at least some immoral orders. LARs could, for example, be programmed in such a way that they never target what they identify as a child. Second, to the extent that LARs are unable to resist immoral orders because they simply act as instructed, they are similarly unable to choose to deviate from moral orders. Hence, the argument of Purves et al. can also be turned on its head as it may always be better for a morally motivated commanding officer to deploy an obedient LAR as opposed to a potentially disobedient human soldier who might choose to ignore a moral order and engage in moral wrongdoing instead. Finally, if it is the point of Purves et al.'s argument that there should always be a check on a commanding officer's orders, this condition could be satisfied by implementing a four-eyes principle with respect to missions that involve the deployment of LARs so that such missions would always need the approval of at least two human beings before being embarked on.

In sum, as long as LARs are carefully deployed by morally motivated human officers, there doesn't have to be anything morally worrisome about their deployment even if the anti-codifiability thesis is true.

A Second Argument Against LARs: Acting for the Right Reasons

For the sake of argument, Purves et al. are willing to concede that LARs could someday become at least as skilled at moral deliberation as the most virtuous human beings. More specifically, they present a second argument against killer robots which aims to establish that there would be something morally objectionable about a killing performed by a robot even if that robot was known to

[24] Note also that if it is reasonable to assume that LARs might someday outperform human soldiers in terms of engaging only in permissible killings, this might provide a moral reason in favor of developing the technology further.

[25] Purves et al., "Autonomous Machines," 858.

be "perfect at making moral decisions" (p. 860 ff.). Their argument runs as follows. First, they put forward the claim that it is impossible for a robot to act for a reason. Their idea is that possessing "an attitude of belief or desire (or some further propositional attitude)" is a conceptual prerequisite of "acting for a reason" and that something which runs on algorithms cannot possess such an attitude (p. 861). Second, they contend that whenever an action lacks the feature of being performed for the right reason, it is morally deficient in at least one respect. They present the case of a "sociopathic soldier" who is "completely unmoved by the harm he causes to other people" and who takes pleasure in killing "scores of enemy soldiers" because he loves following orders (p. 861). According to Purves et al., even if this soldier is never ordered to kill anyone but liable enemy combatants, what he does is nevertheless morally flawed in at least one significant respect. Other things equal, it would be morally preferable to replace the sociopathic soldier with a morally virtuous soldier who understands that while killing enemy combatants is always regrettable, it is nevertheless morally permissible when a goal of sufficient moral value cannot be achieved in a less harmful way.

I believe that Purves et al. are right about the sociopathic soldier. But it seems to me that all the reasons we have to insist that it matters, morally speaking, whether a human person is acting for the right reasons fall away when we are dealing with an LAR that, by assumption, is "perfect at making moral decisions" (p. 860).

Purves et al. do not try to explain why an action is morally flawed when it lacks the feature of having been performed for the right reason. As I see it, there are four different, though to some extent complementary, explanations for why we might appropriately care about the reasons behind an action when the action is performed by a human being.[26] But none of these explanations would seem to apply in the context of robot action.

First, when a human agent acts in accordance with what morality demands but does so for the wrong reasons (or for no reason at all), this seems morally significant because it indicates that the agent followed the demands of morality only coincidentally. In slightly different circumstances, he or she might have performed a morally reprehensible act instead. Consider Purves et al.'s sociopathic soldier. As it happens, the soldier never receives a morally illegitimate order, so he never violates the *in bello* rules. But it is nevertheless true that the soldier would have executed the morally most outrageous orders had he received them.

[26] Judith Jarvis Thomson, "Self-Defense," *Philosophy and Public Affairs* 20 (1991): 293–294, argues that the reasons for which an action is performed are irrelevant to its permissibility. In spirit, Thomson's position is at odds with Purves et al.'s ideas. Strictly speaking, it is nevertheless consistent with Purves et al.'s core contention that an action is morally flawed *in at least one respect* whenever it is performed for the wrong reasons.

When we are dealing with a human agent, we therefore want him or her to act in accordance with what morality demands for the right reasons as this is one of the best available assurances that his or her behavior will robustly track the demands of morality.[27] By contrast, when it comes to robots, Purves et al. are committed to the claim that there is no such close relationship between acting for the right reasons and robustly tracking the demands of morality. Recall that Purves et al. assume that a robot is not the kind of thing that can act for a reason, but they nevertheless grant that a robot could in principle be built in such a way that it would always settle for the morally best alternative. Presumably their idea is that a robot could unerringly settle for the morally best alternative if it ran on sufficiently sophisticated algorithms.

A second explanation for why we might be justified in caring about a human agent's reasons for action centers on the idea of respect. When it is morally permissible to act in a way that will predictably set back others' vital interests, there is something disrespectful about acting in this way for a morally inappropriate reason.

Consider again the sociopathic soldier. When he sets out to kill an enemy combatant without any recognition that the enemy combatant's death is regrettable and without any appreciation of the morally valuable goal that justifies killing the enemy combatant, the sociopathic soldier's attitude toward the enemy combatant is quite plausibly one of reprehensible disrespect. But when an agent is not the kind of agent that acts on reasons, the question of appropriate attitude simply does not arise. There is nothing unduly selfish or inconsiderate about a lion that hunts down its prey, just as there is nothing disrespectful or insensitive about an LAR that has decided to lethally engage an enemy combatant based on the algorithms that were programmed into it.

Against this, it could be argued that a killing performed by an LAR is disrespectful not because the LAR's attitude is disrespectful but because there is something disrespectful about the attitude of whoever decides to deploy the LAR. For many people, there is something deeply unsettling about the thought of finding themselves face to face with an enemy that they know to be unresponsive to reasons, and they would much prefer to be confronted with an enemy who is capable of acting on reasons instead.[28] Hence, there may be something inconsiderate and disrespectful about a decision to utilize LARs. While an argument along these lines is brought forward by Sparrow, it seems to me successfully countered by Jenkins and Purves

[27] See, for example, Alec Walen, "The Doctrine of Illicit Intention," *Philosophy and Public Affairs* 34, no. 1 (2006): 39–67.

[28] See Sparrow, "Robots and Respect," 109–110; also the later discussion under "A Fourth Argument Against LARs."

(2016).[29] Jenkins and Purves (p. 9) argue that a decision to deploy LARs is respectful "in the narrow sense" if it is taken on the reasonable assumption that only liable targets will be engaged and that the decision is respectful "in the wide sense" if it is taken at least to some extent with a view to minimizing civilian casualties.[30] In other words, what would seem to make the deployment of LARs respectful is deploying them in such a way that their behavior can reasonably be expected to conform to the rules of *jus in bello*.

Third, we might insist that actions not performed for the right reasons are morally deficient because they lack moral worth. According to this Kantian idea, actions that are performed for the right reasons are accorded a special moral status—unlike other actions, they have moral worth—because the will behind them is of unconditional moral value.[31]

In my view, it makes sense to call an action morally deficient because it was not performed for the right reasons as long as the action was performed by an agent who is capable of acting on reasons. But if the action was performed by an agent who lacks the capacity to act on reasons, calling it morally deficient because it was not performed for the right reasons seems to me analogous to calling a bicycle deficient because it does not run on four sturdy wheels. It is, of course, possible to argue that the realization of moral worth is morally desirable so that, other things equal, it is preferable to have an action performed for the right reasons as opposed to having it performed by an agent who is incapable of acting on reasons.[32] But even if this is true, it does not imply that an action performed by an agent who is incapable of acting on reasons is thereby necessarily morally deficient. Nor does it imply that there exists a morally weighty reason in favor of employing human soldiers over LARs: if human soldiers frequently act on the wrong reasons or are morally motivated but make empirical mistakes, the disvalue involved in this may well outweigh the moral worth involved in their acting on the right reasons.

Fourth and finally, when a human agent fails to act for the right reasons, we can meaningfully describe his or her conduct as the morally flawed product of a less than fully virtuous character. According to this Aristotelian idea, a person is able to deliberate and act well to the extent that he or she is virtuous: virtues enable one to recognize and balance what is morally at stake in whatever situation

[29] Sparrow, "Robots and Respect"; Ryan Jenkins and Duncan Purves, "Robots and Respect: A Response to Robert Sparrow," *Ethics and International Affairs* 30, no. 3 (2016): 391–400.

[30] By distinguishing between respect in the narrow and the wide senses, Jenkins and Purves follow Jeff McMahan, who applies a similar distinction to proportionality. See *Killing in War* (New York: Oxford University Press, 2009, 20–21.

[31] See Immanuel Kant, *Groundwork of the Metaphysics of Morals* (Cambridge: Cambridge University Press, 1998), esp. sect. 1.

[32] This was pointed out to me by Andreas Carlsson.

that one finds oneself in.[33] On this way of looking at things, each killing performed by Purves et al.'s sociopathic soldier is a morally flawed product of his depraved character.

While it seems reasonable to describe the sociopathic soldier's actions in this way, it would be absurd to characterize a machine's consistent failure to act for the right reasons as the inevitable consequence of its corrupt character. If Purves et al. are right that machines do not act for the right reasons because they do not act for reasons, it seems much more apt to say that a machine's actions do not tell us anything about its—possibly nonexistent—character.

In sum, Purves et al.'s second argument against LARs is not convincing as it stands. While it makes sense to assume that it matters, morally speaking, whether human actions are performed for the right reasons, the same does not seem to hold true of robot actions.

A Third Argument Against LARs: The Responsibility Gap

For Rob Sparrow, the deployment of killer robots is morally problematic because it creates a potential responsibility gap:[34] as long as LARs are in use, there is always a risk that they will inflict wrongful harm for which no one is morally responsible. According to Sparrow (p. 67),

> [it] is a minimal expression of respect due to our enemy . . . that someone should accept responsibility, or be capable of being held responsible, for the decision to take their life. If we fail in this, we treat our enemy like vermin, as though they may be exterminated without moral regard at all. The least we owe our enemies is allowing that their lives are of sufficient worth that someone should accept responsibility for their deaths.

Sparrow contends that a responsibility gap arises when circumstances are such that no human being is morally responsible for the wrongful harm inflicted

[33] See Aristotle, *Nicomachean Ethics*, 2nd ed. (Indianapolis, IN: Hackett 2000), esp. bk. II.

[34] Sparrow, "Killer Robots." The idea that the use of learning machines creates a responsibility gap was first presented by Andreas Matthias, "The Responsibility Gap: Ascribing Responsibility for the Actions of Learning Automata," *Ethics and Information Technology* 6, no. 3 (2004): 175–183. In this chapter, I focus on Sparrow's treatment of the issue because Sparrow, unlike Matthias, argues specifically that the existence of a responsibility gap makes the deployment of LARs necessarily morally problematic.

by an LAR. Sparrow (pp. 71–73) thinks that LARs themselves are never morally responsible for the harm that they inflict, essentially because it is conceptually impossible to punish a machine. Let us take a closer look at these two ideas in turn.

Human Responsibility for Harm Inflicted by LARs

While the relevant passages are somewhat obscure, I take Sparrow (pp. 69–71) to be saying that a human agent is not morally responsible for harm inflicted by an LAR when the harm was not, in some meaningful sense, under the human agent's control. Moreover, harm inflicted by an LAR was not meaningfully under a human agent's control if either

1. The machine behaved in a way that was not foreseeable or
2. The machine in some substantive sense chose to inflict the harm, for example, against an explicit order to desist.

As I see it, the first of these two conditions cannot absolve human agents who had control over the development and deployment of an LAR from their moral responsibility for wrongful harm inflicted by that LAR.

By way of example, consider a programmer who writes a computer program for an LAR that contains a large number of learning algorithms. The basic idea behind the program is to enable an LAR to become increasingly skilled at searching for and lethally engaging human targets whose biometrics it has successfully matched to a record in some database. When put into LAR hardware and tested, the program seems to run smoothly, but it is impossible to predict how the LAR's behavior will evolve once the program's learning algorithms are fed with more and more data. If the programmer—or other individuals working for the same company—decides to hide the fact that the software comes with crucial unpredictabilities, the moral responsibility for any unforeseeable wrongful harm that an LAR running on the software might cause remains with him or her. His or her actions are not only negligent but downright reckless: he or she is pretending that it is relatively safe to use an incredibly dangerous tool.

Alternatively, the relevant individuals might conscientiously inform a potential buyer about the limitations and unpredictabilities of the software. In this case, at least part[35] of the moral responsibility for whatever unforeseeable wrongful

[35] It is conceivable that part of the moral responsibility remains with the developers of the software, simply because they voluntarily decided to create and disseminate something they knew might cause wrongful harm even when handled conscientiously.

harm an LAR running on the program might cause is passed on to the buyer. If an informed buyer decides to put the program to use without first letting it learn and then testing it extensively in a controlled environment, the informed buyer acts recklessly and is morally blameworthy for whatever wrongful harm the LARs cause. Alternatively, the buyer might test and train the program before putting the LARs to use, but he or she might, for example, make the mistake of never testing the program's performance under adverse weather conditions. It might then turn out that the LARs start killing indiscriminately once heavy rain starts to fall. If so, the buyer acted negligently and is once again morally blameworthy for the indiscriminate killings of the LARs.

Finally, the buyer might carefully test and train the program before putting the LARs to use, so he or she might eventually be justified in assuming that the LARs are performing reliably. But the LARs might nevertheless malfunction for some outlandish reason that no one could reasonably have foreseen. This would still not leave us with a responsibility gap.[36] When you decide to use what you know is a dangerous tool to further your own purposes, you are morally responsible for the wrongful harm this causes no matter how many precautions you took to avoid causing wrongful harm.[37] If you took all reasonable precautions and if you were justified in assuming that the risk of wrongful harm was sufficiently small, you are not blameworthy for whatever wrongful harm you happen to cause. But you are still morally responsible: depending on the circumstances, you might have to apologize to your victim, you might owe your victim compensation, or it might be morally permissible for a potential victim to kill you to escape the threatening situation that your actions have put him or her in.[38]

In sum, LARs are dangerous tools, and no one who develops or deploys them can hide behind the excuse that the wrongful harm caused by an LAR came as a complete surprise. Taking due care may absolve the relevant human agents of blameworthiness, but it does not absolve them of their moral responsibility. The second condition is more tricky. If I understand Sparrow correctly, he is saying that artificial intelligence will reach a point where it will cease to be valid

[36] Cf. Jeff McMahan, "The Basis of Moral Liability to Defensive Killing," *Philosophical Issues* 15, no. 1 (2005): 394–395.

[37] As Tom Parr and Andreas Carlsson have pointed out to me, there is an interesting question here about who is morally responsible for wrongful harm an agent causes in the conscientious pursuit not of his or her own purposes but of a morally obligatory aim. Suppose LARs are used in a morally required humanitarian intervention and the LARs inflict wrongful harm despite the fact that all reasonable precautions were taken. In such a case, who is morally responsible for the harm inflicted? Interesting as it is, I won't pursue this question further here as it arises not from the use of LARs in particular but simply from the fact that things can sometimes go wrong when we pursue what we have reason to believe is a morally obligatory end.

[38] McMahan, "The Basis of Moral Liability," 394–404.

to think of an autonomous robot as a mere tool. His idea seems to be that as machines keep learning and become more intelligent, they develop goals and desires of their own. In one of his examples, Sparrow talks about a robot committing a war crime so as to "to revenge the 'deaths' of robot comrades recently destroyed in battle." Elsewhere, he argues that holding "the programmers responsible for the actions of their creation, once it is autonomous, would be analogous to holding parents responsible for the actions of their children once they have left their care."[39]

Nick Bostrom convincingly argues that this anthropomorphizing view of artificial intelligence is false.[40] As machines learn and become increasingly intelligent, they become powerful optimizers: they pursue with skill and ingenuity whatever goals that they were programmed to pursue. But unless they were programmed to do just that, they don't at some point start developing goals of their own. Put differently, artificial intelligence is by construction purely instrumental intelligence—it is skill at pursuing a set of predefined objectives.

Bostrom calls the idea that a machine could become exceedingly skilled at pursuing a narrow set of predefined objectives the *orthogonality thesis.* In his words, "Intelligence and final goals are orthogonal axes along which possible agents can freely vary. In other words, more or less any level of intelligence could in principle be combined with more or less any final goal" (p. 73). Once we keep in mind that learning algorithms simply enable a machine to sort through data to improve the accuracy of its various decision procedures and classification mechanisms (see earlier discussion under "Machine Learning"), it is difficult to doubt the veracity of Bostrom's orthogonality thesis.

But suppose that Sparrow is right, that the orthogonality thesis is false and that learning LARs might someday reach a point at which they develop goals and possibly even desires of their own. If so, Sparrow seems right to claim that when a wrongful killing was in some substantive sense chosen by the machine itself, there might be no human agent who can justly be held responsible for the killing.[41] But it seems to me that in such a case the moral responsibility would lie with the machine itself.

Robot Responsibility for Harm Inflicted by LARs

Sparrow (2007, pp. 71-3) claims that LARs can never be morally responsible for wrongful harm that they inflict, even if they become highly intelligent, very

[39] Sparrow, "Killer Robots," 66, 70.

[40] Nick Bostrom, "The Superintelligent Will: Motivation and Instrumental Rationality in Advanced Artificial Agents," *Minds and Machines* 22, no. 2 (2012): 71–85.

[41] Sparrow, "Killer Robots," 70–71.

powerful, and develop goals and desires of their own.[42] As Sparrow sees it, an agent can be morally responsible only if he or she can be held responsible, and we can hold someone responsible only if it is at least in principle possible to punish him or her. Sparrow then argues that it is conceptually impossible to punish a machine, primarily because punishing someone involves making him or her suffer, while machines are incapable of suffering.

For one thing, I am not convinced that the type of LAR that Sparrow envisages would necessarily be incapable of suffering. Once LARs have goals and desires of their own, why wouldn't they suffer if they had these thwarted?[43] Nor am I entirely convinced that an agent cannot be morally responsible unless it is conceptually possible to hold the agent responsible. Consider the case of a successful suicide bomber who wrongfully blows up ten innocent children along with himself or herself. While it may well be impossible to hold the dead bomber responsible, he or she nevertheless seems morally responsible and blameworthy for what he or she did.

Sparrow might agree that the suicide bomber is morally responsible in some sense, roughly in the sense that makes him or her blameworthy for what he or she did. But he might go on to argue that this is not the sense of moral responsibility that he is interested in. More precisely, his argument seems to be that there is a worrisome responsibility gap whenever no one can justly be held accountable for some wrongdoing. If this is correct, Sparrow's idea would seem to be that if the suicide bomber acted alone, this would confront us with a responsibility gap similar to the gap that he is worried about with respect to LARs.

At least for the sake of argument, I am willing to grant Sparrow that it is morally worrisome if no one can be held accountable for wrongful harm and that LARs acting on their own behalf would be capable of inflicting such harm.[44] The crucial flaw in Sparrow's argument then seems to be that he wrongly assumes that unless we can punish someone by making him or her suffer, it is impossible to hold him or her to account for his or her wrongdoing.

Suppose that Sparrow is right that LARs cannot suffer and that an LAR commits a war crime against the orders of its commanding officer because it aims "to

[42] Sparrow, "Killer Robots," 70–73.

[43] The organization People for the Ethical Treatment of Reinforcement Learners (PETRL) is based on the premise that machines might be capable of suffering. For an argument in favor of this premise, see Brian Tomasik, *Do Artificial Reinforcement-Learning Agents Matter Morally?* Cornell University Library, October 30, 2014, http://arxiv.org/abs/1410.8233. I thank Stefan Schubert for drawing my attention to PETRL.

[44] Once it is no longer appropriate to see LARs as tools in the hands of human agents, an alternative to thinking of them as capable of inflicting wrongful harm is to see them as forces that inflict the type of amoral harm that an earthquake or a wild animal inflicts.

revenge the 'deaths' of robot comrades recently destroyed in battle."[45] It seems to me that we could hold such an LAR responsible, for example, by

- Destroying the machine
- Turning off some of its functions or reprogramming it
- Demanding that the machine apologize or provide some form of compensation to the families and dependents of its victims

In short, while it is difficult to know what would be the most sensible way of holding responsible the type of LARs that Sparrow envisages, it is clear that our practices of holding wrongdoers accountable for their actions are not limited to making them suffer.

A Fourth Argument Against LARs: Heartless Killing

According to a fourth argument against the deployment of killer robots, there ought always to be an element of humanity in lethal targeting decisions. As Mary Ellen O'Connell puts it, "[g]iving up the decision [to kill] entirely to a computer program will . . . remove, literally, the humanity that should come to bear in all cases of justifiable killing."[46] Merel Ekelhof and Miriam Struyk express the idea as follows: "War is about human suffering, the loss of human lives, and consequences for human beings. Killing with machines is the ultimate demoralization of war. Even in the hell of war we find humanity, and that must remain so."[47] As I understand this fourth argument, it proceeds from the assumption that there is something like a morally best way of killing in war. The morally best killings—the most exemplary, the most humane, the most respectful killings—take place when conscientious and empathetic just combatants, feeling the full weight of the decisions before them, eventually and for the right reasons reach the right practical conclusions. The argument against the deployment of LARs is then the following: because there is a morally best way of killing in war, we ought to strive toward it. To deploy LARs, however, is to move away from it. Hence, deploying LARs is always morally problematic in at least one respect.[48] While there may be

[45] Sparrow, "Killer Robots," 66.

[46] "Banning Autonomous Killing," 232.

[47] *Deadly Decisions: 8 Objections to Killer Robots*, PAX, February 26, 2014, 7, http://www.paxforpeace.nl/stay-informed/news/stop-killer-robots-while-we-still-can.

[48] The second argument against LARs that I discussed can be read as a special case of the fourth argument presented here. Read in this way, Purves et al. are claiming that the morally best killings are

something intuitively appealing about this fourth argument, I believe that it falls prey to the following dilemma.[49]

Consider a situation where a commanding officer contemplates sending one of his or her subordinates on a mission, the successful pursuit of which will most likely involve killing a number of enemy combatants. The commanding officer can choose to send a human soldier or to instruct an LAR. Depending on the circumstances of the case, killing the enemy soldiers will be either justified or unjustified. Suppose first that it is unjustified. Then the morally best thing to do for the commanding officer is simply not to send out anyone.

Next, suppose that killing the enemy combatants is justified. Suppose that they are voluntarily fighting an unjust war and that, under the circumstances, killing them would be both proportionate and necessary so that they are liable to be killed.[50] If in this case the commanding officer is morally required to send out a human soldier, then he or she has to put the life of a just soldier at risk so that this soldier might show respect and compassion for a group of liable individuals. In other words, if the commanding officer has to deploy a human soldier so that the enemy soldiers may be killed in the "morally best possible way," then this implies that the morally best possible way of killing liable individuals is one that puts a just combatant in the line of fire. But, quite plausibly, the morally best way of killing liable individuals is one that minimizes the risk of harm to those who are not liable to be harmed. Hence, those who argue that there ought to be an element of humanity "even in the hell of war" owe us an explanation as to why the presence of "humanity" should take precedence over the safety of just combatants.

I am willing to concede that in cases where the risk of harm to a just combatant is very small, the morally best killing of an unjust enemy combatant takes place when a just combatant feels the weight of the decision and finally kills the enemy combatant with empathy and for the right reasons. But even in such cases, it may be morally supererogatory for a just combatant to take on whatever risk of

performed for the right reasons and that a killing performed by an LAR can never be performed for the right reasons.

49 The forcefulness of this dilemma depends on the truth of the revisionary approach to just war theory that is defended by Jeff McMahan and others. While I believe that the revisionary approach to just war theory is correct, I won't try to argue for this here. According to revisionist just war theory, war is not a morally privileged activity: whatever moral principles govern the infliction of harm in ordinary life govern its infliction in the context of war as well. This implies that there is a difference in the moral status of just and unjust soldiers. The former are fighting justly for a just cause and are therefore not liable to be harmed. The latter are fighting unjustly or for an unjust cause and are therefore liable to harmed.

50 If someone is liable to some harm, he or she is not wronged if that harm is imposed on him or her.

harm there remains. Unless a human subordinate volunteers, it may then still be right for a commanding officer to deploy an LAR as opposed to a human soldier. Moreover, while final targeting decisions made by human soldiers can in principle approach some ideal standard, in practice they often won't. To say that we should deploy human soldiers so that some ideal standard will be approximated therefore makes sense only in cases where it is reasonable to assume that the standard may in fact be approximated. Fittingly enough, these will most likely be cases where the risk of harm to just combatants is sufficiently small.[51]

An Argument in Favor of LARs

The basic idea behind the *in bello* principle of necessity is that harm is bad. In the pursuit of sufficiently worthy goals, it is sometimes morally permissible to bring about such harm, but only if we choose the least harmful way in which to pursue these goals. As I see it, the principle of necessity points to an important argument in favor of developing autonomous weapons technology further. Simply put, if we are able to develop LARs that can replace human soldiers in the theater of war, taking a wide perspective on the principle of necessity implies that we should do so as it helps us minimize the extent to which we have to put our soldiers at risk of harm when pursuing just goals.

In light of the general unease about AWS, someone might try to argue that developing autonomous weapons technology further isn't necessary to protect our own soldiers: as long as we develop remotely piloted weapons systems further—or so this argument would go—the need to have human soldiers on the ground will continually decrease anyway.[52] But while it is true that physical harm to soldiers can, at least to some extent,[53] be reduced through the use of remotely piloted weapons systems, the same is not true of mental and emotional harm.

[51] What if the people to be killed are civilians who are not liable to be killed, but it is nevertheless morally permissible to bring about their deaths as a foreseen but unintended side effect? In such a case, it may well be morally appropriate not to prioritize the safety of the just combatants over the interests of the civilians but to take the interests on both sides equally seriously. Yet even if this is correct, it might nevertheless turn out that the just combatants' interest in not being put at risk of harm outweighs whatever interest the civilians have in being killed by a human being as opposed to an LAR.

[52] Cf. Bradley J. Strawser, "Moral Predators: The Duty to Employ Uninhabited Aerial Vehicles," *Journal of Military Ethics* 9, no. 4 (2010): 342–368.

[53] AWS may help reduce the risk of physical harm to human soldiers in places where remotely piloted weapon systems cannot be deployed, for example, in environments where our adversaries are able to make use of electronic jamming to disrupt the wireless data links needed to run remotely piloted systems. I owe this point to Ryan Jenkins. See also Krishnan, *Killer Robots*, 37–42.

According to a study conducted by the US Armed Forces Health Surveillance Center, pilots of remotely piloted aircraft (RPA) report "high levels of stress and fatigue," and there is "no significant difference in the rates of [mental health] diagnoses, including post-traumatic stress disorder, depressive disorders, and anxiety disorders between RPA and [manned aircraft] pilots."[54] In other words, killing by remote control is just as mentally and emotionally burdensome as other types of killing.

In one sense, this is good news. It suggests that RPA pilots are fully aware of what they are doing; they are not under the illusion that they are playing video games. In view of the fact that RPA pilots are killing other human beings, it is perfectly appropriate that their job should turn out to be emotionally and mentally burdensome.

But in another sense, the report brings bad news. Its findings suggest that even if we were to rely exclusively on remotely piloted systems while fighting a just war, we would still expose our soldiers to significant risks of harm.[55] As long as they have to select and lethally engage human targets, their long-term emotional and mental integrity is on the line.[56] It follows that if LARs have the potential to help us shield our soldiers from emotional and mental harm, then this provides us with a valid reason in favor of developing autonomous weapons technology further.

Conclusion

Unease about killer robots is widespread. Many people fear that LARs could easily be abused and that they come with an ineliminable risk of malfunction. Both

[54] Jean L. Otto and Bryant J. Webber, "Mental Health Diagnoses and Counseling Among Pilots of Remotely Piloted Aircraft in the United States Air Force," *Medical Surveillance Monthly Report (MSMR)* 20, no. 3 (2013): 3.

[55] It is possible to doubt that recent statistics on the mental health of US military members are reliable sources of information about the mental health risks that just soldiers are exposed to. Hans Pols and Stephanie Oak, "War and Military Mental Health: The US Psychiatric Response in the 20th Century," *American Journal of Public Health* 97, no. 12 (2007): 2132–2142, describe the mental and emotional harms suffered by American soldiers in World War II as serious and widespread. They report that "in total, there were more than 1 million neuropsychiatric admissions to the medical services of the US armed forces" (p. 2135). Together with the fact that the rates of mental health diagnoses of RPA pilots are similar to those of other pilots, this suggests that RPA pilots fighting for a just cause would be at significant risk of emotional and mental harm.

[56] Nancy Sherman, *Afterwar: Healing the Moral Wounds of Our Soldiers* (Oxford: Oxford University Press, 2015), argues that soldiers' *moral* integrity is on the line as well: as soldiers often fall short of their own moral ideals, they have to somehow come to terms with this failure, as well as with the associated feelings of guilt and shame.

of these worries seem to me well grounded. When thinking about what regulatory framework we should implement with respect to the further development and use of AWSs, we should carefully consider how we can optimally respond to these worries.

In this chapter, I have argued against a third type of AWS-related worry, namely the worry that a final targeting decision made by an LAR would always be morally problematic in at least one respect. I have tried to dismantle four different arguments in favor of this claim. In addition to this, I have suggested that the protective obligations we have toward just soldiers speak in favor of developing autonomous weapon technology further.

As I see it, LARs are tools. They are potentially very sophisticated and potentially very dangerous tools. To develop and deploy them in a morally responsible manner will require much foresight, caution, and care. But, at least in principle, I see no reason why this could not be done.

Acknowledgment

For helpful discussions and comments, I thank Yitzhak Benbaji, Jonathan Birch, Andreas Carlsson, Lars Christie, Ben Ferguson, Johannes Himmelreich, Ryan Jenkins, Bryan Roberts, Stefan Schubert, Tom Parr, and Thomas Seiler.

References

Aristotle. *Nicomachean Ethics*. 2nd ed. Indianapolis, IN: Hackett, 2000.

Arkin, Ronald C. "The Case for Ethical Autonomy in Unmanned Systems." *Journal of Military Ethics* 9, no. 4 (2010): 332–341.

Berreby, David. "Artificial Intelligence Is Already Weirdly Inhuman." *Nautilus* 27 (2015). http://nautil.us/issue/27/dark-matter/_artificial-intelligence-is-already-weirdly-inhuman.

Bostrom, Nick. "The Superintelligent Will: Motivation and Instrumental Rationality in Advanced Artificial Agents." *Minds and Machines* 22, no. 2 (2012): 71–85.

Deng, Boer. "Machine Ethics: The Robot's Dilemma." *Nature* 523 (2015): 24–26.

Docherty, Bonnie. *Losing Humanity: The Case Against Killer Robots*. Human Rights Watch. November 19, 2012. https://www.hrw.org/report/2012/11/19/losing-humanity/case-against-killer-robots.

Ekelhof, Merel, and Miriam Struyk. *Deadly Decisions: 8 Objections to Killer Robots*. PAX. February 26, 2014. http://www.paxforpeace.nl/stay-informed/news/stop-killer-robots-while-we-still-can.

Horowitz, Michael, and Paul Scharre. *An Introduction to Autonomy in Weapon Systems*. February 13, 2015. https://www.cnas.org/publications/reports/an-introduction-to-autonomy-in-weapon-systems.

Jenkins, Ryan, and Duncan Purves. "Robots and Respect: A Response to Robert Sparrow." *Ethics and International Affairs* 30, no. 3 (2016): 391–400.

Kant, Immanuel. *Groundwork of the Metaphysics of Morals*. Cambridge: Cambridge University Press, 1998.

Krishnan, Armin. *Killer Robots: Legality and Ethicality of Autonomous Weapons*. Farnham, UK: Ashgate, 2009.

Matthias, Andreas. "The Responsibility Gap: Ascribing Responsibility for the Actions of Learning Automata." *Ethics and Information Technology* 6, no. 3 (2004): 175–183.

McMahan, Jeff. "The Basis of Moral Liability to Defensive Killing." *Philosophical Issues* 15, no. 1 (2005): 386–405.

McMahan, Jeff. *Killing in War*. New York: Oxford University Press, 2009.

O'Connell, Mary Ellen. "Banning Autonomous Killing: The Legal and Ethical Requirement That Humans Make Near-Time Lethal Decisions." In *The American Way of Bombing: Changing Ethical and Legal Norms from Flying Fortresses to Drones*, edited by Matthew Evangelista and Henry Shue, 224–235. Ithaca, NY: Cornell University Press, 2014.

Open Roboethics Initiative. *The Ethics and Governance of Lethal Autonomous Weapons Systems: An International Public Opinion Poll*. November 9, 2015. http://www.openroboethics.org/category/survey/analysis/analysis-military/.

Otto, Jean L., and Bryant J. Webber. "Mental Health Diagnoses and Counseling Among Pilots of Remotely Piloted Aircraft in the United States Air Force." *Medical Surveillance Monthly Report (MSMR)* 20, no. 3 (2013): 3–8.

Pols, Hans, and Stephanie Oak. "War and Military Mental Health: The US Psychiatric Response in the 20th Century." *American Journal of Public Health* 97, no. 12 (2007): 2132–2142.

Purves, Duncan, Ryan Jenkins, and Bradley J. Strawser. "Autonomous Machines, Moral Judgment, and Acting for the Right Reasons." *Ethical Theory and Moral Practice* 18 (2015): 851–872.

Roff, Heather M. "Killing in War: Responsibility, Liability and Lethal Autonomous Robots." In *Routledge Handbook of Ethics and War: Just War Theory in the Twenty-First Century*, edited by Fritz Allhoff, Nicholas G. Evans, and Adam Henschke, 352–364. New York: Routledge, 2013.

Sherman, Nancy. *Afterwar: Healing the Moral Wounds of Our Soldiers*. Oxford: Oxford University Press, 2015.

Sparrow, Robert. "Killer Robots." *Journal of Applied Philosophy* 24, no. 1 (2007): 62–77.

Sparrow, Robert. "Robots and Respect: Assessing the Case Against Autonomous Weapon Systems." *Ethics & International Affairs* 30, no. 1 (2016): 93–116.

Statman, Daniel. "Drones and Robots: On the Changing Practice of Warfare." In *The Oxford Handbook of Ethics and War*, edited by Seth Lazar and Helen Frowe. Oxford: Oxford University Press, 2015. Availble at: http://www.oxfordhandbooks.com/view/10.1093/oxfordhb/9780199943418.001.0001/oxfordhb-9780199943418-e-9

Strawser, Bradley J. "Moral Predators: The Duty to Employ Uninhabited Aerial Vehicles." *Journal of Military Ethics* 9, no. 4 (2010): 342–368.

Thomson, Judith Jarvis. "Self-Defense." *Philosophy and Public Affairs* 20 (1991): 283–310.

Tomasik, Brian. *Do Artificial Reinforcement-Learning Agents Matter Morally?* Cornell University Library. October 30, 2014. http://arxiv.org/abs/1410.8233.

US Department of Defense. *Directive Number 3000.09 on Autonomy in Weapon Systems*. November 21, 2012. http://www.dtic.mil/whs/directives/corres/pdf/300009p.pdf.

Walen, Alec. "The Doctrine of Illicit Intention." *Philosophy and Public Affairs* 34, no. 1 (2006): 39–67.

Yudkowsky, Eliezer. "Artificial Intelligence as a Positive and Negative Factor in Global Risk." In *Global Catastrophic Risks*, edited by Nick Bostrom and Milan M. Cirkovic, 308–345. Oxford: Oxford University Press, 2008.

9

Distributing Death in Humanitarian Interventions

LARS CHRISTIE

Introduction

The rights and liabilities of combatants have been subject to intense dispute in just war theory. One issue that has been particularly contested is whether combatants have equal rights and liabilities irrespective of which side of the war they are on, as long as they adhere to the *jus in bello* principles. Less attention has been given to the closely related question of the moral equality of noncombatants on either side of the conflict. Some authors have suggested that combatants may favor the lives of fellow noncombatant citizens over enemy noncombatants. One way to attempt to justify such a claim has been advanced by Thomas Hurka, who claims that combatants are under an associative duty to their fellow nationals, which requires them to differentiate between conational noncombatants and noncombatants belonging to an enemy state.[1] This view does not, however, rely on a claim about the unequal moral status of noncombatants on either side of the war but rather on the relationship between a combatant and noncombatants who belong to the same state or political entity. In cases where humanitarian intervention is carried out by a third party with no particular political or institutional relationship to any particular group of noncombatants, this argument has no purchase.

A few authors have directly challenged the idea of the moral equality of noncombatants. Independently, both Gerhard Øverland and Jeff McMahan have claimed that noncombatants differ with respect to an allegedly morally relevant

[1] Thomas Hurka, "Proportionality in the Morality of War," *Philosophy and Public Affairs* 33, no. 1 (2005): 62.

factor: whether or not they stand to benefit from a military intervention.[2] Using this criterion, Øverland and McMahan distinguish between expected beneficiaries of and bystanders to military action.[3] Bystanders to military action do not contribute to either side of the conflict, nor do they stand to benefit from the goal of the military action. Examples of expected beneficiaries of a military intervention can be a persecuted minority within an oppressive regime who would benefit greatly if the regime was overthrown. Examples of neutral bystanders in this scenario can be nonoppressed fellow citizens or citizens of other nations who do not contribute to the oppression and who do not stand to benefit from the intervention. Both Øverland and McMahan claim that the immunity of the former group to collateral harm inflicted as part of a humanitarian intervention is weaker than the immunity of the latter. As McMahan puts it, "it does make a difference to the degree to which noncombatants are morally immune in war whether they are bystanders to military action or expected beneficiaries of it" (2010, p. 363). I will refer to this claim as the *beneficiary thesis*. The beneficiary thesis is not merely relevant in humanitarian interventions but in all cases where a third party has a choice between imposing an unavoidable harm associated with a defensive intervention on one innocent person or group rather than another. For instance, Helen Frowe has defended the relevance of the beneficiary thesis in wars of self-defense, suggesting that combatants must choose tactics that expose their own noncombatants to collateral harm rather than the noncombatants on the unjust side since the former group stands to benefit from their defensive action and not the latter.[4] For reasons of space, I will not consider this extension of the beneficiary thesis here.

In the following two sections I clarify how I understand the beneficiary thesis and contrast it with other justifications of harm imposition. In the fourth section,

[2] Thomas Hurka, "Proportionality in the Morality of War," *Philosophy and Public Affairs* 33, no. 1 (2005): 62; Jeff McMahan, "Humanitarian Intervention, Consent, and Proportionality," in *Ethics and Humanity: Themes from the Philosophy of Jonathan Glover*, ed. N. Ann Davis, Richard Keshen, and Jeff McMahan (New York: Oxford University Press, 2009), 44–74, and "The Just Distribution of Harm Between Combatants and Noncombatants," *Philosophy and Public Affairs* 38, no. 4 (2010): 342–379; Gerhard Øverland, "Contractual Killing," *Ethics* 115, no. 4 (2005): 692–720, and "High-Fliers: Who Should Bear the Risk of Humanitarian Intervention?" in *New Wars and New Soldiers: Military Ethics in the Contemporary World*, ed. Paolo Tripodi and Jessica Wolfendale (Farnham, UK: Ashgate, 2011a), 69–86. Helen Frowe, *Defensive Killing: An Essay on War and Self-Defense* (Oxford: Oxford University Press, 2014), 146–147; and Kai Draper, *War and Individual Rights: The Foundations of Just War Theory* (New York: Oxford University Press, 2015), 160–165, have endorsed similar ideas. As far as I can tell, Frowe and Draper offer no substantial modifications to the view offered by Øverland and McMahan. For that reason, I will focus on Øverland and McMahan in this chapter.

[3] The terms are McMahan's. Øverland uses the terms *to-be-liberated-civilians* and *third parties* to cover the same groups.

[4] Frowe, *Defensive Killing*, 147; McMahan, "Just Distribution of Harm," 364.

I review how the beneficiary thesis interacts with the thesis according to which there is a moral asymmetry between innocent threats and their victims. In this section, I argue that the two views are conceptually related since both are views that allow brute bad luck to determine a person's moral status. At the same time the two views also counterbalance each other: because the potential victim of an innocent threat is also the beneficiary of a defensive act against the threatener, the potential victim will have reduced immunity to the harm associated with this act. In the fifth section, I point out that an expected beneficiary could be defined either relative to a given epistemic perspective or relative to objective probabilities and that either alternative invites serious objections. In the sixth and final section I argue that the beneficiary thesis cannot be applied to war since noncombatants in war will not be expected beneficiaries of risk of collateral harm at the time this risk is imposed. Attempts at accommodating this objection by arguing that such noncombatants nevertheless have reduced immunity because they were expected beneficiaries when the intervention strategy was devised at the outset of the war fail because there is no reason to privilege this time to fix their status as expected beneficiaries. Once the beneficiary thesis is applied to strategies rather than discrete acts, I argue that there is no convincing argument for why this strategy should be individuated at the level of a single war. Since everyone is at risk of becoming exposed to wrongful threats at some point or another in our lives, the strategy we have most reason to accept is a higher-order strategy which minimizes unavoidable harm associated with rescue interventions in general, rather than a lower-level strategy specified on a war-by-war basis.

Between Liability and Lesser Evil

Before evaluating the beneficiary thesis, it is worth clarifying the notion of immunity and how it relates to the justifications for the infliction of nonconsensual harm. In spite of voluminous literature addressing the factors which govern liability to harm, less attention has been devoted to the notion of immunity to harm. One reason for this may be that most authors tie the concept of immunity directly to the concept of rights, either by understanding rights as immunities or by understanding rights as conferring immunities. On this reading, immunity is a statement about a person's moral status, where moral status tracks the moral protection conferred to an agent arising from his or her rights.[5] This is the way the concept of *immunity* will be used here.

[5] This is the way McMahan seems to use the term when he writes "Liability and immunity are different sides of the same coin. To be morally immune to attack is just to be not morally liable to attack. Jeff McMahan, "Liability and Collective Identity: A Response to Walzer," *Philosophia* 34 (2006): 15.

One way in which agents can come to lose their immunity to harm is through rights forfeiture. Such agents are, following McMahan's usage of the term, liable to harm. Since liable agents are not immune to be harmed to avert a threat, harming them for this purpose (provided it is necessary and proportionate) does not wrong them. Exactly what it takes to forfeit one's right against harm is controversial, but standardly forfeiture-based liability is justified by reference to morally relevant internal and external facts about an agent. Internal facts are about the agent's mental state while acting (such as knowledge, intention, and beliefs) and external facts are about an agent's place in the local causal architecture, specifically whether he or she has causally contributed or is the causal antecedent of a threat of harm. Whereas internal facts are relevant to whether the agent fulfills the conditions for moral responsibility, external facts inform us about the causal relationship between an agent and a threat which the agent might be liable to be harmed to prevent.

In contrast to justifications that rely on forfeiture, impositions of harm that appeal to lesser-evil considerations do not appeal to facts about the agent on whom the harm is imposed. Lesser-evil justification appeals to the ratio between the harm averted and the harm caused and the mode of agency with which it is inflicted (especially whether it is foreseen or intended). Although the immunity of a person is overridden when harm justified on lesser-evil grounds is imposed, his or her immunity, as a moral matter, remains intact. For example, to say that lesser-evil consideration can justify imposing proportionate collateral damage on noncombatants in war does not imply that victims of collateral harm have lost their immunity to this harm. To have one's immunity to harm overridden is distinct from having one's immunity undermined or lost through forfeiture, which is why victims of lesser-evil justified harm are entitled to compensation, whereas liable individuals standardly are not.[6]

The novelty of the beneficiary thesis is that it relies on a type of justification which does not invoke lesser evil considerations or the agent's rights forfeiture. Unlike lesser-evil considerations, it appeals to facts about the agent on whom the risk of harm is imposed. But unlike the forfeiture view, the beneficiary thesis only invokes external facts about the expected beneficiary's role in the causal architecture, not internal facts about his or her agency or moral responsibility for occupying this role. [7]

[6] Though the extent to which victims of lesser-evil justified harms are justified in defending themselves is a matter of dispute. See Jeff McMahan, "Self-Defense Against Justified Threateners," in *How We Fight: Ethics in War*, ed. Helen Frowe and Gerald Lang (Oxford: Oxford University Press, 2014), 104–138.

[7] One may think that the type of justification the beneficiary thesis provides is fundamentally different from the type that lesser-evil and liability justifications provide since the beneficiary thesis

By relying on this third type of justification, the beneficiary thesis distinguishes between the permissibility of imposing harms on neutral bystanders and expected beneficiaries, even though individuals in neither group have forfeited their rights and even though lesser-evil consideration gives us no reason to favor imposing harm on one group over the other.

In sum, the beneficiary thesis entails a claim that a person's immunity to harm can be weakened, even if this agent has done nothing to forfeit or waive his or her rights against harm. If the beneficiary thesis is correct, it represents a basis for the justification of harm different from the traditional categories of lesser evil and forfeiture. If sound, the beneficiary thesis establishes a moral asymmetry between innocent agents (bystanders and expected beneficiaries) without appealing to their agency in any shape or form.

Motivating the Beneficiary Thesis

The motivation for the beneficiary thesis is easy to see when we consider a single risk-imposing defensive act. Consider the following case.

> Jones is solely responsible for his wrongful attempt to take innocent Smith's life. Defender can intervene to save Smith, but depending on how she angles her shot, she will impose a risk of paralyzing innocent bystander Brown or innocent bystander Black. If Defender refrains from shooting Jones, there is a significant risk that Jones will proceed to kill Brown. The risk that Jones will kill Brown if he is not stopped is greater than the risk that Defender's shot will kill Brown.[8]

According to the beneficiary thesis, Brown is an expected beneficiary of the preventive killing of Jones since the risk it exposes him to is smaller than the risk Jones would otherwise impose on him. This reasoning is then applied to the distribution of collateral harm in the case of war. McMahan invites the reader to imagine a situation where the NATO forces had to choose between two

does not provide a justification for harm imposition full stop but rather that justification for why one person (an expected beneficiary) rather than another (a bystander) should suffer a given amount of harm. But both lesser-evil and liability justifications are also comparative, providing reason for why an impending threat ought to be redistributed. Neither lesser-evil nor liability justification relies on noncomparative desert-based reasons for imposing harm on a person.

[8] All the proponents of the beneficiary thesis motivate their support for it by invoking analogies to individual cases: Frowe, *Defensive Killing*, 147; Draper, *War and Individual Rights*, 162; Øverland, "High-Fliers," 73; McMahan, "Just Distribution of Harm," 360, 361. This case is based on a similar case offered by Draper.

military options that would have been equally effective in reducing the threat to Kosovo Albanians. One option would have imposed collateral harm on Kosovo Albanians, who are expected beneficiaries of the war; the other would impose an equal amount of collateral harm on Greeks or Bulgarians, who are innocent bystanders to the war.

> In such a case involving genuinely innocent bystanders, it may seem wrong to force Greeks or Bulgarians to pay with their lives for the protection of an equal number of Albanians. It might have been permissible to sacrifice innocent bystanders for the sake of the Albanians, but only if that would have involved significantly fewer killings of innocent people than the alternative.[9]

The idea behind the beneficiary thesis is that agents who are already exposed to a prior risk have a reason to accept a new risk associated with a preventive action that seeks to avert the initial risk, as long as the preventive actions reduce the overall risk to those agents. This reason is not shared by neutral bystanders and gives rise to the claim that the "risks of defensive action ought to be borne by those who stand to benefit from the action rather than imposed on uninvolved third parties."[10] Øverland justifies his claim in the same manner, pointing out that expected beneficiaries "have good reason to accept a certain level of risk [associated with a military intervention] if it means getting rid of the government."[11] Both Øverland and McMahan appeal to reasons of self-interest shared by expected beneficiaries of the military intervention but not by neutral bystanders who do not stand to benefit.

The beneficiary thesis does not claim that the expected beneficiaries have consented to being exposed to collateral harm. If it did, it would collapse into a theory of right waiver, and the notion of expected beneficiary would do no actual normative work in the theory.[12] Moreover, even if a theory that relied on actual consent was theoretically sound, it would be wholly unworkable in the context of military intervention since it is unlikely that all expected beneficiaries

[9] McMahan, "Just Distribution of Harm," 375.

[10] McMahan, "Just Distribution of Harm," 361, see also 363.

[11] Øverland, "High-Fliers," 76. Although Øverland invokes this consideration to justify why soldiers have to take on less risk to themselves in humanitarian interventions than in wars of self-defense, the underlying claim remains the same: that the expected beneficiaries' immunity to collateral harm is less than that of individuals who do not stand to benefit from the military action.

[12] Except, perhaps, if the validity of a subject's consent were conditioned on that subject also being an expected beneficiary. If so, expected beneficiary status would be a constraint on a consent-based justification, not an independently justifying factor. Exploring this theoretical avenue, however, will lead me too far astray from the topic of the chapter.

would actually consent to the military intervention and since it would be impossible to transmit this consent to the intervener.[13] Instead, the beneficiary thesis appeals to the *reasons* which make it rational for an expected beneficiary to consent to the risk of collateral harm, whether or not he or she actually consents to this risk or expresses such consent.

Moral Luck Among Innocent Agents

The beneficiary thesis belongs to a family of views according to which one can establish a moral asymmetry between innocent people wholly on account of their place in the local causal architecture. Another member in this family is the view that there is a moral asymmetry between wholly innocent threateners and their victims. A standard case from the literature of a conflict between an innocent threatener and a victim is the following:

> *Ray Gun*: Falling Person is blown by the wind down a well at the bottom of which Victim is trapped. Falling Person will crush Victim to death unless Victim vaporizes her with his ray gun. If he does not vaporize her, Victim will cushion Falling Person's landing, saving her life.[14]

The standard discussion that accompanies this example is whether there is a moral asymmetry between Victim and Falling Person which grants Victim or a third party the permission to kill Falling Person in self-defense. Many authors believe that innocent agents, such as Falling Person, who through no act or fault of their own threaten someone else can permissibly be killed to avert the threat they pose, in whole or in part because the threatener's immunity to harm is weaker than that of the victim.[15] The claim about the weakened immunity of

[13] While the beneficiary thesis does not require actual consent, it is intended to be compatible with attributing moral relevance to actual dissent of the expected beneficiaries, such that third-party intervention to rescue a victim can be deemed impermissible if the victim, or a sufficiently large number of the victim group, refused to be saved by outside interveners. However, Draper also defends the view that it would be permissible to expose an expected beneficiary to a risk of collateral harm, even if he irrationally dissents to this exposure (*War and Individual Rights*, 162).

[14] The case is taken from Frowe, *Defensive Killing*, 22.

[15] Frowe, *Defensive Killing*, 68–69; Victor Tadros, *The Ends of Harm: The Moral Foundations of Criminal Law* (Oxford: Oxford University Press, 2011), 45; Gerhard Øverland, "Moral Taint: On the Transfer of the Implications of Moral Culpability," *Journal of Applied Philosophy* 28, no. 2 (2011b): 124–125. Tadros, Frowe, and Øverland all argue, roughly along the same lines, that the innocent threateners' immunity to harm is weakened or lost because such agents have an enforceable duty to allow themselves to be harmed in order to avert the threat they pose.

the innocent threatener shares with the beneficiary thesis an assumption that moral luck is a legitimate feature of morality. Both the innocent threatener and the expected beneficiary have no responsibility for the situation they are in; they are merely victims of brute bad luck The moral status of both types of agents is altered by factors entirely beyond their control and indeed even beyond their agency. While it is conceptually coherent for friends of moral luck to hold that brute luck affects the moral status of both innocent threateners and expected beneficiaries, it leaves open the question of how a conflict between them ought to be solved, whether one party's bad luck cancels out the other or whether the bad luck of one party is attributed greater moral relevance than the other (and if so, why). Consider a version of the Ray Gun, where a third party can avert Falling Person from killing Victim by seriously harming either of the two. In alleged favor of imposing the preventive harm on the Falling Person is the causal fact that the threatener is threatening to harm the Victim. However, since the beneficiary of a potential defensive act would be the Victim, the beneficiary thesis would indicate that the Victim also has weakened immunity. A virtue of the view that innocent threateners have weakened immunity against harm is that it conforms to the apparently widespread intuitive judgment that there is a moral asymmetry between the innocent threatener and the innocent threatener's victim. Yet once the view is combined with the beneficiary thesis, we are pushed back toward accepting a symmetry between the innocent threat and the victim, given that both would seem to have a weakened immunity to harm.

Those who deny that innocent threateners have weakened immunity against defensive harm just by virtue of their bad brute luck, like McMahan, are faced with both a conceptual and an intuitive problem if they also want to hold on to the beneficiary thesis. To see the conceptual problem, consider how McMahan rejects the idea that the immunity of innocent threateners can be weakened by the mere fact that they pose a threat.

> Although she [the innocent threatener] is causally implicated in the threat to you, that is a wholly external fact about her position in the local causal architecture. It has no more moral significance than the fact that an innocent bystander might, through no fault of her own, occupy a position in the causal architecture that makes your killing the only means by which you could save your own life.[16]

This explanation of the irrelevance of causation to the moral status of the innocent threatener invites the following question: If external facts about one's

[16] Jeff McMahan, "The Ethics of Killing in War," *Ethics* 114, no. 4 (2004): 720.

position in the causal architecture cannot establish a moral asymmetry between innocent threateners and bystanders, how can they establish an asymmetry between expected beneficiaries and bystanders? In virtue of what does one's place in the local causal architecture acquire moral relevance in cases where we compare bystander with beneficiary cases but does not when we compare bystanders with innocent threateners? The intuitive problem is this: if the immunity of innocent threateners is wholly intact and on par with that of a neutral bystander, as McMahan claims, while the immunity of expected beneficiaries is not, then a third party ought to direct the harm associated with a preventive action to Victim and not Falling Person. The view that there's a symmetry between innocent threateners and their victims is normally thought, even by proponents of the symmetry view, to be counterintuitive. The view that there's an asymmetry to the victim's disfavor (on account that he would benefit from the defense, whereas the innocent threatener would not) is presumably even harder to swallow.

Whose Expectations?

Unfortunately, adherents to the beneficiary thesis do not properly spell out how we are to understand the notion of "expected beneficiary." One obvious question is, *Expected by whom?* At first glance, the notion "expected beneficiaries" seems to presuppose the epistemic vantage point of a subject, yet it is not entirely clear which epistemic vantage point is privileged.[17] One option would be to privilege the victim's perspective and define a person as an expected beneficiary of a given risky action if that person believed that the act in question would reduce the overall risk he or she is exposed to. This does not seem like a promising strategy, however, for at least two reasons. Firstly, we can easily imagine cases where a person is reasonably mistaken about whether a given act will benefit him or her or not. If the third-party defender realizes this mistake, he or she clearly cannot justify exposing a person to risk by reference to that person's mistaken belief. Once this constraint is admitted, we have also admitted that the victim's epistemic perspective cannot be what determines his or her status as an expected beneficiary. Secondly, it would severely restrict the beneficiary thesis and make

[17] One could try to avoid this, as Draper does, by referring to "expectable" rather than "expected" beneficiaries (*War and Individual Rights*, 160). But trying to distinguish an expectable from an expected beneficiary runs into the same problem as distinguishing a foreseen consequence from a foreseeable consequence. Expecting, like foreseeing, cannot be given a meaning in the abstract without specifying a subject doing the foreseeing or expecting. What is expectable to one agent might not be expectable to another.

it inapplicable to cases where the victim is unaware that he or she is exposed to a prior risk or is wholly unconscious and unable to form any beliefs. Rather than privileging the victim's epistemic perspective, it may seem more promising to privilege the intervener's epistemic perspective. Some of the adherents to the beneficiary thesis invoke the concept of *intended beneficiary* interchangeably with the concept of *expected beneficiary*.[18] The concept of "intended beneficiary" suggests that it is the intentions of the intervener the beneficiary thesis tracks and, consequently, that the intervener's epistemic perspective is privileged. Understood this way, the concepts of *intended* and *expected* beneficiary invite other objections. The most serious is this: if a person's status as expected beneficiary is determined by the intervener's reasonable belief, a person would have no right to defend himself or herself against an intervener who imposes a grave risk of harm on him or her on the mistaken but epistemically justified assumption that he or she was an expected beneficiary of this intervention. On the conceptual level, it is hard to see how people's immunity to harm can be determined by the intentions or epistemic perspective of others. What determines a person's moral status is presumably facts about this person (whatever they be), not facts about the intentions or epistemic perspective of others.

One response to the problem of choosing which epistemic perspective to privilege is to insist that a person's immunity is reduced only insofar as he or she *actually*, in terms of objective probabilities, stands to benefit from the defenders' action—irrespective of what anyone may believe about this.[19] The notion of objective probabilities, chances, as mind- and perspective-independent features of the world is controversial, largely because it is seen as incompatible with a deterministic universe. As I cannot hope to make any progress on the metaphysical debate over the soundness of objective chances and their compatibility with determinism, I will limit my comment to another complication that arises from relying on the notion of objective probabilities.[20] Even if we grant

[18] McMahan, "Just Distribution of Harm," 366, 373; Draper, *War and Individual Rights*, 160).

[19] McMahan, "Just Distribution of Harm," 360, 363, explicitly formulates his version of the beneficiary thesis in terms of objective probabilities, whereas Draper grants that "the probability that a risk will be realized is always relative to an epistemic situation and so must be subjective in that sense" (*War and Individual Rights*, 99). It's not entirely obvious what Drapers means by this, however, since he also claims that "intended beneficiaries, even the ones who will ultimately be killed, are actually better off (in terms of expectable benefit) at the outset of the war, because, for each individual, the small chance of being killed as a side effect of the liberation effort is more than compensated for by the high likelihood of reaping the benefits of liberation" (p. 160). These formulations seem to presuppose the existence of objective probabilities since reduction in the merely subjectively ascribed probability that the beneficiary will be killed presumably cannot be a compensation for anything.

[20] For a discussion on whether objective chance are compatible with a deterministic world, see Jonathan Schaffer, "Deterministic Chance?" *British Journal for the Philosophy of Science* 58, no. 2 (2007): 113–140.

that the expected beneficiaries are defined relative to objective probabilities, actual verdicts about expected benefits will always be made by epistemically limited agents. As such, the theory owes us an explanation of how we should address the possibility of reasonable mistakes. There are essentially two types of reasonable mistakes a third-party intervener can make: he or she can mistake expected beneficiaries for neutral bystanders—call this group *merely apparent bystanders*—and mistake neutral bystanders for expected beneficiaries—call this group *merely apparent beneficiaries*. To illustrate the case of a merely apparent bystander, consider the case introduced at the beginning of the section "Motivating the Beneficiary Thesis." As described, Defender's intervention to stop Jones is expected to benefit both Smith and Brown. We may easily imagine, however, that unbeknown to Defender, Jones also harbors the undisclosed but clear intention to kill Black. In this scenario, Black is merely an apparent bystander. The problem of merely apparent bystanders also applies in war. A successful reversal for armed aggression might deter the same aggressor from going to war again later or deter other aggressors. Consider the Second World War: if German aggression had been stopped and reversed when Germany first annexed Sudetenland, it would at the time have been reasonable to believe that expected beneficiaries primarily would have been the Czechoslovakian inhabitants facing immediate threat of occupation. The much larger threat that the German regime posed to Europe as evidenced by the later actual turn of events was hardly recognized by anyone (thus the weak response to Germany's first aggressive moves). The fact that the reduction in risk to a great number of people that would have resulted from an early reversal of German aggression would be spread across time and space does not undermine the fact that these benefits would in fact be highly significant. If allied forces had decided to defeat the German army in 1938, thereby preventing the war from escalating, Jews, who later turned out to be among the primary victims of the ensuing war, might have appeared at the time as neutral bystanders. Yet they would in fact be expected beneficiaries of such a war and, by the light of the beneficiary thesis, therefore have weakened immunity to collateral harm of such a war. If the notion of expected beneficiaries relies on objective and not epistemic probabilities, causally and temporally remote beneficiaries cannot be excluded from the group of expected beneficiaries just because they may *appear* as neutral bystanders. A defender of the beneficiary thesis may argue that the problem of merely apparent bystanders is unproblematic since it leads us to treat people as if their immunity to harm is higher than what their actual but unforeseeable status as expected beneficiaries would imply. Yet this type of move is not available to the adherents of the beneficiary thesis since the consequence of this mistake would be that genuine bystanders were made to bear the risk that by the light of the beneficiary thesis should have been borne by the merely apparent bystanders. To see this, imagine a third party who imposes an equal amount of collateral risk on two individuals on account of his or her reasonable but mistaken belief that both are neutral bystanders. If only one is in fact a neutral bystander, whereas the other is a merely apparent bystander, and the actual neutral bystander somehow is aware of this mistake, then the beneficiary thesis owes us a story as to what the actual bystander may do to avoid being exposed to a risk that ought to have been shifted toward the merely apparent bystander.

This second problem, that of mistaking a neutral bystander for an expected beneficiary is more severe. Most accounts of liability to lethal harm hold that agents can themselves become liable when they impose a risk of harm on another person on the mistaken assumption that this person is liable to that risk of harm. On McMahan's own account of liability to defensive harm, for instance, a person who innocently mistakes a merely apparent aggressor for an actual aggressor and then engages in mistaken self-defense becomes liable to defensive harm from the apparent aggressor or a third party as a means of averting the threat from the innocently mistaken defender.[21] Does a third-party defender who mistakes a bystander for an expected beneficiary become liable just like he or she would if he or she mistook the same person for an aggressor? If reasonably mistaken third-party defenders are deemed liable, the beneficiary thesis will dramatically sanction defenders for unavoidable and blameless mistakes they occasionally will make in the course of trying to follow the beneficiary thesis.

Any moral theory of defensive harm that in part relies on objective probabilities must confront some version of the dilemma described above. Yet the dilemma is more pressing for the beneficiary thesis, at least if the notion of expected beneficiary is exclusively defined in terms of probabilities. Moreover, unlike agents who act in self-defense, third-party defenders act in accordance with a moral duty or in a supererogatory manner. Stripping agents who act in line with a moral duty, or beyond the call of duty, of immunity to harm whenever their reasonable beliefs turns out false seems unduly harsh. At the very minimum, we are owed an account by the proponents of the beneficiary thesis of how this implication of the thesis can be justified or how it can be avoided. It seems to me the only way this implication can be avoided is to revert to the notion of subjective probabilities, but this would invite the objections raised at the beginning of this section back in.

[21] For others who share this view, see Michael Otsuka, "Killing the Innocent in Self-Defense," *Philosophy and Public Affairs* 23, no. 1 (1994): 74–94; Jonathan Quong, "Liability to Defensive Harm," *Philosophy and Public Affairs* 40, no. 1 (2012): 45–771; Saba Bazargan, "Complicitous Liability in War," *Philosophical Studies* 165, no. 1 (2013): 177–195; and Victor Tadros, "Orwell's Battle with Brittain: Vicarious Liability for Unjust Aggression," *Philosophy and Public Affairs* 42, no. 1 (2014): 42–77.

Act-Relative and Strategy-Relative Expected Beneficiaries

Before focusing the application of the beneficiary thesis on the context of war, it is necessary to distinguish more clearly between two ways of understanding the notion of *expected beneficiary*. The first way is relative to a single defensive act, as illustrated by the example with Smith, Jones, Brown, and Black. On this understanding, a person is an expected beneficiary of an act if this act diminishes the overall expected risk of harm to that person. The other way the notion of expected beneficiary can be understood is relative to an overall strategy. On this understanding, a person is an expected beneficiary if the strategy will reduce the overall expected risk of harm to this person. As McMahan points out, if the beneficiary thesis could only be applied in contexts where noncombatants were expected beneficiaries in the act-relative sense, the thesis would have little purchase in war:

> Suppose that at the time a decision has to be made about whether to fight a war in defense of a group of non-combatants, all those non-combatants are expected beneficiaries of the war, even if the war will be fought in a way that will expose them to new risks. They all have reason, at that time, to want the war to be fought. They know that the strategy will later require acts that will convert some of them from expected beneficiaries into expected or actual victims. They also know that if it were a constraint on the implementation of the strategy that no individual act of war could be done unless all those non-combatants it would expose to risk would be expected beneficiaries [in the act-relative sense] of it, it would be impossible to implement the strategy.[22]

As McMahan points out in this quote, individual acts of war often expose noncombatants to extremely high degrees of risk, turning those noncombatants into expected victims rather than expected beneficiaries. The challenge is to justify how someone's prior status as an expected beneficiary can justify imposing a risk of harm on that person, after that person has become an expected victim of that act. This challenge is met, according to McMahan, by switching to the strategy-relative notion of expected beneficiary: "what is relevant to the justification of the strategy is whether those whom it will expose to risk are expected beneficiaries when it is adopted, rather than later during its implementation"

[22] McMahan, "Just Distribution of Harm," 363.

(p. 363). The quote makes clear that the notion of expected beneficiary, as it is applies in war, is to be defined relative to a strategy. But the strategy-relative notion of expected beneficiary invites new objections. To see this, let's call the time at which we decide the strategy for how collateral harm should be distributed *t0* and the times when the subsequent risk is imposed through discrete acts (and sometimes materialized) *t1, t2,* etc. McMahan suggest that *t0* should be made to overlap with the time when "a decision has to be made" about going to war. The problem with this approach can be illustrated by the following example. Suppose that minority group A is among the several minority groups expected to benefit from an intervention at time *t0,* the time when the decision to go to war is undertaken. Suppose that after some years, due to changing war dynamics, they are no longer expected beneficiaries of a continuation of the war but that repressed minority group B, which initially appeared to be made up of neutral bystanders of the war, now emerges as being made up of expected beneficiaries. What reason do we have to keep treating minority group A as expected beneficiaries and group B as neutral bystanders, even after it is apparent that their statuses have been reversed? To fix their moral immunity to collateral harm by their status as expected beneficiaries or neutral bystanders at the very beginning of the war and not adjust these categories as probabilities change seems difficult to defend. McMahan argues that fixing the label "expected beneficiary" at the outset of the war is justified because "they [those for whom the intervention is conducted] all have reason, at that time, to want the war to be fought." The reasons McMahan refers to are based on the probabilities that apply at that time, but these probabilities change over time; and when the probabilities change, so do the reasons. It is difficult to see how past reasons that no longer apply can be binding on a person absent that person's consent. Given that the beneficiary thesis does not rely on consent-based justifications, it seems odd to claim that the probabilities that gave an individual a reason at a previous point in time can be relevant to that person's moral status at a later point, when those probabilities have changed. It might be thought that this problem can be avoided by pushing *t0* forward in time, reassessing the category of expected beneficiaries continually as the war progresses, essentially shrinking the temporal distance between *t0* and the subsequent individual acts of war. But once we engage in this adjustment, we realize that there is no non-arbitrary stopping point until we have reached a point where soldiers assess the expected beneficiaries of each of their discrete actions. This would collapse the distinction between act-relative and strategy-relative beneficiaries and constrain the beneficiary thesis, as McMahan observes, in a way that would make it inapplicable to war.

The arbitrariness of fixing the strategy-relative notion of expected beneficiaries at the outset of the war can be illustrated in another way. Consider what an adherent of the beneficiary thesis would answer someone who is exposed to a high risk of collateral harm on account of his or her prior status as a strategy-relative expected beneficiary at the outbreak of the war. We can imagine this person complaining, asking what justifies exposing him or her, rather than a neutral bystander, to a risk of collateral harm, when it is clear that he or she has become an expected victim of this act. The response the adherent of the beneficiary thesis gives is that he or she had reasons to accept the strategy of which this action is a part at the outbreak of the war, before it became clear he or she would become an expected victim of the strategy. But if this is a legitimate answer to strategy-relative expected beneficiaries, then presumably we could say the same to neutral bystanders. Imagine a neutral bystander complaining about being exposed to a high risk of collateral harm when this risk could, at a small increase, be shifted to a strategy-relative expected beneficiary of the intervention. To him or her we could also say that he or she, at an earlier point in time, before it became clear who would become in need of humanitarian intervention, had reasons to accept a strategy that distributes collateral harm in a way that strictly minimizes collateral harm irrespective of the noncombatants' status as expected beneficiary or neutral bystander relative to that specific intervention as this generalized strategy would reduce the overall risk he or she was exposed to at that time. Perhaps it may be thought that the strategy-relative notion of expected beneficiary can be made sense of through the idea of risk pooling. Expected beneficiaries at the outset of the war have reason to pool their risk and accept a strategy that lowers the risk that they all face at that point. But this reply invites the same objection. Once we appeal to the reasons people have for pooling involuntarily and morally arbitrary risk of harm, it does not seem optimal to pool risks at the level of specific wars. Given that we are all at risk of accidental or wrongful harm at some point or another in our lives, the risk-pooling strategy would seem to suggest that we pool all such risks at a general level and adopt a strategy for averting such risk in a manner which minimizes overall risk of harm to innocents.

In sum, even if we, contrary to the argument in the previous sections, accept the beneficiary thesis with respect to discrete risk-imposing defensive acts, we should reject the attempt at applying the thesis to arbitrarily individuated risk-imposing strategies. Once we appeal to agents' interests in accepting general strategies that reduce the overall risk those agents are exposed to, we need a criterion by which to identify when such reasons should be consulted. The beneficiary thesis fails to provide any justification for why we should privilege the reasons that apply to agents at the onset of a specific humanitarian intervention. Once this failure is recognized, the moral relevance of the distinction between strategy-relative beneficiaries and strategy-relative bystanders individuated on a war-by-war basis disappears.

Acknowledgment

I am very grateful to the Stockholm Centre for the Ethics of War and Peace, which awarded me a Summer Fellowship in June 2016, enabling me to present this work and develop the arguments in this chapter. I also thank the participants at the CELPA seminar in Warwick for helpful comments to previous version of this chapter.

References

Bazargan, Saba. "Complicitous Liability in War." *Philosophical Studies* 165, no. 1 (2013): 177–195.

Draper, Kai. *War and Individual Rights: The Foundations of Just War Theory*. New York: Oxford University Press, 2015.

Frowe, Helen. *Defensive Killing: An Essay on War and Self-Defense*. Oxford: Oxford University Press, 2014.

Hurka, Thomas. "Proportionality in the Morality of War." *Philosophy and Public Affairs* 33, no. 1 (2005): 34–66.

McMahan, Jeff. "The Ethics of Killing in War." *Ethics* 114, no. 4 (2004): 693–733.

McMahan, Jeff. "Liability and Collective Identity: A Response to Walzer." *Philosophia* 34 (2006): 13–17.

McMahan, Jeff. "Humanitarian Intervention, Consent, and Proportionality." In *Ethics and Humanity: Themes from the Philosophy of Jonathan Glover*, edited by N. Ann Davis, Richard Keshen, and Jeff McMahan, 44–74. New York: Oxford University Press, 2009.

McMahan, Jeff. "The Just Distribution of Harm Between Combatants and Noncombatants." *Philosophy and Public Affairs* 38, no. 4 (2010): 342–379.

McMahan, Jeff. "Self-Defense Against Justified Threateners." In *How We Fight: Ethics in War*, edited by Helen Frowe and Gerald Lang, 104–138. Oxford: Oxford University Press, 2014.

Otsuka, Michael. "Killing the Innocent in Self-Defense." *Philosophy and Public Affairs* 23, no. 1 (1994): 74–94.

Øverland, Gerhard. "Contractual Killing." *Ethics* 115, no. 4 (2005): 692–720.

Øverland, Gerhard. "High-Fliers: Who Should Bear the Risk of Humanitarian Intervention?" In *New Wars and New Soldiers: Military Ethics in the Contemporary World*, edited by Paolo Tripodi and Jessica Wolfendale, 69–86. Farnham, UK: Ashgate, 2011a.

Øverland, Gerhard. "Moral Taint: On the Transfer of the Implications of Moral Culpability." *Journal of Applied Philosophy* 28, no. 2 (2011b): 122–136.

Quong, Jonathan. "Liability to Defensive Harm." *Philosophy and Public Affairs* 40, no. 1 (2012): 45–77.

Schaffer, J. "Deterministic Chance?" *British Journal for the Philosophy of Science* 58, no. 2 (2007): 113–140.

Tadros, Victor. *The Ends of Harm: The Moral Foundations of Criminal Law*. Oxford: Oxford University Press, 2011.

Tadros, Victor. "Orwell's Battle with Brittain: Vicarious Liability for Unjust Aggression." *Philosophy and Public Affairs* 42, no. 1 (2014): 42–77.

10

Legalism, Justice, and the War on Terrorism

LIONEL K. MCPHERSON

Let's start with a blunt contention: neither the ethics nor the laws of war take noncombatant casualties seriously enough. This is not to deny that the standard norms offer some guidance: namely, they rule out intentionally targeting ordinary noncombatants. The requirement of discrimination holds that combatants must restrict their attacks to legitimate targets; its corollary is the so-called noncombatant immunity principle, which represents a (limited) prohibition on deliberate use of force against noncombatants. The other rule focused on protecting noncombatants is the requirement of proportionality, according to which the military utility of legitimate attacks in war must outweigh the harms done to noncombatants (and perhaps to combatants).

The noncombatant immunity principle is supposed to be critical in morally and legally distinguishing terrorism from justified conventional warfare. I have argued elsewhere that this dominant view is in tension with "the brute reality of war for noncombatants."[1] Typically in war, there are extensive noncombatant deaths; many of them cannot be construed as merely accidental since they are foreseeable, likely, and avoidable; and the margin of noncombatant to combatant deaths has only grown as weapons technology has become more sophisticated. I find that the noncombatant immunity principle overly relies on the notion that whether there is intention to harm noncombatants makes an essential moral difference. But I will not be pressing a controversial moral comparison of terrorism and conventional warfare.

My central aim here is to caution against just war legalism, as I call it, whereby the standard norms permit many noncombatants to be harmed routinely in the

[1] Lionel K. McPherson, "Is Terrorism Distinctively Wrong?" *Ethics* 117 (2007): 529. See also Virginia Held, *How Terrorism Is Wrong* (New York: Oxford University Press, 2008), 71–90.

course of military actions. The pragmatic question will be this: *How can a military power, such as the United States, expect to win sympathy among foreign populations that are a home to insurgents or terrorists?* Plausible answers are not to be found mainly in technocratic reconstruction schemes, much less in esoteric psychological operations (i.e., PSYOP). The key lies in certain existential truths: in general, people deeply value their own lives and the lives of persons for whom they have special concern, such as family, friends, and fellow members of their national or religious group; they are offended by practices betraying a sense that their lives somehow count for less than those of members of other groups; and they have reasonable enough moral sensibilities about what counts as merely accidental as compared to reckless, negligent, or callous harm to them as ordinary noncombatants. I will argue that the standard norms of conduct in war do not adequately reflect these existential truths, the last most explicitly.

"Hearts and Minds"

Political and military leaders have long understood the need to build local sympathy for war or counterinsurgency efforts amid foreign populations. For example, President Lyndon Johnson famously declared, "So we must be ready to fight in Vietnam, but the ultimate victory will depend upon the hearts and the minds of the people who actually live out there. By helping to bring them hope and electricity you are also striking a very important blow for the cause of freedom throughout the world."[2] Johnson's words and subsequent approach to the Vietnam War illustrate the conviction that intensifying a war at the cost of greater noncombatant casualties can be compatible with also trying to "pacify" an unsympathetic population through "civil affairs" programs. A similar conviction persists to this day. As a cursory survey of literature on US "hearts and minds" strategy shows, there is a curious lack of attention paid to the issue of harm to noncombatants.

Consider a state-of-the-art "economic theory of insurgency":

> The consensus among scholars and practitioners on how to most effectively conduct such conflicts [e.g., Iraq and Afghanistan] is reflected in the U.S. Army's counterinsurgency doctrine. This doctrine . . . places a heavy emphasis on influencing "human factors," for example, the

[2] Lyndon B. Johnson, "Remarks at a Dinner Meeting of the Texas Electric Cooperatives, Inc." (speech, Washington Hotel, Washington, DC, May 4, 1965). Gerhard Peters and John T. Woolley, The American Presidency Project, accessed February 1, 2016, http://www.presidency.ucsb.edu/ws/?pid=26942.

> populations' tolerance for insurgent activities, by combining benign measures such as economic reconstruction with carefully targeted strikes against violent actors.
>
> While this combined approach makes intuitive sense, existing discussions of it are not grounded in a coherent social scientific theory of insurgency . . . . Some argue that reconstruction addresses grievances; others claim that reconstruction raises the opportunity cost of rebellion for potential recruits by improving local labor market opportunities; still others view reconstruction as a method of buttressing allies . . . . [W]e develop a fourth approach: modeling insurgency as a three-way interaction between rebels seeking political change through violence, a [foreign or foreign-sponsored] government trying to minimize violence through some combination of service provision and hard counterinsurgency, and civilians deciding whether or not to share information about insurgents with government forces.[3]

Evidently missing from the Army's counterinsurgency doctrine and scholarly variations of it is an emphasis on a civilian population's "tolerance" for noncombatant casualties due to "hard" counterinsurgency.

We might hope that psychologists would be better attuned to "human factors." In the early days of the wars in Iraq and Afghanistan, the American Psychological Association published this news:

> The military has increasingly turned to psychological operations (PSYOP) during wartime to try to influence [foreign] civilians' and troops' emotions, motives and behaviors through carefully planned persuasion campaigns. The key to success in these campaigns, PSYOP experts say, is tapping into social psychology research, such as the literature on learning, motivation, cognition, culture and persuasion . . . .
>
> To effectively persuade citizens to change their political allegiances, lay down their arms and the like, the military must target their vulnerabilities and susceptibilities, [Lt. Col. R. Scott] Rodgers notes. That's why many PSYOP messages contain an "if–then" approach. In the war with Iraq, one of the leaflets dropped illustrates a coalition plane destroying an Iraqi tank with a caption in Arabic warning: "Take an offensive posture, and you will be destroyed." Another photo showed

[3] Eli Berman, Jacob N. Shapiro, and Joseph H. Felter, "Can Hearts and Minds Be Bought? The Economics of Counterinsurgency in Iraq," *Journal of Political Economy* 119 (2011): 768.

> the Iraqi tank intact and read: "Do not take an offensive posture, and you will not be destroyed."[4]

Of course, "citizens" include noncombatants. Broadly threatening them with harm, under the guise of targeting combatants, is not a promising approach to winning their sympathy. But the American Psychological Association's advocacy of violent intimidation was not an anomaly (attached to the article is the statement "APA's Public Policy Office advocates on Capitol Hill for all psychological research programs within the Department of Defense").[5] *The Economist* reports,

> APA psychologists did indeed work with officials from the Defense Department and the CIA to facilitate the torture of detainees [in the War on Terror]. This involved issuing loose ethical guidelines that endorsed existing DoD interrogation policies and permitted psychologists to participate at Guantanamo Bay and elsewhere—unlike their colleagues in the field of psychiatry, who refused to back the government's evolving interrogation tactics. Though the APA's policies adhered to US law, they violated medical ethics.[6]

The use of torture that is an open secret cannot be expected to win local sympathy, either—especially when the torture's victims are known to include ordinary noncombatants caught in the dragnet.[7]

Another obstacle to effective "hearts and minds" strategy is resistance to buy-in from the military. In a recent example, the United States sent "human terrain teams" to Iraq and Afghanistan as part of the "Human Terrain System" (HTS) military program. The stated goal of HTS was to use social science experts, especially anthropologists, to "recruit, train, deploy, and support an embedded . . . sociocultural capability; conduct . . . sociocultural research and analysis; develop and maintain a sociocultural knowledge base to support operational decision making, enhance operational effectiveness, and preserve and share

[4] Melissa Dittmann, "Operation Hearts and Minds: Psychological Operations Are Becoming a Regular Part of Military Strategy," *Monitor on Psychology* 34 (2003): 32, accessed February 1, 2016, http://www.apa.org/monitor/jun03/operation.aspx.

[5] Dittmann, "Operation Hearts and Minds."

[6] E.W., "Terror, Torture and Psychology: How America's Psychologists Ended Up Endorsing Torture," *Economist*, July 28, 2015, accessed February 3, 2016, http://www.economist.com/blogs/democracyinamerica/2015/07/terror-torture-and-psychology.

[7] See, for example, David Leigh, James Ball, Ian Cobain, and Jason Burke, "Guantanamo Leaks Lift Lid on World's Most Controversial Prison," *Guardian*, April 24, 2011, accessed February 4, 2016, http://www.theguardian.com/world/2011/apr/25/guantanamo-files-lift-lid-prison.

sociocultural institutional knowledge."[8] Military leaders in the field were wary. The following perspective, for instance, comes from "a former brigade commander" with "a social science advanced degree" and "well versed with . . . counterinsurgency doctrine," who "was also a strong advocate of night raids . . . in which Special Forces and other specialized combat units enter Afghan villages to capture or kill [suspected] Taliban or other anti-government forces":

> If [human terrain teams] accepted that we are going to do night raids, then they could give useful advice on how to mitigate some of the adverse effects. They might say "Here is how you follow up. Here is how you make them less contentious . . . . Show respect to the elders. If you did damage, pay restitution . . . . "
>
> But you have to remember this: due to our raids, we dropped the average age of insurgent leaders from 34 to 26 . . . . That's a real plus for our side. And I think the population appreciates the increased security that is provided.
>
> [Interviewer] So, at least in this case, there is no significant role for HTS?
>
> Only if they accept that we are going to do night raids.[9]

Entertaining the notion that Afghan civilians were on balance appreciative beneficiaries of night raids almost requires discounting noncombatant deaths. In reality,

> U.S. Special Operations Forces (SOF) killed well over 1,500 civilians in night raids in less than 10 months in 2010 and early 2011, analysis of official statistics on the raids released by the U.S.-NATO command reveals.
>
> That number would make U.S. night raids by far the largest cause of civilian casualties in the war in Afghanistan. [T]he U.N. Assistance Mission in Afghanistan . . . had said the use of Improvised Explosive

[8] Sharon R. Hamilton, "HTS Director's Message," *Military Intelligence Professional Bulletin* 37 (2011): inside front cover, accessed February 3, 2016, http://fas.org/irp/agency/army/mipb/2011_04.pdf. The HTS program, which started in 2007, was quietly ended in 2014 amid protest over professional ethics by social scientists as well as a host of problems with the program itself; see, for example, Ryan Evans, "The Seven Deadly Sins of the Human Terrain System: An Insider's Perspective," *Geopoliticus: The FPRI Blog*, July 13, 2015, accessed February 3, 2016, http://www.fpri.org/geopoliticus/2015/07/seven-deadly-sins-human-terrain-system-insiders-perspective.

[9] Paul Joseph, *"Soft" Counterinsurgency: Human Terrain Teams and US Military Strategy in Iraq and Afghanistan* (New York: Palgrave Macmillan, 2014), 88–89.

> Devices (IEDs) by insurgents was the leading cause of civilian deaths, with 904 . . . .
>
> [T]he total number of alleged insurgents killed in the raids was 2,844 . . . .
>
> [A] minimum number of 1,588 people . . . were killed in the raids even though they weren't targeted.
>
> Not every one of the untargeted individuals killed in night raids was a noncombatant civilian. But the socio-cultural and physical setting of the raids guarantees that the percentage of civilians in that total is extremely high.[10]

With the United States as a case study, a broad conclusion to draw is that civil pacification efforts often have given way to conventional warfare or "hard" counterinsurgency that routinely subjects ordinary noncombatants to violence. The United States operates the world's most sophisticated military, with by far the world's largest military expenditures, and has the world's greatest university system (from which to draw psychologists and anthropologists). With all of these resources at its disposal, this country presumably is in the most favorable position to field effective counterinsurgency operations; and if recent results represent its best practices, that is further reason to be pessimistic about civil pacification. Extensive noncombatant deaths, caused intentionally or not, are an affront to the existential truths I earlier cited. The issue is not merely that people prefer not to be threatened or harmed. There is a pressing question as to whether the standard norms of conduct in war run afoul of moral sensibilities—particularly from the perspective of people in populations made vulnerable to noncombatant casualties the norms would permit. The letter of the law is cold comfort.

I have argued elsewhere that the standard norms of conduct in war are not morally sound.[11] Yet my treatment of noncombatant casualties here ultimately does not depend on controversial, revisionist views about the morality of war. Present purposes call only for showing why, concerning noncombatants, revisionist views resonate with moral sensibilities that can be rooted in a global common sense. Proponents of the roughly standard theory of the just war have reason to care about these sensibilities, which call attention to how just war legalism can make a moral mockery of the standard norms. Moreover, the trumpeted goal of military powers to win hearts and minds in unsympathetic populations cannot

[10] Gareth Porter, "ISAF Data Show Night Raids Killed over 1,500 Afghan Civilians," *Inter Press Service*, November 2, 2011, accessed February 3, 2016, http://www.ipsnews.net/2011/11/isaf-data-show-night-raids-killed-over-1500-afghan-civilians/.

[11] See Lionel K. McPherson, "Innocence and Responsibility in War," *Canadian Journal of Philosophy* 34 (2004): 485–506.

be done with much prospect of success when perhaps technically legal—or, as I will put it, "legalistic"—military actions kill or maim many ordinary noncombatants in those populations. Prudential, if not expressly moral, considerations are reason enough to do better.

Doubts About Standard Noncombatant Immunity and Proportionality

Around the turn of the new millennium, a body of thought known as "revisionist just war theory" began to take shape.[12] Revisionists have pushed back against the standard view that the principles governing just cause for war (*jus ad bellum*) and just conduct in war (*jus in bello*) are strictly "independent." As Michael Walzer elaborates the doctrine of independence, "It is perfectly possible for a just war to be fought unjustly and for an unjust war to be fought in strict accordance with the rules," even as he acknowledges that "this independence . . . is nevertheless puzzling."[13] The puzzle is partly generated by eliding a third possibility: although an unjust war can of course be fought according to the rules recognized in the laws of war, this does not entail that morality permits citizens to fight in the service of an unjust war. What law permits and what morality permits can come apart, which is not unique to the domain of war. For example, while the Fugitive Slave Act legally required that escaped slaves be returned to their "masters," chattel slavery never had serious moral standing.

The laws of war are far from morally akin to the likes of the Fugitive Slave Act. Just war theorists of any type believe that war can be properly subject to ethical limits. Norms of conduct in war have a practical, morally salient rationale: they impose actionable constraints on who can be legitimately attacked given the reality of a war already underway; and these constraints are supposed to help protect noncombatants and reduce gratuitous harms to combatants. Revisionists are not generally committed to the view that the laws of war must be thoroughly modified so as to correspond with morality's requirements. Jeff McMahan succinctly makes the point: "It is, indeed, entirely clear that the laws of war must diverge significantly from the deep morality of war . . . . Perhaps most obviously, the fact that most combatants believe that their cause is just means that the laws of war

[12] See, for example, Jeff McMahan, "Innocence, Self-Defense and Killing in War," *Journal of Political Philosophy* 2 (1994): 193–221, and "The Ethics of Killing in War," *Ethics* 114 (2004): 693–733; Igor Primoratz, "Michael Walzer's Just War Theory: Some Issues of Responsibility," *Ethical Theory and Moral Practice* 5 (2002): 221–243; and McPherson, "Innocence and Responsibility in War."

[13] Michael Walzer, *Just and Unjust Wars*, 3rd ed. (New York: Basic Books, 1977), 21.

must be neutral [in practice] between just combatants and unjust combatants [re *jus ad bellum*]."[14] This point primarily concerns the doctrine of battlefield equality—also known more tendentiously as "the doctrine of the moral equality of combatants"—according to which combatants have an equal right to fight and kill. The doctrine of independence paves the way for the doctrine of battlefield equality. I would argue, contrary to these doctrines, that fighting in the service of an unjust war changes the moral calculus of foreseeably inflicting harms on noncombatants. To avoid this complication for present purposes, I proceed on the assumption that combatants are fighting in the service of a just war.

My focus is on two *in bello* rules: the noncombatant immunity principle and the requirement of proportionality, which are recognized in international law. Article 51(2) of the 1977 Geneva Protocol I states, "The civilian population as such, as well as individual civilians, shall not be the object of attack." This represents the noncombatant immunity principle. Article 51(5)(b) prohibits "an attack [of the type] which may be expected to cause incidental loss of civilian life, injury to civilians, damage to civilian objects, or a combination thereof, which would be excessive in relation to the concrete and direct military advantage anticipated."[15] This represents the proportionality requirement. Whether separately or together, I suggest, these rules do not offer nearly enough protection to noncombatants.

The noncombatant immunity principle can be more accurately characterized as the *limited* noncombatant immunity principle (LNI). As I have observed elsewhere, "Noncombatants, according to LNI, rightfully are immune from deliberate use of force against them. They are not broadly immune from use of force through legitimate acts of war that can be expected to harm them."[16] The proportionality requirement is also in effect more modest than specified. As one commentator observes,

> In the final analysis, it appears that the interpretation by the United States and its allies of their legal obligations concerning the prevention of collateral casualties and the concept of proportionality comprehends prohibiting only two types of attacks: first, those that intentionally target civilians; and second, those that involve negligent behavior in ascertaining the nature of a target or the conduct of the attack itself.[17]

[14] McMahan, "Ethics of Killing in War," 730.

[15] Adam Roberts and Richard Guelff, eds., *Documents on the Laws of War*, 3rd ed. (Oxford: Oxford University Press, 2000), 448–449.

[16] McPherson, "Is Terrorism Distinctively Wrong?" 533.

[17] Judith Gail Gardam, "Proportionality and Force in International Law," *American Journal of International Law* 87 (1993): 410.

A partial explanation for this proportionality minimalism, which includes recognition of limited noncombatant immunity, is the real difficulty that would be involved in trying to weigh expected harms to innocent civilians and civilian infrastructure against anticipated military advantage. In addition to the issue of incommensurable values, there is a puzzle as to how military advantage in the service of an unjust war could ever be worth the loss of ordinary noncombatant lives. I have proposed a subjective "golden rule test" for how to think about assessing proportionality (plus noncombatant immunity) in particular instances.[18] Before returning to that later, I want to raise doubts about standard noncombatant immunity and proportionality.

The reality of noncombatant deaths through conventional warfare is a moral embarrassment to standard noncombatant immunity. In the 1990s, for example, noncombatants constituted 75% to 90% of war and war-related deaths.[19] The ongoing conflicts in Iraq and Afghanistan yield comparable numbers.[20] Many noncombatants who die are not directly killed by combatants, and many combatants try to fight within the rules. But the basic problem for the noncombatant immunity principle remains: namely, the intentions of users of force cannot carry as much moral weight as commonly believed with respect to noncombatants. The source of this problem is the doctrine of double effect (DDE). As applied by standard just war theory, the DDE can be described as follows:

> [O]ne may never intend to cause an evil, even to achieve a greater good. One may pursue a good end through neutral means, even if foreseeing that this will have evil effects, provided that the evil is proportionate to the good and that there is no better way of achieving the good. . . . [Individual acts of] war that unintentionally harm noncombatants are not necessarily ruled out, since such acts have only military targets. The DDE is applied in a manner internal to the standard theory's account of neutral means of fighting . . . . From this perspective, [*ad bellum*] justice is irrelevant to the conception of a good end and neutral means.[21]

[18] See Lionel K. McPherson, "Excessive Force in War: A 'Golden Rule' Test," *Theoretical Inquiries in Law* 7 (2006): 81–95.

[19] Chris Hedges, *What Every Person Should Know About War* (New York: Free Press, 2003), 7.

[20] See, for example, Iraq Body Count, accessed February 13, 2016, www.iraqbodycount.org, which currently estimates 152,000 to 172,000 civilian deaths, among 242,000 total deaths including combatants, from violence since the 2003 invasion of Iraq.

[21] McPherson, "Is Terrorism Distinctively Wrong?" 534.

This version of the DDE is oddly indifferent to whether individual acts of war would promote the success of an unjust war.[22] Bracketing that, it still goes beyond moral plausibility.

The DDE is helpful in distinguishing plain accidents from morally culpable acts—that is, in distinguishing simple harm-doing, so to speak, from actual wrongdoing. For example, you might be driving soberly and safely when momentarily blinded by glare as a woman crosses the street; your car hits and kills her. We recognize that your causal role in the event does not mean you have acted wrongly: this is a clear case of plain accident. Circumstances were outside the boundaries of your reasonable control. By contrast, circumstances surrounding plain accidents can be very unlike circumstances that lead to noncombatant casualties in war. Second-person scenarios help make the discussion less abstract.

Let's say you believe you are acting within the rules as you fight to protect yourself and your fellow combatants and as you fight to gain military advantage. Often, especially in going after insurgents or terrorists, you know that you or combatants under your command almost certainly will injure or kill noncombatants, perhaps many of them—as the US commander of night raids in Afghanistan knew. This is consistent with your rules of engagement, which seem to be legally compatible with the standard norms of conduct in war. Hard choices have to be made. You may ask how you, whether following or giving orders, could be expected to act otherwise under the circumstances. Your government-designated job is to fight well, and your priority is for your side to win the war.

The challenge is to understand these hard choices in moral and not exclusively legal terms. In the scenario described, noncombatant casualties cannot be construed as plain accidents. Rather, the harms to noncombatants are foreseeable, likely, and avoidable. You, your fellow combatants, and your nation could accept greater personal and collective risk in fighting if you were to undertake a different course (e.g., a limited ground rather than a massive air campaign) or means (e.g., lower-altitude bombing), in the interest of harming far fewer noncombatants on the other side. This obviously would make fighting more difficult and risky for your side. There would be greater concern for noncombatant immunity.

However, you might recall the scholarly counsel of US Lieutenant General James Dubik. He argues in effect that "command responsibility"—according to which "a commander is not only responsible for protecting the rights of [another people's] civilians, but also for protecting the rights of [his or her] soldiers, to

[22] See, for example, Walzer, *Just and Unjust Wars*, 151–156, 39–41; and Brian Orend, *The Morality of War*, 2nd ed. (Peterborough: Broadview Press, 2013), 121–125.

ensure that [his or her soldiers] are only exposed to due risk"—permits shifting a lot of injury and death onto another people's innocent civilians; exercising "due care" for their civilians becomes secondary to a "responsibility to protect his soldiers' rights," predominantly the right to life.[23] In other words, a so-called role obligation might actually require commanders to give priority to the lives of their own citizen-combatants at the expense of another people's ordinary noncombatants. Such a requirement, as we have seen, fits a minimalist interpretation of the proportionality requirement, which includes recognition of limited noncombatant immunity.

Standard just war theory's version of the DDE almost invites a minimalist approach to *in bello* rules. This DDE is not largely passive before ethical dilemmas (e.g., saving a woman's life at the cost of losing the fetus) are referred to it for adjudication. It actively shapes conduct in war by enabling standard noncombatant immunity and proportionality to not support protecting noncombatants as a priority in comparison to narrow military advantage and protecting the lives of a nation's own combatants. Maybe the laws of war cannot be expected to do better than try to extend such limited protection to noncombatants, which is still far better than none. My central aim here does not call for more fully elaborating a revisionist critique.[24] The basic point is that many of the harms routinely done in war to noncombatants cannot plausibly be construed as anything like plain accidents. Ordinary noncombatants would not be unreasonable to think that their lives warrant greater moral consideration than the standard norms require, particularly when these norms are indifferent to *ad bellum* considerations.

In sum, persons are not always morally culpable when they cause unwarranted harm. Accidents or circumstances beyond our reasonable control do happen. Yet when persons could well expect their actions to cause unwarranted harm, any appeal to plain accident goes out the window. In this event, the harmdoer's intentions do not seem to make an essential moral difference to the permissibility of an action. As David Rodin observes,

> one may fail to observe a reasonable standard of care either by possessing a direct intention to cause harm, by possessing an oblique intention to cause harm, or by possessing no intentional attitude toward the harm at all, as when one fails to foresee a harmful consequence of one's action that one could have been reasonably expected to foresee and avoid. Considerations of recklessness and negligence threaten not to

[23] James M. Dubik, "Human Rights, Command Responsibility, and Walzer's Just War Theory," *Philosophy and Public Affairs* 11 (1982): 370.

[24] See McPherson, "Is Terrorism Distinctively Wrong?" 534–539.

> disprove the principle of double effect but rather in certain contexts to render it irrelevant.[25]

To clarify, we can distinguish two issues. First, which I am not pressing here, appeal to double effect is morally implausible when killing in the service of an unjust war since "the good" being sought (namely, unjust victory) is morally indefensible. Second, appeal to double effect when killing in the service of a just war too often extends morally implausible permissions to harm noncombatants since there is an evident lack of due care for their lives. Even if we are skeptical about Rodin's quasi-pacifist view that ordinary noncombatants have a fundamental, overriding right not to have likely, foreseeable, and avoidable harms inflicted on them in war, we can acknowledge that such a view poses a serious challenge to the permissiveness of standard noncombatant immunity and proportionality. What I have characterized as a global common sense is not nearly as permissive.

Justice Grievances over Noncombatant Casualties

More than a few theorists and practitioners might believe that what matters in conduct in war cannot be framed in some morally idealist manner. They might maintain that established laws of war set the limits since these laws supply rules geared to realistic circumstances of war. In broad outline, the laws of war can be seen as having the worthy purpose of making the nature and the extent of political violence less horrific than they otherwise would be and historically have been. I understand and largely share this perspective. Nonetheless, we would make a mistake in not also thinking about conduct in war apart from the limits of legal interpretation—a moral and pragmatic mistake. As an American, the "we" I explicitly have in mind now are citizens of the United States and its allies. We underestimate the importance of the political morality of war at our own peril, given our strategic foreign policy interests as a nation. This political morality often concerns justice grievances.

Many Western observers apparently believe that religious extremism is at the root of terrorism coming from the Muslim world. More progressive observers have emphasized the influence of political repression, underemployment, poverty, et cetera. Presumably, religious extremism and these other factors have all played a role in inciting and sustaining the terrorism that the United States and its allies declared global war on after 9/11. But I would propose that a typical

[25] David Rodin, "Terrorism Without Intention," *Ethics* 114 (2004): 765.

root cause of terrorism and insurgency, and of social environments that do not unequivocally reject nonstate political violence, is a deep sense of being victimized by foreign or foreign-sponsored powers. In addition to the transnational al-Qaeda network, for example, consider nationalist movements such as Palestine's Hamas and the Algerian National Liberation Front of the 1950s and 1960s. The looming threat or reality that ordinary noncombatants will become collateral casualties of a military power's legalistic tactics, such as heavy urban bombardment and drone attacks, only exacerbates a feeling of loss of self-determination as a people.

Populations made vulnerable to legalistic violence are not merely laboring under a misunderstanding about intentions. Indeed, the authors of the "rapid dominance" doctrine embrace the view that "the appropriate balance of Shock and Awe must cause . . . the threat and fear of action that may shut down all or part of the adversary's society or render his ability to fight useless short of complete physical destruction."[26] This statement, readily available on the World Wide Web, does not bother making a pretense of due care for noncombatants. (Shortly after the start of the Iraq War, one of the authors expressed disappointment that the doctrine's execution in Baghdad was not shocking and awesome enough.[27]) If we are honest with ourselves, we cannot truly believe, for instance, that Muslim suicide attackers, who include an increasing number of women, are mainly motivated by a clerical promise of "72 virgins" in the afterlife. As Michael Scheuer, a former senior CIA analyst and chief of its bin Laden unit, writes in a blurb for *Messages to the World*, "Western media . . . fail[ed] to give their audience the words that put [Osama bin Laden's] thoughts and actions in cultural and historical context. . . . Bin Laden has been precise in telling America the reasons he is waging war on us. None of the reasons have anything to do with our freedom, liberty and democracy, but have everything to do with US policies and actions in the Muslim world."[28]

To recognize that justice grievances are often a root cause of terrorism and insurgency is not thereby to grant that the various grievances are reasonable on the whole, let alone urgent enough to warrant resort to some form of political violence. Fortunately, my argument here does not lead us into thorny political debates. There will be no discussion of which causes on which sides are right or reasonable. My argument is restricted to justice grievances over conduct in war regarding noncombatants. Bin Laden featured the issue in a November 2001

[26] Harlan K. Ullman and James P. Wade, *Shock and Awe: Achieving Rapid Dominance* (Washington, DC: National Defense University, 1996), 92.

[27] Timothy Nash, "Meet Mr. 'Shock and Awe,'" *Slate*, April 1, 2003.

[28] Osama bin Laden, *Messages to the World: The Statements of Osama Bin Laden*, ed. Bruce Lawrence, trans. James Howarth (London: Verso, 2005), back cover.

letter: "We should therefore see events not as isolated incidents . . . . On the pretext of reconstruction, 13,000 of our brothers were killed in Somalia. In southern Sudan hundreds of thousands were killed . . . . More than a million children have been killed in Iraq, and the killing continues . . . . No one, not even animals, would put up with what is going on [in Palestine]."[29] Questions about the accuracy of his numbers aside, bin Laden was referencing the reality of extensive noncombatant deaths in connection with US or US-allied military actions.

As we learned, bin Laden believed in the political primacy of power and violence, with ideal morality a weak player. This type of orientation is shared by mainstream political theorists, foreign policy and military practitioners, and their fellow travelers, for whom political realism is the prevalent view. Roughly, political realism denies that morality has any fundamental place in international relations. Political realists can be unclear about the relation between their descriptive and prescriptive claims, that is, about the extent to which moral norms do figure into international relations as compared to the extent to which they should.[30] (Since I want to set up a pragmatic argument, I will not address prescriptive realism.) Descriptive realists are under the seventeenth-century influence of Thomas Hobbes. Through the model of international relations as a state of nature, they argue that we more reliably can predict how states will act once we evaluate what is in their national interest, or at least what states take to be in their national interest (or political elites take to be in their own interests). If we are optimistic that states will do the right thing because it is the right thing to do, descriptive realists caution, we usually will be disappointed and, worse, unprepared to cope with the economic and military advantages competitor states seek and the strategic threats they pose. Simply put, descriptive realists believe that having strong moral expectations in international relations is a fool's hope, that the dynamics of state power are crucial.

No one would deny that being prudent is a virtue in international relations. While efforts toward negotiation and compromise must reflect some sensitivity to fairness, these efforts presuppose that the parties are rational enough to be motivated primarily by their respective interests. Political realism, however, with its assumption that the principal actors in international relations are competing states, has trouble accounting for nonstate actors, particularly when their motivations suggest a kind of moral idealism that emphasizes a people's self-determination and self-respect. (Bin Laden, a Saudi son of privilege, joined the US-supported mujahideen resistance in the Soviet war in Afghanistan because, he said, "I felt outraged that an injustice had been committed against the people

[29] Osama bin Laden, *Messages to the World*, 137.

[30] See Charles R. Beitz, *Political Theory and International Relations* (Princeton, NJ: Princeton University Press, 1979), pt. 1.

of Afghanistan. It made me realise that people who take power in the world use their power under different names to subvert others and to force their opinions on them."[31]) The apparent deviation of these nonstate actors from pursuit of selfish interests might help explain a tendency to characterize their motivations as "extremism," an anomaly that defies the realist model of state-oriented power politics.

A statist conception of international relations has grave limitations in a post-9/11 world. The relevance and global influence of nonstate actors tied to the Muslim world should be evident by now, as should the perils of policies and actions that they and we know take a severe toll on ordinary noncombatants in their populations. These actors—whether terrorist or insurgent groups, locals who shelter or tolerate them, or many Muslims worldwide who do not endorse certain means of "militant" political violence but might well endorse some of the stated political aims of that violence—have reasonable enough moral sensibilities regarding noncombatant casualties. They care no less about their peoples' lives than we care about ours. The motivations and sympathies of these nonstate actors—relatively few of whom the United States and its allies are trying to defeat directly through the use of force—cannot summarily be reduced to selfish interests or fanatical religious or racist visions.

An approach to fighting terrorism and counterinsurgency that depends on widely employing legalistic violence is almost bound not to succeed: its deeply negative impact on hearts and minds in unsympathetic populations is no less foreseeable, likely, and avoidable than the extensive noncombatant casualties it generates. This will be true apart from the question of whether our major foreign policy goals are just. To reiterate, my discussion is restricted to conduct in war, though broader issues of justice of course lie in the background.

Not-So-Hypothetical Case Studies

I am contending that conduct in war—even when falling within standard legal limits—is too often legalistic, taking inadequate account, pragmatically speaking, of harms to ordinary noncombatants. In this context, what is pragmatic is informed, not determined, by reasonable enough moral sensibilities; so the charge of unrealistic idealism would be misplaced. I am not interested in assigning blame but in arguing generally for a more productive approach, regardless of the military powers in question.

[31] Robert Fisk, *The Great War for Civilisation: The Conquest of the Middle East* (New York: Vintage Books, 2007), 8.

Consider a hypothetical case around which to focus our attention:

> Stationed in the state of Nevada, you're an Air Force commander in charge of combat drone operations in and around Iraq. A drone camera operator, looking at her video screen, has sighted a vehicle of a type that, according to the crew intelligence coordinator, ISIS fighters use to travel under guise of civilian commuter buses. The camera operator asks for confirmation that this is an ISIS bus. You order the drone pilot to be ready to fire on the vehicle if and when they get confirmation.
>
> There's no question destroying an ISIS transport would be permissible under your rules of engagement and international law. Moments later, they have confirmation that an ISIS mid-value target is in the vehicle. But the vehicle is not an ISIS transport but a commuter bus carrying twenty to thirty innocent civilians, heading away from the battle area, yet still well within ISIS-controlled territory.
>
> What should you do? How should you think about what to do?[32]

Let's stipulate that with no further, timely information available, you have authority to make the call. The drone camera operator only knows that the ISIS fighter got on the bus with the twenty to thirty innocent civilians and didn't get off; she can't locate him in the bus. You have two options: order your pilot to fire on the commuter bus or not to fire on the bus.

The dilemma is obvious: you'd almost surely be killing all twenty to thirty civilians on board the commuter bus in order to kill the ISIS fighter; and your drone pilot would be aiming at the bus, not at the fighter. You might wonder if the benefits could be worth the cost in innocent civilian lives. But schooled as you are in just war theory, the laws of war, and common sense morality, you quickly reach three provisional conclusions. First, cost–benefit calculation is not permitted in this case: the standard theory's version of the DDE rules out intentionally harming ordinary noncombatants, even for the sake of substantial military gain, and thus voids any appeal to proportionality. (Proportionality is only relevant when targeting persons who permissibly can be killed and harming innocent persons is foreseen. In the hypothetical case, since you're aiming at the bus, you cannot plausibly invoke proportionality by arguing that you're aiming at the one, mid-value ISIS fighter and not also at the innocent civilians on the

[32] Cf., for example, "The source [of secret government documents] described official U.S. government statements minimizing the number of civilian casualties inflicted by drone strikes as 'exaggerating at best, if not outright lies'": Jeremy Scahill, "The Assassination Complex: Secret Military Documents Expose the Inner Workings of Obama's Drone Wars," *Intercept*, October 15, 2015, accessed June 7, 2016, https://theintercept.com/drone-papers/the-assassination-complex/.

bus with him.) Second, your resolute belief that your country has a just cause is irrelevant: the standard view that *jus ad bellum* and *jus in bello* are strictly independent means that rules of war cannot be violated in the service of a just cause. (The laws of war re *jus in bello* are supposed to be inviolable and thus are indifferent to just cause.) Third, the spirit of the golden rule seems to tell against firing on the bus: you realize that were many American civilians, including friends of yours, on board, you wouldn't order the pilot to fire and wouldn't think anyone else should.

Having arrived at these provisional conclusions, you might be unable to shake the feeling that this is one of those hard choices in war that may demand tough but necessary decisions. You begin to wonder if you were under the influence of a faulty premise. Reconsidering the requirement of discrimination between combatants and noncombatants, you now have this thought: you wouldn't be intending to kill the twenty to thirty innocent civilians on board the commuter bus; you would only be intending to kill the ISIS mid-value target. Perhaps, then, it is permissible within the limits of legal interpretation to order the drone pilot to fire on the bus to kill the fighter, with the likely result that the twenty to thirty innocent civilians also on board will be collaterally killed. You would not regard these civilian casualties as a welcome side effect as might be envisioned by proponents of "shock and awe" tactics. You know you would avoid harming the civilians if you could still manage to kill the mid-value target.

As for other qualms, you are confident that the benefits of killing this ISIS fighter would be worth the immediate cost in innocent Iraqi civilian lives, in the sense that killing him would represent a direct military advantage: a capable fighter and leader would no longer pose a threat to US and allied troops. So the proportionality requirement, on a typically minimalist legal interpretation, would be satisfied. You remain bothered by the golden rule, though you are prepared to dismiss this worry as counterfactual speculation of a kind that suits humanitarians, not military commanders delegated the responsibility of protecting the security of their nation's citizens, including citizen-combatants. Anyway, you remember thinking that such a test—which would have us ask, "Could we legitimately be subjected, under similar circumstances, to a use of force comparable in its effects to the use of force that we are prepared to employ against other people?"[33]—does not deliver objective verdicts about moral, let alone legal, permissibility. The test is valuable as a tool for measuring sincerity of deliberation. If the worst you can be charged with under the circumstances is a double standard in deliberation, you are willing to take that chance for the sake of better serving your country. Such are the burdens of command responsibility.

[33] McPherson, "Excessive Force in War," 90.

I am not sure whether international law governing conduct in war can accommodate the reconsidered line of reasoning. The answer, I suspect, is yes. Whether we think that intention sometimes matters in assessing the permissibility of actions that can be expected to cause unwarranted harm, our hypothetical case does not look like one of those times. If firing on the commuter bus is morally or legally permissible, the reason presumably cannot depend on the claim that the commander did not intend to kill the civilians and was not, say, using them as a means—that the actual target was not the bus itself but the ISIS fighter, though the drone pilot could not even attempt a "precision strike" on him and could only fire on the bus. Any such claim would border on making a mockery out of morality, law, and common sense. The issue is not whether you would, if you could, kill the mid-value ISIS fighter without also killing the innocent civilians who happen to be on the bus with him: you can't. Knowing that the specific effect you'd "aim at" (namely, killing the ISIS fighter) is permissible and would explain why you fired on the bus cannot explain away that you know you'd also be killing the innocent civilians. (Moreover, your drone pilot would literally be aiming at the bus and not specifically at the ISIS fighter on it.) Concern for justice is not a function of loopholes by way of casuistry or legalism: the spirit and not merely the letter of norms of conduct can make an important difference.

Imagine how, as the drone commander, you might try explaining your decision to the civilian victims' survivors. Would you tell them you were acting in strict compliance with the law given that these victims were not intended targets; and while you regret their deaths and recognize that they cannot really be characterized as tragic accidents, you would make the same decision again? Do you believe that if the victims' survivors are reasonable enough, they have reason to care about some technical distinction between intending and not intending to harm innocent civilians, even when the harms would be foreseeable, likely, and avoidable and nothing directly critical is at stake? Are you prepared to tacitly dismiss their common-sense objections driven by the interest we all have in not suffering unwarranted grave injury for the benefit of other people of no special relation to us?[34] I am not suggesting that the perspective of innocent victims and their survivors is a sound indicator of permissibility in this type of case or any other. Rather, I am arguing that intention cannot carry nearly the moral weight the standard theory and the laws of war have supposed it does. The alchemy of intention distorts conduct in war, predictably fueling deep justice grievances over noncombatant casualties.

In certain moods, proponents of the standard norms seem inclined to agree. Take the following scenario:

[34] Cf. Rodin, "Terrorism Without Intention," 764.

A national liberation group is greatly overmatched militarily. Its militants have low-tech rockets and sporadically fire them into the adversary's home territory. Upwards of 90% of these rockets are shot down or fall harmlessly in the desert. Occasionally, the rockets injure or kill civilians, no more than a few dozen or so since their introduction roughly 15 years ago.

These rocket attacks are widely condemned in the Western world as acts of terrorism. Yet the militants insist that they do not intentionally target civilians, explaining that they intend to hit military targets. Indeed, their rockets lack sophistication, range, and accuracy; very few now get through the adversary's missile-defense system. Criticizing their rocket attacks as acts of terrorism is political propaganda, the militants say. They claim that these attacks are no different with respect to *jus in bello* than ostensibly permissible missile and bomb attacks launched on their densely populated territory by the adversary—that the real difference is the adversary's attacks cause many multiples greater civilian casualties and damage to civilian infrastructure.

That is the scenario. The militants could easily find evidence that their critics are hypocritical or disingenuous in condemning their rocket attacks as acts of terrorism. For example, the *New York Times* published the following from one of its leading columnists (to reduce political distraction, I have redacted the names of the parties to the conflict):

> [Country X's] counterstrategy was to use its Air Force to pummel [militant group B] and, while not directly targeting [country A's] civilians with whom [militant group B] was intertwined, to inflict substantial property damage and collateral casualties on [country A] at large. It was not pretty, but it was logical . . . . [T]he only long-term source of deterrence was to exact enough pain on the civilians—the families and employers of the militants—to restrain [militant group B] in the future.[35]

To be clear, the columnist made these observations not in condemnation but in support of country X, a close ally of the United States. Nor does this represent the mere opinion of a prominent journalist, who expounds the case above as a model for dealing with territory Z. "[Country X's] aim," its president is reported

[35] Thomas L. Friedman, "Israel's Goals in Gaza," *New York Times*, January 13, 2009.

to have said, "was to provide a strong blow to the people of [territory Z] so that they would lose their appetite for shooting at [country X]."[36]

Whether the columnist and the president are correct in their strategic assessments is, without recourse to legalism, irrelevant to the permissibility of intending to cause "enough pain" to civilians. Any political entity or partisan can always try to argue that the ends justify the means, such that the laws governing conduct in war are rendered functionally irrelevant. The question becomes how seriously we are going to take these laws, particularly concerning noncombatant immunity. The answer surely cannot be to take refuge in legalistic claims that are transparent in their moral absurdity and bad faith. Populations made vulnerable to extensive noncombatant casualties will find not only that many of the harms are an affront to justice but also that the enabling rationalizations are an affront to their self-respect. These populations know we are attaching lower value to their lives than to ours since they recognize that we would regard such treatment of our ordinary noncombatants as unacceptable in terms of justice. A subjective golden rule test is supposed to make this obvious.

At some point, there is no fooling common sense about the relatively equal value and priority that innocent persons expect, as their due, to be placed on their lives. The reasonable response to the not-so-hypothetical cases would be to concede that intending to destroy the commuter bus with civilians in order to kill an ISIS fighter is impermissible, on any plausible interpretations of the relevant international laws, as are "shock and awe"–type tactics that intend to harm civilians without intentionally targeting them. Less dramatic versions of such conduct are not uncommon in contemporary warfare. Remember: the brute reality of war is that far more noncombatants than combatants are killed. The ratio is only getting worse as military technology becomes more sophisticated, the battle space increasingly overlaps with the domestic sphere, and domestic pressures lead military powers to prioritize reducing risk to their own combatants to ever lower levels.

A Pragmatic Conclusion

Apart from the moral dimensions of my argument, I have argued that causing extensive noncombatant casualties in populations whose cooperation is needed will predictably be counterproductive. Such a lesson, which has a history of marginalization under the influence of sheer military power, now seems

[36] Greer Fay Cashman, "'Solidarity During War Is Israel's Finest Hour'," *Jerusalem Post*, January 14, 2009.

underappreciated with respect to the strategic aims of the United States and its allies. Our political and military leaders have sounded blasé about the impact of our political violence on these populations. US General Tommy Franks set a tone when stating that "we don't do body counts" of combatants or noncombatants in Afghanistan: thus we hear, for instance, " 'Ultimately, the numbers are not knowable,' said Capt. Frank Thorp of the Navy, who is Central Command's chief spokesman. 'And besides, that number may not be an indication of anything.' "[37] Of course, "that number" is an indication of something important. Presumably, a government has the responsibility to try to count and publicly acknowledge the persons, at least and especially noncombatants, it is killing—despite the negative impact, at home or abroad, this information might have on support for the military actions in question.

We cannot expect to win hearts and minds among Muslim peoples when our government's conduct in war seems to highlight that we attach much greater value to American and ally lives and interests. In general, people deeply resent being disrespected through action and attitude. In the Muslim world, our just war legalism has material consequences known locally and publicized via the World Wide Web and Arab satellite news outlets like Al Jazeera and Al Arabiya. The number of noncombatant casualties we cause, often for apparently modest military gain, is a powerful indicator of our priorities. If the war on terrorism is to have any realistic chance of success, we must give up legalistic approaches to killing.

The spirit of the laws governing conduct in war, not some contrived letter, should be our guide going forward. The overarching aim in fighting terrorism and insurgency is not to win battles or conventional wars, nor to hunt down "bad actors" in technologically sophisticated fashion. There is the short-term perception of progress, and there is real progress, which is long term. This means that as far as the *jus in bello* part of a justice equation is concerned, we need to fight to a much higher standard. Greatly reducing noncombatant casualties, rather than taking satisfaction in the knowledge that we could have injured and killed far more, is a pragmatic imperative and not simply a moral one.

Acknowledgment

This chapter is structured around a talk I gave at the US Military Academy at West Point in 2009. I'd like to thank the hosting officers and cadets for their

[37] John M. Broder, "A Nation at War: The Casualties; U.S. Military Has No Count of Iraqi Dead in Fighting," *New York Times*, April 2, 2003.

generous spirit of inquiry. I thank Erin Kelly, Debbie Mann, and the editors of this volume for very helpful comments.

References

Beitz, Charles R. *Political Theory and International Relations*. Princeton, NJ: Princeton University Press, 1979.

Berman, Eli, Jacob N. Shapiro, and Joseph H. Felter. "Can Hearts and Minds Be Bought? The Economics of Counterinsurgency in Iraq." *Journal of Political* Economy 119 (2011): 766–819.

bin Laden, Osama. *Messages to the World: The Statements of Osama Bin Laden*, edited by Bruce Lawrence, translated by James Howarth. London: Verso, 2005.

Broder, John M. "A Nation at War: The Casualties; U.S. Military Has No Count of Iraqi Dead in Fighting." *New York Times*, April 2, 2003.

Cashman, Greer Fay. "'Solidarity During War Is Israel's Finest Hour.'" *Jerusalem Post*, January 14, 2009.

Dittmann, Melissa. "Operation Hearts and Minds: Psychological Operations Are Becoming a Regular Part of Military Strategy." *Monitor on Psychology* 34 (2003): 32. Accessed February 1, 2016. http://www.apa.org/monitor/jun03/operation.aspx.

Dubik, James M. "Human Rights, Command Responsibility, and Walzer's Just War Theory." *Philosophy and Public Affairs* 11 (1982): 354–371.

Evans, Ryan. "The Seven Deadly Sins of the Human Terrain System: An Insider's Perspective." *Geopoliticus: The FPRI Blog*, July 13, 2015. Accessed February 3, 2016. http://www.fpri.org/2015/07/the-seven-deadly-sins-of-the-human-terrain-system-an-insiders-perspective/.

E.W., "Terror, Torture and Psychology: How America's Psychologists Ended Up Endorsing Torture." *Economist*, July 28, 2015. Accessed February 3, 2016. http://www.economist.com/blogs/democracyinamerica/2015/07/terror-torture-and-psychology.

Fisk, Robert. *The Great War for Civilisation: The Conquest of the Middle East*. New York: Vintage Books, 2007.

Friedman, Thomas L. "Israel's Goals in Gaza." *New York Times*, January 13, 2009.

Gardam, Judith Gail. "Proportionality and Force in International Law." *American Journal of International Law* 87 (1993): 391–413.

Hamilton, Sharon R. "HTS Director's Message." *Military Intelligence Professional Bulletin* 37 (2011): inside front cover. Accessed February 3, 2016. http://fas.org/irp/agency/army/mipb/2011_04.pdf.

Hedges, Chris. *What Every Person Should Know About War*. New York: Free Press, 2003.

Held, Virginia. *How Terrorism Is Wrong*. New York: Oxford University Press, 2008.

Iraqbodycount.org. Accessed February 13, 2016. www.iraqbodycount.org.

Johnson, Lyndon B. "Remarks at a Dinner Meeting of the Texas Electric Cooperatives, Inc." Speech. Washington Hotel, Washington, DC, May 4, 1965.

Joseph, Paul. *"Soft" Counterinsurgency: Human Terrain Teams and US Military Strategy in Iraq and Afghanistan*. New York: Palgrave Macmillan, 2014.

Leigh, David, James Ball, Ian Cobain, and Jason Burke. "Guantanamo Leaks Lift Lid on World's Most Controversial Prison." *Guardian*, April 24, 2011. Accessed February 4, 2016. http://www.theguardian.com/world/2011/apr/25/guantanamo-files-lift-lid-prison.

McMahan, Jeff. "Innocence, Self-Defense and Killing in War." *Journal of Political Philosophy* 2 (1994): 193–221.

McMahan, Jeff. "The Ethics of Killing in War." *Ethics* 114 (2004): 693–733.

McPherson, Lionel K. "Innocence and Responsibility in War." *Canadian Journal of Philosophy* 34 (2004): 485–506.

McPherson, Lionel K. "Excessive Force in War: A 'Golden Rule' Test." *Theoretical Inquiries in Law* 7 (2006): 81–95.

McPherson, Lionel K. "Is Terrorism Distinctively Wrong?" *Ethics* 117 (2007): 524–546.

Nash, Timothy. "Meet Mr. 'Shock and Awe.'" *Slate*, April 1, 2003.

Orend, Brian. *The Morality of War*. 2nd ed. Peterborough, UK: Broadview Press, 2013.

Peters, Gerhard, and John T. Wooley. The American Presidency Project. Accessed February 1, 2016. http://www.presidency.ucsb.edu/ws/?pid=26942.

Porter, Gareth. "ISAF Data Show Night Raids Killed over 1,500 Afghan Civilians." *Inter Press Service*, November 2, 2011. Accessed February 3, 2016. http://www.ipsnews.net/2011/11/isaf-data-show-night-raids-killed-over-1500-afghan-civilians/.

Primoratz, Igor. "Michael Walzer's Just War Theory: Some Issues of Responsibility." *Ethical Theory and Moral Practice* 5 (2002): 221–243.

Roberts, Adam, and Richard Guelff, eds. *Documents on the Laws of War*. 3rd ed. Oxford: Oxford University Press, 2000.

Rodin, David. "Terrorism Without Intention." *Ethics* 114 (2004): 752–771.

Scahill, Jeremy. "The Assassination Complex: Secret Military Documents Expose the Inner Workings of Obama's Drone Wars." *Intercept*, October 15, 2015. Accessed June 7, 2016. https://theintercept.com/drone-papers/the-assassination-complex/.

Ullman, Harlan K., and James P. Wade. *Shock and Awe: Achieving Rapid Dominance*. Washington, DC: National Defense University, 1996.

Walzer, Michael. *Just and Unjust Wars*. 3rd ed. New York: Basic Books, 1977.

Postscript

JEFF MCMAHAN

As the splendid essays in this book attest, just war theory, as a moral rather than a legal theory, has largely abandoned the view that whether a person is a morally legitimate target of attack in war depends on whether he or she has the status of being in a certain category, such as the category of soldiers or the category of civilians. Most contemporary just war theorists have come to believe that the idea that people can be liable to attack simply by virtue of being a member of a group, such as a military organization, is too much like the idea, common among terrorists, that people can be liable to attack simply by virtue of being citizens of a certain state or members of a certain national group, independently of what they actually *do*. Accordingly, many just war theorists now accept that whether people are morally liable to attack is a matter of what they, as individuals, have *done* or are *doing*. On this view, merely being a member of a military organization is not sufficient to make a person liable to attack in war; nor is having civilian status sufficient to exempt a person from liability to harm in war.

I interpret this shift in understanding as a belated recognition of the principle to which Thomas Nagel appealed forty-five years ago in his seminal essay, "War and Massacre," that "hostile treatment of any person must be justified in terms of something *about that person* which makes the treatment appropriate."[1] A person's mere membership in a group does not necessarily make hostile treatment of that person appropriate even if such treatment is appropriate for members who act in ways that are characteristic of the group and its purposes. Thus, while members of a military organization characteristically strive during a state of war to kill or injure members of the opposing military organization, some, such as military lawyers, may instead devote all their efforts to constraining the violent and destructive action of their fellow members. It is simply a mistake to suppose

[1] Thomas Nagel, "War and Massacre," *Philosophy & Public Affairs* 1, no. 2 (1972): 123–144.

that their membership in the organization alone makes hostile treatment of them by enemy soldiers morally appropriate. Similarly, hostile treatment of a civilian physicist in Nazi Germany who is working to provide Hitler with an atom bomb would be entirely appropriate, even though hostile treatment of other civilians who are uninvolved in the war would not be. What matters to liability in these and other cases is what people do—for example, whether they are morally responsible for threats of unjustified harm—not whether they are properly classifiable as members of some group.

In some moods, traditional just war theorists seemed to endorse a doctrine of liability and to want their criterion of liability to attack in war to be action-based rather than status-based. Walzer, for example, wrote that the "problem is not to describe how immunity is gained, but how it is lost. We are all immune to start with; our right not to be attacked . . . is lost by those who bear arms . . . because they pose a danger to other people."[2] According to this view, the criterion of liability to attack in war is, in effect, posing a threat to others. Those who pose a threat are combatants; those who do not are noncombatants. The former are liable to attack; the latter are not but retain their immunity.

Yet this view does not coincide with the received view that all members of the military on both sides in a war are legitimate targets of attack while no civilians are (with the exception, perhaps, of members of the government at the head of the military chain of command). As revisionist just war theorists have pointed out and as I noted earlier, not all members of the military pose a threat or contribute to threats posed by others; and many civilians make vital contributions to threats directly posed by others. Suppose, moreover, that a group of civilians is intentionally and wrongly attacked by soldiers in a time of war and that they resort to self-defensive violence in an effort to save themselves. No one, not even a traditional just war theorist, supposes that they thereby make themselves liable to attack. Yet "because they pose a danger to other people," they satisfy Walzer's suggested criterion of liability in just the way that combatants fighting for a just cause do. So it turns out that, to the extent that traditional just war theory has a criterion of liability to attack, it is status-based rather than action-based. It is, rather like the means of discrimination favored by terrorists, a doctrine of liability by association, combined with a doctrine of immunity by association.

The failure of traditional just war theory to offer a plausible account of what makes a person a morally legitimate target of attack in war has left contemporary just war theorists the formidable task of trying to develop one. Many of these theorists have sought to build from the ground up, starting with the general question of what can make a person liable to attack in contexts other than

[2] Michael Walzer, *Just and Unjust Wars* (New York: Basic Books, 2015), 145.

war—for example, in self-defense or third-party defense of another ("other-defense"). The literature on the ethics of self- and other-defense has therefore burgeoned, with the discussions becoming ever more probing, sophisticated, subtle, and rigorous in argumentation.

The questions are legion. Is culpability necessary for liability? Is moral responsibility necessary for liability? Is it even necessary for liability that one make a causal contribution to a threat? Is threatening to violate a right necessary for liability? Or might a person be liable to be harmed as a means of preventing him or her from acting in a way that would be impersonally bad though not worse for anyone? Can a person become liable to defensive harming by acting in a way that will *justifiably* infringe or override a right? Can someone who only *appears* to pose a threat or bluffs about posing a threat be liable to be harmed? Is someone who reasonably but mistakenly believes he or she is threatened and takes what he or she believes to be necessary defensive action then liable to defensive harm? Does a defender who threatens to harm an aggressor in a way that is unnecessary or disproportionate thereby make himself or herself liable to defensive harming by the aggressor or a third party? Do the constraints of proportionality and necessity have to be satisfied for a person to be liable to be harmed, or can a person be liable to be harmed even when harming him or her would be unnecessary or disproportionate?

These are only a few of the questions that are being debated in discussions of the morality of self- and other-defense. All are difficult, and all are relevant in one way or another to issues of liability in war. None has been decisively answered. So the debates continue. The essays gathered in this book address some of these questions and make important advances (on occasion by correcting mistakes that I have made!). And, of course, they address other important questions as well. Although much remains to be done, the progress these essays make provides renewed grounds for optimism that we will continue to enhance our understanding of the morality both of defensive harming generally and of war in particular. And it is reasonable to hope that a deeper and clearer understanding of the morality of war will eventually inform the practice of war, both by reducing the incidence of war and by diminishing the wrongful harms inflicted by the participants.

Reference

Nagel, Thomas. "War and Massacre." *Philosophy & Public Affairs* 1, no. 2 (1972): 123–144.Walzer, Michael. *Just and Unjust Wars*. New York: Basic Books, 2015.

INDEX

Note: Page references followed by a "*t*" indicate table; "*f*" indicate figure.

Printed in the USA/Agawam, MA
July 10, 2018

678387.004